D1737430

ART CENTER COLLEGE OF DESIGN
3 3220 00258 0186

The Roman Years of a South Carolina Artist

Women's Diaries and Letters of the South
Carol Bleser, Series Editor

A Woman Doctor's Civil War: Esther Hill Hawks' Diary
Edited by Gerald Schwartz

A Rebel Came Home: The Diary and Letters of Floride Clemson, 1863–1866
Edited by Ernest McPherson Lander, Jr., and Charles M. McGee, Jr.

The Shattered Dream: The Day Book of Margaret Sloan, 1900–1902
Edited by Harold Woodell

The Letters of a Victorian Madwoman
Edited by John S. Hughes

A Confederate Nurse: The Diary of Ada W. Bacot, 1860–1863
Edited by Jean V. Berlin

A Plantation Mistress on the Eve of the Civil War: The Diary of Keziah Goodwyn Hopkins Brevard, 1860–1861
Edited by John Hammond Moore

Lucy Breckinridge of Grove Hill: The Journal of a Virginia Girl, 1862–1864
Edited by Mary D. Robertson

George Washington's Beautiful Nelly: The Letters of Eleanor Parke Curtis Lewis to Elizabeth Bordley Gibson, 1794–1851
Edited by Patricia Brady

A Confederate Lady Comes of Age: The Journal of Pauline DeCaradeuc Heyward, 1863–1888
Edited by Mary D. Robertson

A Northern Woman in the Plantation South: Letters of Tryphena Blanche Holder Fox, 1856–1876
Edited by Wilma King

Best Companions: Letters of Eliza Middleton Fisher and Her Mother, Mary Hering Middleton, from Charleston, Philadelphia, and Newport, 1839–1846
Edited by Eliza Cope Harrison

Stateside Soldier: Life in the Women's Army Corps, 1944–1945
Aileen Kilgore Henderson

From the Pen of a She-Rebel: The Civil War Diary of Emilie Riley McKinley
Edited by Gordon A. Cotton

Between North and South: The Letters of Emily Wharton Sinkler, 1842–1865
Edited by Anne Sinkler Whaley LeClercq

A Southern Woman of Letters: The Correspondence of Augusta Jane Evans Wilson
Edited by Rebecca Grant Sexton

Southern Women at Vassar: The Poppenheim Family Letters, 1882–1916
Edited by Joan Marie Johnson

Live Your Own Life: The Family Papers of Mary Bayard Clarke, 1854–1886
Edited by Terrell Armistead Crow and Mary Moulton Barden

The Roman Years of a South Carolina Artist: Caroline Carson's Letters Home, 1872–1892
Edited with an Introduction by William H. Pease and Jane H. Pease

The Roman Years of a South Carolina Artist

Caroline Carson's Letters Home, 1872–1892

Edited with an Introduction by
William H. Pease and Jane H. Pease

University of South Carolina Press

Published in Columbia, South Carolina, by the
University of South Carolina Press

Manufactured in the United States of America

07 06 05 04 03 5 4 3 2 1

Library of Congress Cataloging-in-Publication Data

Carson, Caroline, 1820–1892.
The Roman years of a South Carolina artist : Caroline Carson's letters home, 1872–1892 / edited with an introduction by William H. Pease and Jane H. Pease.
p. cm. — (Women's diaries and letters of the South)
Includes index.
ISBN 1-57003-500-8 (cloth : alk. paper)
1. Rome (Italy)—Description and travel. 2. Carson, Caroline, 1820–1892—Journeys—Italy—Rome. I. Pease, William Henry, 1924– II. Pease, Jane H. III. Title. IV. Series.
DG806.2 .C377 2003
914.5'6320484—dc21 2003000798

This is Caroline Carson's book. Were she alive, she would, in all probability, dedicate it to her father. Therefore, we dedicate it to the spirit of James Louis Petigru.

Contents

Part III

The Gradual Disintegration of a Dream World, 1883–1892

Illustrations

Caroline Carson provided the titles in italics. The editors have supplied the titles in quotation marks.

Figures

Plates

following page 192

Series Editor's Preface

The Roman Years of a South Carolina Artist: Caroline Carson's Letters Home, 1872–1892, edited with an introduction by William H. Pease and Jane H. Pease, is the eighteenth volume in what had been the Women's Diaries and Letters of the Nineteenth-Century South series. This series has been redefined and is now titled Women's Diaries and Letters of the South, enabling us to include some remarkably fine works from the twentieth century. This series includes a number of never-before-published diaries, some collections of unpublished correspondence, and a few reprints of published diaries—a potpourri of nineteenth-century and, now, twentieth-century Southern women's writings.

The series enables women to speak for themselves, providing readers with a rarely opened window into Southern society before, during, and after the American Civil War and into the twentieth century. The significance of these letters and journals lies not only in the personal revelations and the writing talent of these women authors but also in the range and versatility of the documents' contents. Taken together, these publications will tell us much about the heyday and the fall of the Cotton Kingdom, the mature years of the "peculiar institution," the war years, the adjustment of the South to a new social order following the defeat of the Confederacy, and the New South of the twentieth century. Through these writings, the reader will also be presented with firsthand accounts of everyday life and social events, courtships and marriages, family life and travels, religion and education, and the life-and-death matters that made up the ordinary and extraordinary world of the American South.

Jane and William Pease are also authors of the magnificent biography, *James Louis Petigru: Southern Conservative, Southern Dissenter* (USC Press, 2002), which details the life of the brilliant lawyer and leading Charleston unionist in the thirty years preceding the Civil War. Caroline Petigru Carson (1820–1892), James Petigru's elder daughter, paid a very high price for her father's staunch unionism in the antebellum years. However, for the last twenty years of her life, she would experience exuberant freedom living as an artist in Rome.

Raised in a well-connected and intellectual lowcountry family, for half her life Caroline led a conventional existence as a southern woman of the Victorian era. For the second half of her life, until her death in 1892, her existence was much more unconventional and controversial. In 1837, Caroline—a debutante and much-sought-after belle despite her father's politics—appeared to be facing the brightest of futures as a plantation mistress, until her marriage to William Carson, an alcoholic rice planter twice her age by whom she bore two sons. William Carson died in 1856 and Caroline, at age thirty-six, embarked on the life of a merry widow, supported by her father's thriving law practice. When the Civil War came in 1861, Caroline left South Carolina and took up residence in New York City. After her father's death in 1863, his many supporters in the North raised money to assist his rebellious daughter and her children. It was while Caroline was in New York City that she began her life as a painter. In 1872, at the age of fifty-two, Caroline made her great leap into the unknown, traveling abroad and settling in Rome with hopes of establishing a successful career there as an artist. It is astonishing that this child of the Old South, destined to be a southern belle in perpetuity, embarked alone on the life of an expatriate artist. The Peases have meticulously edited Caroline Petigru Carson's letters to her favorite son James in which she vividly describes the expatriate culture of Rome, the artists, the writers, and all the famous Gilded Age visitors who came to the Eternal City and attended her Saturday afternoon *salon*. The eventful chronicle of her twenty Roman years is a legacy well worth preserving.

CAROL BLESER

Acknowledgments

BECAUSE THE ORIGINALS of all the letters reproduced in this volume are from the Vanderhorst Family Papers in the South Carolina Historical Society, the society deserves our deepest thanks for permission to publish the letters, granted by its acting director, W. Eric Emerson. The texts from which we worked were copied and made available to us by the then director, Alexander Moore, who almost providentially had become acquisitions editor for the University of South Carolina Press when our manuscript was ready for publication. Without his aid, encouragement, and support, *The Roman Years* might never have gone to press.

Furthermore, this volume would not contain illustrations of Carson's paintings were it not for the generosity of the Phillips family. Ted Phillips called us long distance to share his excitement when he first discovered a collection of the hundred or so Carson paintings, sketches, and drawings that subsequently became the Phillips Collection. And since they acquired these works, Ashton and LaVonne Phillips have allowed us to view, study, and photograph them without restriction. Moreover, LaVonne has fed us and eased our labors in innumerable ways on the many days we have worked in her home.

For modern photographs of Italian sites, William Pease alone is responsible. But Constance Schulz, whose own books demonstrate her expertise in copying images, exceeded the bonds of friendship when she offered to and did photograph Carson's watercolors reproduced here. She deserves and has our sincere thanks. We are also grateful to the South Carolina Historical Society for furnishing photographs of Carson's copy of Thomas Sully's portrait of James Louis Petigru and of the photo portrait of the artist taken early in her Roman years. The University of South Carolina School of Law has again granted us permission to use the warmest of Carson's various oil portraits of her father.

We must also thank the Davis, Health Sciences, Sloane and Botany Libraries of the University of North Carolina and their librarians who helped us run down obscure leads as we tried to identify the people and pictures mentioned in Carson's letters. In addition, the late Jean Cooke helped us identify some of the flowers in Carson's paintings; Raimondo Luraghi came to the rescue when obscure Italian words stumped us; Joy Kassen shared with us her own work on nineteenth-century American sculptors in Rome; Robert Seymour confirmed our conviction that Carson's biblical paraphrasing was her own; Judith Hunt clarified Bentivoglio Middleton's Italian connections; Tom Brown elucidated the fate of A. E. Harnisch's Calhoun monument; and Carmine Berton gave us an extended tour of Sorrento's Bellevue Hotel Syrene, enhanced with his own historical insights, to help us visualize the quarters Carson might have occupied and to experience her responses to viewing Mount Vesuvius from her balcony, and contemplating the precipitous drop to the sea immediately below. We thank them all not just for their specific aid but for making the world in which Caroline Carson lived become yet more comprehensible.

CHAPEL HILL, JANUARY 2002

Editorial Note

BECAUSE THERE ARE WELL over three hundred letters from Caroline Carson to James Carson among the Vanderhorst Family Papers in the South Carolina Historical Society, we have had to cull extensively. Our guideline for inclusion was to keep the texts that exhibited Caroline Carson's personal, social, and artistic life with as little cutting as possible. Our guidelines for exclusion were imposed by the sheer quantity of the collection. We have eliminated duplication except when two versions of an event or circumstance differ. For three categories of letters we have selected only the essential minimum. Most correspondence dealing with her Carolina kin and the New York friends with whom she had little contact after 1872 is omitted. So, too, is the extensive record of her legal battles to regain Dean Hall, carried on through the trial and appellate courts at both the state and federal levels, revealing her impatience, as the daughter of a skilled lawyer, with her attorneys' inattention to her instructions and her fury when they failed to meet deadlines or refer to essential documents. The most sweeping cuts are from her lengthy and repetitive advice to James: how he should care for his health; how he should woo and win a rich wife; to whom he ought to apply for jobs and from whom he should seek personal advice; why he ought never again to take a job in South America; and, always, why he should smoke and drink less. In addition, much fascinating gossip about New York socialites, her own unusual recommendations for redeeming plantation agriculture, and her praise and prescriptions for homeopathic medicines had to be omitted. Observing such relatively clearly defined guidelines has allowed us to keep the focus on Caroline Carson in Rome and has imposed a more objective editing protocol than would personal value judgments about what was important and what insignificant in all her observations.

Most challenging of all, however, were Carson's handwriting and punctuation. Perhaps because she hated paying postage, there are precious few paragraph breaks in her letters. Simply for readability we have imposed a paragraphing that reflects shifts in subject content. When her periods, commas, and dashes are clearly made, we have transcribed them as they appear in the manuscript. Most of the time, when there is little to distinguish one from the other, we have interpreted them according to modern usage. Occasionally, when there was no punctuation mark at all and the meaning was unclear without it, we have inserted one in brackets. Totally illegible words we have indicated by a question mark in brackets; when we were unsure about the word we thought was there, we have followed our best reading by a question mark in brackets.

Carson's unusual punctuation of contractions we have transcribed just as it occurs. We have also retained all punctuated abbreviations as they occur, but for uncommon and unpunctuated ones we have generally supplied the missing letters. Where her handwriting made no distinction between capital and lowercase letters, we have simply guessed on the basis of customary usage—hers when we could detect a pattern, ours when we could not. Finally, where she has clearly misspelled a word we have left it as she wrote it except where clarity of meaning required us to bracket a correction or attach a footnoted explanation.

Note on Carson's Paintings

Ashton and LaVonne Phillips of Charleston, South Carolina, own the most extensive collection of Carson's sketches and paintings, mostly watercolors, numbering over one hundred. Among them are eighteen images of flowers and plants, over fifty landscapes (all but two of which were done in Europe), and fourteen portraits (at least half of which were painted before 1872). The Gibbes Museum of Art in Charleston owns fewer than a dozen identifiable finished Carson works, including eight small watercolor portraits painted in the 1850s and one larger portrait of a woman done in Rome in May 1873. Its unique holding is a collection of designs for fans that she produced on parchment or silk by tracing her original sketches.

The Morris Museum of Art in Augusta, Georgia, owns an 1878 watercolor of an Italian rural scene and an 1862 watercolor, *Portrait of a Lady,* which is very likely a portrayal of Angelica Hamilton Blatchford. The Greenville County Museum of Art in Greenville, South Carolina, has another watercolor portrait of an unidentified woman, dated October 1870. Of her several oil portraits of James Louis Petigru, one, a copy of a Thomas Sully painting, is owned by the South Carolina Historical Society in Charleston; another by the University of South Carolina School of Law in Columbia; and a third, the only full-length one, hangs in the South Carolina Supreme Court building in Columbia. An extensive search of other museums that seemed likely to own a Carson work has proved futile. A number of Charlestonians, however, are reputed to own one or more of her flower paintings.

Caroline Petigru Carson in Rome. Courtesy of the South Carolina Historical Society.

Introduction

When, in December 1872, Caroline Petigru Carson arrived in Rome, she little imagined that she would live the rest of her life abroad. She had come intending only to view the art treasures of Europe and to perfect her skills as a painter. She had chosen Rome because for more than a century foreign artists and connoisseurs had matured their talents there. But after she had spent a very lonely two weeks visiting art galleries in Florence she hesitated to go on. Nonetheless, her first month in Rome changed her mind. There she was made welcome in the studios and the social circles of a well-established community of American sculptors and painters. And, having arrived at the height of the touring season, she enjoyed mingling with a good number of Americans whom she already knew and with the new acquaintances to whom they introduced her. By March the dual promise of artistic fulfillment and a congenial social life convinced her to settle in and act out her long-held aspiration to live a painter's life.

Carson was fifty-two years old when she rented her first apartment near the Spanish Steps, an area where American tourists congregated and artists of all nationalities maintained studios. Doing so marked another sharp change in a life that had already endured several abrupt upheavals. Born in 1820, she was the first daughter and second child of James Louis Petigru, a Charleston, South Carolina, lawyer already well on his way to professional and political prominence, and his plantation-born wife. When she was only six, the death of her eight-year-old brother, until then the focus of her parents' aspirations for their progeny, opened the way for her to become the child closest to her father, fulfilling his demanding educational and behavioral expectations as her younger siblings did not. Early on she learned to negotiate difficult home situations to master the skills that allowed her, as a woman grown, to pursue unusual goals while avoiding social condemnation. "Patience and Perseverance," the motto she had first written on her school slates, guided both her intellectual growth and her interaction with others. So, although her formal schooling ended when she was fifteen, her education did not. During the single year she had spent in a fashionable New York school, her letters home as well as her English compositions embodied both keen observation and the easy writing style that marked her later correspondence. Like similar finishing schools, Mme Binsse's taught sketching and painting, but only as ladylike accomplishments, which encouraged the superficiality of her early sketches of family and friends. On the other hand, its serious language instruction and insistence that all classes except English be conducted in French polished Caroline's ability to speak and write a language she had already studied at the Misses Robertsons' school in Charleston. And after she returned home, she continued to hone her mastery of language. She learned Latin under the tutelage of a Catholic priest who was a friend of her father. Still later, when she was in her twenties, Giulio Posi, a Roman-born teacher, taught her Italian so expertly that within a few years she was making polished translations of Dante's sonnets. Her omnivorous reading in all these languages drove her to collect an extensive personal library spanning philosophy, religion, history, literature, and art. Indeed, of the languages commonly taught in American colleges at that time, only German and Greek remained outside her ken.

Never, however, did Carson's intellectual interests deter her from the active social life she began as a belle in Charleston and later pursued in New York, Rome, and a variety of American and European resorts. Her easy conversational style was lightened by wit, as was her voluminous correspondence. She readily turned out doggerel verses to celebrate birthdays and festive gatherings—even to ask a friend to tea. And so she got on in the world, following the behavioral maxim she constantly urged on her sons: "Suaviter in modo, fortiter in re" (Gentle in manner, resolute in execution). Accordingly, her smooth style was balanced by serious study and unyielding tenaciousness when she faced those practical circumstances over which she could not triumph and that sometimes excluded her from the world she wished to inhabit.

Part of her life as an outsider stemmed from her father's situation. Although his extraordinary legal skills won him social prestige as well as financial rewards, his persistent unionism left him politically isolated after he led the opposition to South Carolina's attempted nullification of federal laws in the early 1830s. Despite her youth at the time, the loyalties her father's politics then shaped left Caroline forever out of step with her fellow Carolinians. Moreover, when she became a debutante in 1837, her father's rash financial speculations and generous loans to friends exploded in a national economic downturn and abruptly ended his family's comfortable prosperity. Obliged to turn over all his property except his Charleston residence to creditors, James could only lament that never had his home "been so gloomy as at the very time when people brush up and look as smart as they can to bring out a daughter."* Although Caroline became a much sought-after belle despite her family's financial woes, she failed to fall in love with any of her many suitors.

By the time she was twenty-one, she was an easy target for her mother's resentment at her own reduced circumstances and her insistence that her daughters marry soon and well. So, in a state whose laws forbade divorce, she embarked on a loveless marriage to William Carson, an alcoholic rice planter twice her age. The birth of two sons did little to alleviate her miseries at his isolated Dean Hall plantation from which, by 1850, she escaped whenever she could to her parents' home in Charleston or to New York, where she achieved a measure of personal freedom. Only in 1856, however, did her marriage end. Mired in debt and worn down by drink, William died. Free at last from his abusive behavior, Caroline, a thirty-six-year-old widow, discovered that the settlement of his much diminished estate left her only very limited means to support herself, educate two adolescent sons, and cope with serious illness.

For the next four years, however, her father's thriving law practice supported Caroline's life as a very merry widow surrounded by the social elite to which his professional standing in the South and his political prominence in the North introduced her. Among the many notable men whose attention she attracted was Edward Everett, whose terms as professor of literature and president of Harvard College attested to his intellect, while his service as Massachusetts governor, American senator, minister to England, and secretary of state reflected his access to power. From the spring of 1858 until December 1860 their emotional relationship seemed to promise Caroline the affection, social position, intellectual companionship, and financial security she so desperately wanted. But after his defeat as the

* William H. Pease and Jane H. Pease, *James Louis Petigru: Southern Conservative, Southern Dissenter* (Athens: University of Georgia Press, 1995), 93.

vice presidential candidate on the Constitutional Union party ticket in 1860 he abruptly broke off their engagement just as South Carolina seceded and the turmoil leading to the Civil War began.

Deeply hurt by Everett's rejection but sharing her father's loyalty to the Union, Carson chose wartime exile in New York, where, ever since 1850, she had cultivated an active social life while she sought medical attention for uterine tumors, severe eye infections and various dermatological disorders. One cousin had condemned her indulgence there as a "race for fashion & excitement" at her father's expense.* Other than among critical kin, however, her reputation was apparently undamaged. And still, in June 1861, however unsettling her apprehension that all their lives would be drastically changed by the war, Caroline did nothing to rein in her extravagance. Within weeks of leaving Charleston that month, she embarked on a ten-week tour of England and the continent, paying her way with the last substantial sum her father could give her, a gift of two hundred dollars from Edward Everett (perhaps conscience money), and a subsidy from the New York friends whose daughter she accompanied. On her return to New York, she lived for months at a time in the town houses or on the country estates of her own or her father's friends, who willingly entertained the daughter of James Petigru. Despite his daughter's urgings that he would enjoy a similar welcome in the North, the old lawyer refused to leave Charleston. There he challenged Confederate confiscation of the property of Carolinians exiled in the North, an unremunerated service that could not replace his customary professional income, decimated as it was by the wartime closing of most courts.

With all her income from the South cut off by the war, and aware that she could not rely on the hospitality of friends forever, Carson watched the very limited funds she had brought north with her drain away. Because no hoarding of them could make them last, she sought a way to support herself by turning her amateur talent for painting into a paying proposition. She was, however, ill prepared to do so. Charleston had offered little in the way of art education. Of the artists she knew there, only one, the miniaturist Charles Fraser, had made art a profession and still retained upper-class status. Those who hoped to fulfill both social

* Caroline North Pettigrew to Louise North, 13 August 1859, Pettigrew Family Papers, Southern Historical Collection, University of North Carolina, Chapel Hill.

and financial aspirations had, like portrait painter Thomas Sully, left town. Others, like businessman-painter Henry Bounetheau and banker-sculptor John Cogdell, had to content themselves with art as a hobby. The rest, whether residents or transients, pursued their crafts in the same social rank as carpenters and shoemakers.

The city's commitment to art education had lived and died with an Academy of Fine Arts, which had lasted only two or three years after its founding in 1821. The Carolina Art Association, not founded until 1858, confined itself to annual displays of the European paintings, either original or copied, owned by its members. So although in the 1850s Carson had dabbled in watercolors, copied miniature portraits done by others, and drawn portraits of family members in charcoal and pastels, she had earned no money by her efforts. Her Charleston friends scorned the very notion that a lady would become a professional artist. Only in New York, where she had taken drawing classes at Cooper Union before the war, had Caroline ever received significant instruction. Nonetheless, shortly before April 1862 she set up shop as a portrait painter, wielding her brushes six hours a day in a rented studio.

No matter how diligently she worked, Carson never became truly self-supporting. Her wartime financial dependence on friends continued, for it was they, almost alone, who bought her drawings and commissioned portraits. Some even subsidized her art more directly, raising two thousand dollars to cover the rent for her studio and apartment and to pay the wages of her English maid. As a result, realizing that portrait painting would remain unprofitable, Carson learned to tint photographs, recognizing that this newly available form of portraiture was "the only lucrative business open" to her.* Yet she also continued to paint more marketable watercolors of flowers that put to artistic use the knowledge gained from the "botanizing" expeditions so popular among antebellum Charleston ladies.

In March 1863 James Petigru, who had remained his daughter's staunchest psychological support, died. By April her small backlog of funds was exhausted. And by May she was so ill that she was forced to rely completely on her friends for personal care as well as material support.

* Caroline Petigru Carson to James Louis Petigru, 25 November 1862, Vanderhorst Family Papers, South Carolina Historical Society, Charleston.

Perversely, however, it was her father's death that ended that entire dependence by opening the way for his admiring friends to honor him with a memorial fund to benefit his daughter. In Boston an anonymous group of "Gentlemen" raised ten thousand dollars and placed it in trust for her. New Yorkers gathered a similar sum that bought Carson a house on West Twenty-sixth Street. In December her son William came home from his four-year European commercial education to live with his mother and help with her expenses. A year and a half later, her younger son, James, who had stayed in South Carolina and served in the Confederate army, came north to live with his mother while he pursued an engineering degree at Columbia College for which, however, she had to pay by selling her diamonds. That she had so long retained her wedding diamonds, had fairly constantly employed a maid, and had constantly received material support from her father's and her own friends, all argue that Carson's fear of destitution was excessive. On the other hand, although she never experienced real poverty, she never felt solidly secure. She was forever haunted by the priority her mother had assigned to wealth, by her memories of her husband's physical and psychological abuse, by the deprivations that the debts of others had imposed upon her, by the humiliating conclusion of her hoped-for second marriage to Everett, and by the recurrence of potentially fatal illnesses. Yet she met the fears those specters induced with the patience and perseverance to which she had pledged herself as a child. From 1863 until 1870, while she was intermittently an invalid, she tinted photos and painted salable pictures whenever she was able to do so. When she was not, she knitted fancy articles for sale. Merging the small returns such exertions brought with Willie's contributions, her small but regular income from the Boston gentlemen's trust fund, and, after 1866, a tiny income from the few South Carolina stocks she regained after the war, she made a go of it.

Then, in 1870, with both sons employed far from New York and her illness, probably cancer, in remission, Carson's independent life resumed. Once again she tinted photographs. She exhibited enough watercolors for the *New York Post* to commend her as an aquarellist. She taught drawing classes and took lessons in perspective to gain expertise in landscape painting. Still, even her steady efforts did not produce a wholly reliable income. She continued to count on her friends' willingness to be her patrons—though some of them confused those roles, asking as gifts the very work they had commissioned. Such frustrations sharpened her readiness in 1872 to chaperone the nieces of an acquaintance on their grand tour of Europe.

When, however, that plan collapsed but she was paid thirteen hundred dollars for the time and effort she had already expended, she embarked on the trip alone. And when she arrived in Rome that December, she was prepared for another transformation in her life as great as that imposed by the Civil War. Despite the trials and loneliness the next twenty years would impose, she was ready to follow the often rocky path toward a new autonomy and artistic fulfillment. By March 1873, she had found Gustavo Simoni, a young and affordable painter who promised to teach her all that she had so long wished to learn. Her future virtually glowed before her. "I am going to begin to paint. I shall feel more contented."*

Even so, Carson hoped eventually to return to the United States and live with or near her children. But the failure of either son to achieve the steady employment and settled life that would have made it possible became a disappointment that loomed over her until she died. So, too, did her endless and unsuccessful litigation to regain Dean Hall, the Carson plantation.

Carson and her sons had sold the place in 1858 but held the buyer's mortgage. Then, although the mortgage deed specified that the debt must be paid in United States funds, her former factor, acting as her agent, accepted payment in Confederate money when the property was resold in 1863. The original mortgagee and his successors contended that that payment had settled the debt. Carson, never having consented to the deal, initiated legal maneuvers to regain Dean Hall in lieu of a cash settlement the year after the war ended. Thereafter, legal costs soared as suits and countersuits jockeyed back and forth from state to federal courts and up and down from law to appeals courts, taxing Carson's purse for the rest of her life. And so, both because she wanted the plantation only for her sons and because she could live better and more cheaply in Italy, she stayed in Rome. Even there, however, her finances were always tight. She believed she needed at least two thousand dollars a year to cover the rent on her large apartment, wages for two servants, and her and her maid's expenses

* Caroline Petigru Carson to James Petigru Carson, 16 March 1873, Vanderhorst Family Papers.

for summer travel and resort living. Her American capital, which produced her only reliable income, never paid her more than eighteen hundred dollars annually. For the rest she depended on the highly variable sale of her art and on gifts from friends. In the best years her sales yielded a comfortable one thousand dollars; in the worst, they fell below two hundred dollars.

Financial insecurity, though it often depressed her, never stifled Carson's social style or her enthusiasm for living in Rome. Before the first year was out, she moved from the Piazza di Spagna area, where Italian and European artists clustered, to an apartment facing the Palazzo Barberini, the geographic center of the established American art colony. At its center was the elaborate apartment where wealthy Yankee sculptor William Wetmore Story and his Boston-born wife, Emelyn, entertained resident artists and distinguished visitors likely to become their patrons. Though Story had first come to Rome in 1847, it was not until 1856 that his settlement there made the Barberini a magnet for American artists living and working in Rome—among them the much respected landscape painter William S. Haseltine and John Rollin Tilton, whose popular landscapes had long since become repetitive. Carson soon cemented friendships within the circle they and their wives formed. Not far away a rival magnet for American artists centered around Luther Terry, an undistinguished painter, and his wife, Louisa, whose fortune came from the Ward family of New York and whose standing in Rome had been established by her first husband, Thomas Crawford, whose sculpture had become immensely popular in the United States before he died in 1857. Equally important for Caroline's social circle, Crawford, from the time he had arrived in Rome in 1837, had cultivated ties with Italians of all political persuasions as well as with artists of all nationalities. As a result, the Terry apartment in the Palazzo Odescalchi was an even more cosmopolitan meeting place than the Storys', one where Rome's bitterly divided papal and secular factions mingled freely and where American artists interacted with the Italian elite under Louisa's encouraging eye.

From the start, Carson moved easily within and across these social and professional circles. But she was never bound by them. Although she kept her Protestant orientation and was a committed worshipper at St. Paul's Episcopal Church, she was nonetheless fascinated by Catholic ritual and endlessly studied the religious art that adorned Roman churches. She

La Societá degli Acquarellisti in Roma
Sig.ra Carolina Carson
Il Presente Diploma
Il Presidente
Il Segretario

Certificate of Caroline Carson's membership in the Societá degli Acquarellisti in Roma, 1876. Courtesy of Ashton and LaVonne Phillips.

readily associated with struggling Italian artists like her first teacher there, the young Simoni. Later, she shared models and exchanged advice with established artists regardless of nationality, such as the German Otto Brandt, the Englishman Jim Pole, and the important Italian naturalist painter Giovanni (Nino) Costa. It was not surprising, then, that when the Societá degli Acquerallisti was formed in 1876, she was the only woman and only foreigner elected to its membership. Equally important to her were the socially prestigious Italians she cultivated, some of whom she met through their rich American wives whom she had known in the States. As a result, guests of different nationalities, including many of the diplomats accredited to Rome, came regularly to the Saturday afternoon receptions she held in her studio. Some did no more than drink her tea and converse. Others bought finished pictures on display or commissioned new pieces. A number became steady patrons. Still others became warm friends.

By the mid 1880s, when the medieval and Renaissance art of Florence drew both artists and tourists away from classical Rome, Carson was tempted to move with them. But she never did. The expenses of moving restrained her. She feared losing the accustomed attentions provided by her servants, Lorenzo and Esterina Servadei Pizzuti, whose young son, christened Giacomo Carlo in honor of both James and Caroline Carson, had become her surrogate grandchild.

Perhaps most important, her persistent ill health and her disappointment in her sons immobilized her. James, her clear favorite, never lived up to her lofty expectations either in his engineering profession or in making a good marriage. Only twice did she see him after she had left New York in 1872. Once she spent several weeks with him when she visited the United States in the summer of 1877. And in 1883 she financed his disappointing two-month visit to Rome. Willie, whose improving business career as an independent accountant took him to London several times in the 1880s did, in 1890, visit his mother in Rome. Most opportunely, he was on another such trip in 1892 and able to spend time with her before she died of cancer on August 15.

It was therefore William, in association with her Roman banker, James C. Hooker, who arranged for her burial in Rome's Protestant cemetery, closed her apartment, sold her furniture and clothes, and shipped her jewelry, laces, correspondence, and paintings back to the United States, where he and his brother divided them as their mother's will specified. William died, apparently of cancer, in 1894. James lived on until 1923 at Dean Hall, which the brothers had regained shortly after their mother's death. It was there that he fulfilled at least one of her aspirations by writing a life-and-letters biography of his grandfather and her father, James Louis Petigru.

The almost monthly letters his mother wrote James during the twenty years she lived in Rome form the substance of this book. In them her friends and associates come alive as she catches the essence of a life in a brief sketch or follows the story of a friend's woes and triumphs over time. In them her artist's eye informs her articulate pen to portray scenes from both city and countryside. Her letters take us with her to the ruins and churches that American tourists regularly saw in nineteenth-century Rome, as well as to parties in impressive palaces and into street life glimpsed from a window or balcony. She tracks the spa and resort life of rich Americans who mingled with Europe's reduced nobility or gaped at those who still flourished. Whether describing the triumphs and frustrations of her climbing adventures in the Swiss Alps or her horror at seeing a man plunge to his death from a Sorrento cliff, Carson draws verbal pictures.

Read as a whole, her letters chronicle the life of a mature and talented lady of the old school who spent twenty years in Rome as an artist. Whether consciously or not, she paints the warts as well as the dimples. The letters testify that she was a social snob and a domineering mother. Her insistence on a comfortable life led her to sponge on more fortunate friends. Her pride sometimes led her to revenge herself on those who thwarted her persevering though sometimes impatient will. Long ago she had herself realized that she was a woman "warring" with herself, one torn between pleasure and conscience in a battle that conscience often lost. But whatever her faults, the Caroline Carson of her letters is a woman who charmed many of those she met into close friendships, who gave generously of time and spirit to sick strangers as well as suffering friends, whose mind remained engaged in the events and intellectual concerns of her time, and whose pursuit of art never ceased. In the end, the chronicle of her Roman years opens the door on a flawed but brave and thoughtful person and to the world in which she lived.

Part I

The Excitement of a New World, 1872–1877

1872–1873

December 22, 1872, Rome, 74 Via della Croce.

The Christmas is nothing now in Rome. The Pope[1] is determined to sulk and so all the festivals and processions are suspended, or carried on with no more pomp than in any other place. N[ew] York for instance. There is the music but nothing more. By the way in all the Roman churches women's voices are banished, and none but men with those artificial voices[2] are permitted. The Catholics maintain that for many years the supply for the Popes quire is no doing of the Pope's—how then the numbers are kept up is unexplained as it is certainly not an inherited gift. Any way I think the voices are unpleasant to listen to. I cannot divest myself of the idea of these unnatural creatures. I don't imagine the angelic hosts such at all, and I really feel embarrassed when anyone says (as they do) would'nt you suppose that was a woman singing? The whole world is agreed that the miserere[3] sung in the Sistine chapel the Good Friday ev[enin]g is the most moving and solemn thing in the world. But I have not heard that, (nor shall, for the Pope has shut that off too) but I do not believe I should forget the singers in the music.

I left off here however to go to Vespers at St Peter's. One must go often to begin to understand St Peter's. But the Gothic Cathedrals seem to me more beautiful. I suppose partly because twenty years ago the style of building was to run up flimsy wooden and brick buildings in the Greek style distorted with columns like temples, with wooden pediments, and all sorts of angles that looked mean and common. So that when the real thing appears the old disgust hinders the mind from approving it. I am very glad that the church builders in N York have adopted the Gothic. The porticos and arches are too cold and naked for a northern climate. They grew up naturally here, and when the warm weather comes, I expect better to appreciate their beauty and fitness.

The climate, (as I expected) is so like Carolina that I detest it. Chilly, and damp. You make a fire in a sort of stove which smokes and goes out. So you are first suffocated and then chilled. No good glowing fire. Over head is beautiful blue & sailing white clouds. But your feet slip on reeking damp pavements, and you are one minute bathed in perspiration, and the next chilled to the marrow. Every body exclaims what a lovely day, gazing up at the sky. And I go shivering along just in the old Carolina way. If I put on a warm cloak I have to unbutton or slip it off in quarter of an hour, and then I take cold. I wonder what makes this sort of climate pleasant? I have no doubt it is lovely in the Spring. But in winter give me N York.

Here comes Christmas. I wonder where you are spending it. My heart is with you all the while. I go Christmas eve to a reception at Mr Hooker's.[4] Miss Cleveland (my Boston friend) accompanies me. There is to be music. He lives in apartments in the Palazzo Buonaparte. . . . Mr & Mrs Bunch[5] are here. Helen whom I saw at Vevey is finishing off in Paris, to be presented in the Spring, & then they return to Santa Fé de Bogota. The Bunches are very friendly & have introduced me to some nice English. They had a grand interview with the Pope through Mrs Bunch being first cousin of the Archbishop of Balt[imore]. She says the Pope is fascinating and heavenly, & Robert immediately ordered for her a cameo ring the Pope's likeness in commemoration of the occasion. I have been sadly behind hand in getting letters of introduction feeling quite indifferent. Now however I have written to Bishop Lynch[6] for some.

1. Pius IX, pope 1846–1878. In 1870, after Rome became the capital of newly united Italy and was no longer a papal domain, Pius IX refused to recognize the secular government and retreated to the Vatican.
2. Castrati.
3. Psalm 51 in the Douay Version of the Bible; Psalm 50 in the King James Version.
4. James Clinton Hooker (1818–94), secretary of the American legation in Rome in the 1850s. From his arrival in 1847 he served as a banker for Americans in Rome. At this time he was a partner in the banking firm of Maquay and Hooker.
5. Robert Bunch, in the 1850s the British consul in Charleston, was a friend of the Petigru family. Currently he was posted in South America. Helen was the Bunches' daughter.

6. Patrick Neeson Lynch (1817–82), Irish-born Catholic bishop of Charleston, who had taught Latin to CPC (this abbreviation in the notes indicates Caroline Petigru Carson).

January 12, 1873, Rome.

I went Sat[urday] 4th (my birthday) to be presented to the Pope. Miss Healy[1] daughter of the artist accompanied me, they being all Catholics & in favour the Pope having posed for Healy. The dress required is black silk & a bl[ack] lace veil on the head—no bonnet, nor gloves. I took as any one does a lot of rosaries to be blessed by the Pope. We ascended the great staircase of the Vatican wh[ich] has for sides perfect yellow marble, wh[ich] our marbled hall[2] perfectly imitates. The papal guards stand around in their striped yellow & black costumes just as Michael Angelo[3] designed their dress, in the anteroom a servant in crimson velvet suit ushered us in to the presence chamber—which is a long lofty apartment about the size St Andrew's Hall Charleston was. The ceiling finely gilded and three large pictures of martyrdoms &c opposite the windows, wh[ich] are all on the south side. The Throne was a simple red velvet chair with heavy gilding of a plain pattern & dingy, placed on a small platform covered by crimson velvet and that on two more steps covered with plain red cloth. Over head hung a lofty baldaquin of plain & rusty crimson cloth. The walls were covered by cotton cloth of the kind called Turkey red & the window curtains of the same material. The carpet plain green velveteen corduroy. Two large & handsome brass braziers in the center of the room warmed it, chimney there was none. Round the walls were wooden benches with backs and marked off like chairs each one inscribed Pius IX. On these sat the guests about 50 in number.

We waited about half an hour [until at] 11½—a side door opened and all the guests went upon their knees while the Pope entered accompanied by a Cardinal in his scarlet vestments and a number of monsignori in violet cloaks. The Pope wears a white sort of coat down to his heels with a large white cape—and a broad white sash of watered ribbon, a white scull cap & white slippers. A priest carried after him his hat a large round scarlet affair with a gold cockade but flat, and turned up on one side. He did not put it on. He looked just as you know him by the pictures—very brisk and quite lively in his air. He is 80 years old but he moves as lightly but more gracefully than Uncle Gov.[4] He immediately began to move round the circle and the usher of the chamber preceded him taking from each person his ticket of presentation and reading aloud the name to which the Pope listened as if he intended to remember it and return the call next day. He then gave his hand to have the ring kissed by each in turn, and to every three or four persons he addressed some remark to one. To Miss Healy he spoke quite affably so I had a good chance to see his countenance. His hand is very handsome and as cold as a frog. When he had completed the tour he stepped into the middle and in French blessed each and all there present and all they had on them (that for the rosaries) and their families (that for you & Willie[5]) and he said this blessing would be particularly valuable to us in the present bad condition of human affairs. Then He gave the apostolic blessing in Latin and retired—and we came away. I shall send one of the rosaries to dear Margaret.[6]

That same PM I drove with Mrs Sumner[7] to the Villa Borghese and saw Canova's[8] famous statue of Pauline Buonaparte, Princess Borghese, & many splendid ancient statues & busts. Nothing as superb as Mrs Sumner's own head. In the ev[enin]g to a little gathering at Mrs Wister's with Mrs Kemble.[9] Thursday Miss Greenough[10] drove me out to the meet at the tomb of Cecilia Metella on the Campagna.[11] There I saw Gus Schermerhorn[12] following the hounds with Prince Humbert[13] and all the finest Italian grandees and strangers pell mell. It was very gay, and [though] I don't care to go again as far as the chase is concerned, the drive is always enchanting.

Friday Mrs Kemble took me to drive. Sat[urday] I dined with Mrs Hicks[14] at a grand banquet given by her to Mr Bancroft[15] who has been taking a tour into Egypt & stopped at Rome on his way back to his post. He came to see me Friday, but I think he bears me a grudge on account of the Schuylers, and he was not as graciously overpowering as in the old time. Mrs Hicks was very splendid. The Hon George [Lee Schuyler][16] sat between her & me. After dinner I took Miss Healy and went with Mr Hooker to the Opera. The house looks very shabby in comparison of N Y Academy of Music. Today I went to church. Then to walk in a lovely garden of which I have the freedom. Mrs Bunch introduced an Englishman, Mr Esmeade who has bought himself a piece of ground for his delectation, and he has offered me to walk there and gather the flowers and make sketches as much as I please.

1. Mary Healy, later Bigot, lived in Rome with her father, French-trained Boston portrait painter George Peter Alexander Healy (1813–94), from 1867 to 1873. He was known for his portraits of distinguished Europeans, including King Louis Philippe of France, and famous Americans such as Daniel Webster and Henry W. Longfellow.
2. The South Carolina Carson plantation, Dean Hall, apparently had followed the nineteenth-century pattern of painting plaster walls to resemble marble.
3. Michelangelo Buonarroti (1475–1564), Tuscan-born sculptor, painter, architect, and poet, much of whose work was done in Rome.
4. Robert Francis Withers Allston (1801–64), CPC's uncle, was a politically active Georgetown rice planter who had served as governor of South Carolina (1856–57).
5. William Carson (1843–94), CPC's elder son.
6. A servant CPC had employed when she lived in New York in the 1860s.
7. Alice Mason Hooper Sumner (1838–90), the alienated wife of Sen. Charles Sumner (1811–74) of Massachusetts, who, after her divorce, used her maiden name, Alice Mason.
8. Antonio Canova (1757–1822) led the revival of classical sculpture in Italy.
9. Frances Anne Kemble (1809–93), the famous English actress who had married and divorced Pierce Butler, a Georgia planter, and later published a journal indicting the slavery practiced on Butler's plantation. Mrs. Wister was her daughter, Sarah Butler Wister.
10. Probably the daughter of Richard Saltonstall Greenough (1819–1904), a sculptor long resident in Rome.
11. A massive circular tower faced with marble and topped with an elegant frieze. An inscription dedicates it to the wife of M. Licinius Crassus, one of Julius Caesar's generals in Gaul. In the thirteenth century the Caetani family transformed the tomb into a defensive tower for their castle. The flat land surrounding Rome to the north, east, and south was, though malarial in the summer, a favorite locale for foxhunting and country excursions.
12. Augustus Schermerhorn, a wealthy New York socialite whose mother was CPC's friend.
13. The Italian crown prince.
14. Anette Schenck Hicks, a wealthy American expatriate.
15. George Bancroft (1800–1891), American historian and United States minister to Prussia, 1867–74. The nature of the grudge is unclear.
16. George Lee Schuyler, a wealthy and socially prominent New Yorker, often advised CPC on business matters. His first and second wives, Eliza Hamilton and her sister Mary Morris Hamilton, were both CPC's close friends. George and Mary Schuyler were traveling with his daughters Georgine and Louise.

February 2, 1873, Rome.

I find that the damp of Rome and Italy generally produces in me a variety of colds which take me on one hand or another. I inadvertently get my feet damp and the bowels undergo a tremendous commotion. I slime my feet by india rubbers and my head dissolves in water. I walk out in a velvet mantle, am racked to the bones with chill, I put on a cloak, and am bathed in perspiration. I am however going presently to put on my prophylactics and cloak and sally forth with Ostensacken[1] for a morning on the Palatine to explore the heaps of ruins which were once the palaces of the Caesars. The Porta del Populo through which one must pass to go to the Am[erican] Chapel is the exit from the superb piazza del Populo, built by Michael Angelo, but outside it is a cattle & pig market, so the slush and dirt are enormous. I got my last cold trudging through two Sundays ago. So this Sunday I turn my steps instead to the heights of the Palatine. It is not despizable to have Ostensacken for a cicerone for he is so full of knowledge, and one wants so much of that to look at Rome. . . .

I passed last ev[enin]g at Mrs Wister's. She receives every Sat[urday] ev[enin]g and I go pretty often. It is always pleasant there; unlike the Storys' which is notoriously dull. Mr Story (the Boston sculptor) is very bright and social—but some how Mrs Story is ponderous, and Miss Story plants herself about in attitudes as if her business were to furnish her father with models all her life.[2] Mrs Sumner is here looking very handsome. I find her very friendly. But I think she chafes at Sumner's taking so long to die.[3] He has outlived his prestige and his own importance and surely it would better become him to remove, and give her another chance. Mrs Kemble is grand. Mrs Hicks moves in another orbit. . . .

I had yesterday a lovely letter from Mrs Blodgett[4] from Thebes on board their Nile boat. It was very kind of her to write. I had not done so. I am so busy all day sight seeing, and painting that after I have finished my dinner I fall asleep from weariness, and letters never get written. I am shocked at doing so little. But really I don't think I get enough nourishing food. I have ate so much bread and butter since I came to Europe I am disgusted. For breakfast I have a cup of coffee, two boiled eggs, two slices of bread & butter. One O'clock Esterina[5] boils a little kettle on a spirit lamp & makes tea, another slice of bread & butter. Dinner sent from the

Trattoria at 6 PM. ½ pint that thin potage you know, a portion of fish or some thing equivalent—2 portions of roast (wh[ich] means 2 slices of beef or mutton) same one vegetable, & 2 spoonfulls of some sweet thing. This is for me & my maid. She has some cheese, a sausage or thing with a hunk of bread midday. I have plenty of wine at about 5 cents a bottle. But I don't find myself strong. If I were to order more roast sent to put up for breakfast I don't think I would eat either breakfast or dinner because it is all so much alike. When I dine out I feel better for two days. But to dine out the carriage costs lire 5 that is $1—and every time I go out in the ev[enin]g the same. I long for that coupé of our crowning aspirations. I am going this ev[enin]g to Mrs Terry's, tomorrow ev[enin]g to Mrs Harnden, who is wife of the London correspondent of the Times, whose acquaintance I made through Mrs Bunch.

Tuesday ev[enin]g Mrs Terry has a musical party at which our Miss Ried of NY is the great voice. Mrs Terry was formerly Mrs Crawford wife of the sculptor who made the statue of Washington at Richmond, the best of American things. Crawford died and left his fame to Story, and his wife to Terry a painter and a gentle kindly man. Miss Crawford is full of talent & we have painting mornings together. Mrs Terry is sister of Mrs Julia Ward Howe and of the immortal Sam [Ward]. By the way they tell me Sam made his only visit to Rome a few years ago. He dropped upon them one morning about 10 AM. Emily Crawford appeared first and he gave her a beautiful ring, and then had nothing for the others.[6] He talked brilliantly all breakfast, posted around Rome all day, was the life of a dinner party they [g]ot up for him, and went off at 11 PM saying he had seen Rome, and had <u>business</u> at Palermo, or some where—and never came back. He had merely taken Rome en passant, a man so absorbed in business, could'nt travel for pleasure!

I have come back from the Palatine having walked on and under masses of brick work that look like the crumbling old rocks you see showing up in a wild country, and then there are remains of beautiful inlaid floors, frescoed walls and mighty arches, to which the learned have affixed the names of Augustus, Nero, Tiberius, Caligula & Vespasian, as being their respective palaces—but all a mass of ruin in which the ignorant can discern little resemblance to regular habitations. There are some of the most intricate passages between enormous walls leading into little rooms mere cells, and even the three or four definite apartments are very small for all the mighty mass of building. They must have been dreadfully uncomfortable. The atrium you know was a square open to the sky with a drain just as in the yard with us. Imagine for instance the yard of 149[7] that would be a large Atrium, paved with mosaic marbles—all around open rooms long narrow and high with the walls painted beautifully in fresco—but no light except from the door opening into the atrium, down into which the rain pours at pleasure. When there are upper stories they are reached by solid marble steps and into those rooms are pierced a few small windows. But their splendour must have been in their porticoes adorned with rows of pillars and statues and fountains. There they must have lived, and have gone into the house proper only to sleep in these cells, as you may suppose prisoners disport themselves in the jail yard, & are locked up at night. There was a fountain struck me it had been flowing since the Caesar's time, but I suppose the distribution of the water may be modern, it comes through a pipe so opened that the water flies spread out like a glass globe under it is placed always a fresh bouquet of flowers and flowers grow all around the marble brim where the water falls.

1. Baron Carl R. Romanovich von der Osten Sacken (1828–1906), entomologist and diplomat who was Russian consul general in New York from 1862 to 1871, after which time he interrupted his diplomatic career to pursue his studies of insects.
2. William Wetmore Story (1819–95), Massachusetts-born sculptor and writer, had given up his law practice to practice his art in 1847 and had lived in Rome with his family since 1856. He had married Emelyn Eldredge in 1843. Edith Story had been born in the United States but grew up in Italy.
3. Charles Sumner died in 1874.
4. Probably New York socialite Elinor B. (Mrs. William T.) Blodgett.
5. Esterina Servadei was CPC's maid during her twenty years in Rome.
6. Louisa Cutler Ward (1823–97) lived in Rome with her first husband, Thomas Crawford (1813–57), an American sculptor, from 1846 until he died. In 1861 she married their mutual friend, Luther Terry (1813–1900), an American painter resident in Rome. Her brother Samuel Ward (1814–84) was a well-known political lobbyist. Emily is a misheard reference to Mimoli, the nickname of her daughter Mary Crawford. Miss Crawford is her eldest daughter, Annie.
7. CPC's New York home on West Twenty-Sixth Street from 1864 until she left in 1872.

February 16, 1873, 74 Via della Croce, Rome.

The Carnival[1] began yesterday. There was no carnival to mention last year the Papal adherents determining to sulk at the coming of the King to Rome.[2] They hold out in opposition more than ever—and the Pope asserts in all his speeches that there are no strangers in Rome and nothing going on! The hotels are all as full as they can hold, and the Government is making an effort to get up the Carnival by subsidizing to promote festivities. I have invitations to go to the balconies of many friends.

The whole parade goes on in the Corso, and people hire for the two days the little balconies and parlours adjoining of the shop keepers and hotels on the street. Mr Hooker has given me his apartment in the Palazzo Buonaparte for tomorrow, and asked me to invite all my own party to go. So I have asked Staigg & his wife,[3] Posi & Elinor.[4] The whole Greenough family, brother of Mrs Huntington & Henry Huntington[5] who has come for a little trip. Yesterday I went to Mrs Hicks's balcony. She had displayed the American flag—& got Mrs ex Sec of the Treasury McCulloch,[6] & a lot of people. She had tea and cake & wine & liquor. The street was crowded with people, and the cars with the mummers came along & were hailed as they passed. There were not many masks out, but the throwing of confetti & bouquets was pretty brisk. Mrs Edward Cooper[7] had the next balcony but one—& Miss Cooper looked very pretty in her domino and seemed delighted to pelt every body with confetti & got also pelted in return. I'll go one day to them. Mrs Sumner has asked me too, and young Mr Wurts Sec of Legation & cousin of my friend Mrs R Lenox Kennedy[8] has asked me to occupy his balcony at the Legation. So I shall see the Carnival if there is any thing to see.

Feb[ruary] 18th . . .

I am enjoying Rome now tho' half a hundred years old,—and a woman. How much more will you find that time has for you. Plod away now and keep your mind bright and your heart clean, and you will find 40 is plenty soon enough for marrying and enjoying life. As you say having but one life we must enjoy that—so never do you make the fatal mistake of marrying any woman on any account but that you love her and want to pass your time with her. Where would be the joy of riches with a disagreeable or tiresome woman tacked to you. And as for counting on dropping an uncomfortable wife—that is not to be done. One gives up position and loses the advantages either of marriage or freedom.

What avails to poor Detmold[9] his riches with such a fly in his pot of honey. He married Phoebe thinking he was gaining a step socially. If he had relied on his own talents & industry he could have climbed to any post and plucked the best flower. It is very hard to think one's youth is passing in drudgery & others are enjoying life in its heyday. . . . Now I too see people I could envy. Here is Mrs Schermerhorn with her excellent Augustus. But strange as it may seem, Gus can't please either Miss Goodman or a lovely Miss Shaw he went to America after last summer. She has taken another man— & Gus rides desperate fox hunts over the Campagna, while his mother shuts herself up and quakes. In all probability he will drop off and leave her without the coveted grandchildren for which there is such ample provision. Then I travelled with Mrs Huntington & her son—and I could not but contrast her happiness in so much, with my solitude. But I find he can't go on with the study of his profession, medicine, because he has had two or three attacks of the brain, and has to give up study. Surely I think myself more happy than Mrs Huntington.

I shall convey your declarations to the fair Anette [Hicks] as she writes her name, with only one n—which is unlucky for with the French accent circumflex it makes a—little ass. She is, the malicious say, fairer than ever. I don't know how that may be—but she is very good natured and as pleased with her riches as a child with its toys, and like a free handed child she spreads them around, delighted with the show.

You will be amazed to hear I am going to make my first appearance on the stage. Mr Story the sculptor (his family leaders of ton here & in Boston)—has written a little play Cross Purposes, and they pitched upon me to take the part of the Mamma of a jealous young wife. As I have no way of returning my obligations to society, I hold myself bound to do the things I am asked to do. So I consented to try—warning them that as soon as I began they would find me quite inadequate and dismiss me. Then came out what I did not know, that Mrs Kemble had offered to supervise the acting of the play, and hear each person their part. Mine was sent me—I read it over attentively and went quaking to Mrs Kemble but sustained by the expectation of her saying—"my dear Lady, I respect you very much, but you are quite unfit to act any part"—Instead of which I had no sooner uttered my first sentence than she stopped me to say—"It is refreshing to hear one speak who speaks with expression and knows how to use an accent in the right place!" And so on to the end. I was more surprised than I ever was in my life. The part is not at all a striking one, so you need not expect to hear of my coming out as a great actress; but it is troublesome enough. With Mrs Kemble's approval however I feel so strong that I shall face the audience with composure. The rehearsals are daily—I was there all the morning—Tomorrow rehearse at 11 AM. Lunch at Mrs Terry's at 1 PM to meet Admiral Alden.[10] Carnival at 3 with Mrs Sumner.

Thursday—Rehearsal at Storys—Carnival at Mr Wurts'. Friday dinner at Mrs Tiltons.[11] Then to supper at Mrs Hicks' to go to the Opera house ball in mask & domino. Sunday to church where Archbishop French will preach. Monday grand Lunch with Mrs Hicks. Play to come off Monday ev[enin]g. Tuesday grand Carnival. Ash Wed[nesday]—shut up. Detmold & P[hoebe] & Harriette[12] came this morning in force to see me. P has relaxed in her severity—it seems she disapproved of my coming abroad and wished to mark it by her manner! Wh[ich] of course I did not see.

1. Pre-Lenten festival culminating on Mardi Gras.
2. King Victor Emmanuel I had converted the Quirinal (built 1574–1740), formerly the pope's residence, into a residence for the royal family, which they used from 1870 to 1945.
3. Richard Morell Staigg (1817–81), American miniaturist.
4. Giulio Posi, who had taught CPC Italian in Charleston, had returned to his native Rome with his American wife, Elinor Bellinger, frequently referred to as Elena.
5. Mrs. Adèle Greenough Huntington was the sister of the sculptor Richard S. Greenough (1819–1904).
6. Susan Mann McCulloch, whose husband, Hugh (1808–95), had been Andrew Johnson's secretary of treasury but was now a private banker in Rome.
7. Cornelia Redmond Cooper, whose husband, Edward (1824–1905), was a wealthy New York manufacturer.
8. George Washington Wurts. Mrs. Kennedy was a New York socialite.
9. Christian Edward Detmold (1810–87), German-born engineer who had worked in Charleston as a railroad surveyor in the late 1820s and later became a successful manufacturer and the chief architect for the New York Crystal Palace (1853). His wife was Phoebe Crary Detmold.
10. James Alden (1810–77), newly appointed American consul general in Rome.

11. Caroline Tilton, wife of John Rollin Tilton (1828–88), an internationally recognized American landscape painter resident in Italy since 1852 and known for his landscapes in both oil and watercolors.
12. Probably a sister of Phoebe Crary Detmold.

March 7, 1873, Naples, Hotel Grande Bretagne.

Here I am in Naples on a visit to Mrs Hicks. You will be especially interested to have your letter from this spot and in this atmosphere where the fair Anette spreads her magnificence around. I must prepare you for a heart break. I do believe she is going to marry an English Lord, whom she has kept dangling after her 18 months. She won't let him come where she is, because then she must decide. Now he writes to bring her to book and she is sorely vexed. She don't want to lose a splendid position, and she don't like to put on the yoke again. But she will marry him no doubt. She won't tell his name yet even to me. But she says Gov Dix[1] knew about it & Chas O'Conor[2] and they both approve. She is really very funny about it all. And I hope that if she does take this step it will be for her happiness, for she is a good creature and like a child in her enjoyment of her riches, but with a very strong will, and very decided notions about things. I had no idea I sh[oul]d find so much interest in studying her character. She declares a great affection for you, and as I am the confidante of yours for her it is of course highly interesting to me.

I came Tuesday 4th March to stay till next Tuesday. I left Esterina in my apartment with a lira a day for her food—and I made the journey of 7 hours alone. Brig Gen Kiddor was introduced to me as a fellow passenger & he was at hand in case of need. Mrs Hicks's courier met me at the station and conveyed me safely from there. I found the fair Anette and Mrs Meagher[3] waiting for me and supper. Naples is you know one of the most beautiful spots on earth, there is an Italian proverb: Vedere Napoli & poi morire, that is See Naples and die. Earth has nothing more beautiful to offer. But it likewise might be applied to the viciousness of the dirt. Mrs Hicks however has the finest rooms in a new open part of the city, where the air is pure. And I have smelt no bad things to mention in driving through the streets, wh[ich] are twice as broad and bright as Rome and full of the liveliest looking population. Here you see just as you expect the lazzaroni[4] lolling in the sun, the shopkeepers of convenience[?] things sitting out on the side walks doing all their household work. Women & children knitting. Men tinkering pots or making nets. A woman with masses of black hair flowing over her shoulders combing away, a fellow with a hole in the knee of his trousers cracking[?] something there. The funniest little open carriages with little horses like our marsh tackies covered by old harnesses all plated with brass and brass saddles glittering in the sun. There are many handsome shops too and superb equipages and capital horses and the drive is up and down by this hotel every afternoon very like the battery in the old palmy days of Charleston. There is a park beyond this wide street where the carriages drive up or down and in the park the equestrians and walkers circulate and outside that is the sea—bounded by Vesuvius in his smoky nightcap.

Our Anette is no seer of sights. She has been here before & gone the rounds & she prefers resting after the business of the Carnival at Rome. Mrs Meagher & I took the courier and went to Pompeii. I was carried in a chaise a porteurs all around without the least fatigue, and saw everything in that wonderful place. There is the site of the temple of Jupiter, with the altar standing and many of the marble columns, and you stand on the eminence and before you stretch the line of the marble columns and Pompeii—the blue waters of the bay and the mountains like a great wing spread out opposite and the mountains covered with snow far off to the left. You feel it is a spot where one must build an altar and light incense. We got back by 3 PM—& I rested till dinner. Then came a superb English Catholic bishop. He had been all over US. & knew Bishop Lynch. Today we are going to drive[,] see the museum of Sculptures, and [go] to the San Carlo[5] this ev[enin]g. Tomorrow we go to Sorrento and I hope to visit the Blue Grotto. Tuesday I return to Rome.

1. John Adams Dix (1798–1879), former governor of New York.
2. Charles O'Conor (1804–84), prominent New York lawyer active in Democratic politics.
3. Elizabeth Townsend Meagher, widow of Thomas Francis Meagher (1823–67), who emigrated from Ireland to the United States where he was appointed secretary of the Montana Territory.
4. Loafers or beggars.
5. Teatro San Carlo, the largest opera house in Italy, was built in Naples in 1737.

March 16, 1873, Rome.

I returned 12th from Naples, where I left the fair Annette still undecided what she w[oul]d do about her lover—whose name she will not disclose yet. He is cruising in a yacht in the Mediterranean & wants to join & escort her round. She telegraphed me 13th she had decided to go to Athens & Constantinople up to Vienna & Paris. If I had consented she would have dispatched Mrs Meagher back to Paris, and taken me on the round. But I did not feel willing to put myself between the bark & the tree in that way. . . .

But I really became quite interested in Mrs H when I saw her nearer. Her idea now is that she will announce her engagement at Paris, go to NY this spring & be married & return and in July invite me to come and spend the summer at her castle—in the air of England. I confide this to you as too far away to tell any body, and as a thing I hav'nt the least idea of seeing come to pass. . . .

I am glad to get back to Rome, it has a sort of home feeling now. I am going to begin to paint—Mrs Aug Schermerhorn gave me an order too—& Mrs Edward Cooper a little order. I shall feel more contented doubtless when I have my brushes in my hand. Today I went after church to walk in Mr Esmeade's garden & took the two Greenoughs with me. They are lovely girls nieces of Mrs Huntington. We gathered large bunches of violets, mignonette & Anemones. I stopped in coming back to call on Mrs Gouv[ernor] Wilkins & the Screvens.[1] Eliza (Adele's niece) travels with them. They are quite nice girls & Mr Screven seems a jolly good fellow, very Carolina of course.

1. Gouvernor Morris Wilkins was an Episcopal clergyman. The Screvens were a South Carolina family. James Carson later courted Mary Screven.

April 22, 1873. Rome.

I am beginning to think homeopathy will have to be tried on your fever. I find people here practice it with good success, and I mean to inquire into it and let you know. Dr Barker sent a card to me this winter in one of dear Mrs Barker's letters,[1] introducing me to a young Scotch physician assistant of Simpson[2] the great surgeon & specialist in Dr Barker's line, & Dr B asked me to recommend him! I had some difficulty in finding him, as he seemed quite unknown to fame in Rome. But I heard by chance of a lady lending her teapot to Dr Aitkin & I sent Dr Barker's introduction together with my card. In a few days I r[e]c[eive]d the visit of a very nice young man, who if he had not a teapot, put a good face on the matter and was very presentable and agreeable enough. I dare say he was disappointed not to find in me a lucrative patient, but he put a good face on that to[o], & showed no disappointment, whatever he may have felt. But the other day I had a note from Miss Story asking me to come to see her mother who was ill, & sending the carriage for me, quite as if I were a doctor-in-the-middle-of-the-night. (I join this, that you may not suppose I was sent for in the middle of the night) I found Mrs Story suffering and frightened at having no good adviser, and in her strait she had sent for me as one who might know what she ought to do. I at once recommended Aitken, and she sent for him that ev[enin]g. Next day I got an elegant note from him thanking me, & saying he would call to do so in person—and he was here today, but I was out. It is likely it may be the beginning of his career in Rome. Funny is'nt it? I declare I sometimes wonder how the Romans got on before I came, I am in such demand for every thing.

I beg you will not think my vanity is blooming out, but I am really pleased and surprised to find myself in the place this society has made for me. Mr Sam Ward[3] (he who went over in the Russia with me) has a daughter married to a very agreeable little german baron Von Hoffmann who made a fortune in America & has bought a beautiful villa here at Rome. Both are in very delicate health, but they live very handsomely & give dinner parties. I dined there this winter & Mrs George Cabot Ward (aunt of Mrs V Hoffmann and next door neighbour in 10th St to Phoebe [Detmold]) drove me out. I had the post of honour by the master of the house. Monday I was invited to dinner there, & went with Mr Tilton the Painter. It was a company of 18 and the guests of the day were Matthew Arnold[4] & his wife, and to my surprise he was appointed to take me in

Matthew Arnold is wonderfully like Mr Schuyler, not so graceful, but square and stronger looking, and singularly the likeness continues in the manner too. He is quite delightful and his wife is very pretty, small and nice. After a while I told Arnold how I had laid hold on the Rugby sermons of his father as my anchor and leader when I found myself set down with two boys to bring up and never a pattern of a great boy to go by. I told him I did'nt believe the sermons had done you & Willie much good, but they did me—and put me on the track of what to expect and what to aim at. He was quite delighted to have still another instance of the widespread influence of his father's life and teachings, and then he asked minutely about each of you just as if he meant some day to know you.

Yesterday was the anniversary of the foundation of Rome, & to make up to the people for the Pope depriving them of all the religious shows, the municipality illuminated the city & hung out flags. I took an open barouche at 8 PM with Posi Elinor, Baron Ostensacken & Miss Dewey[5] as company. We drove to the Coliseum, to which long before we reached our carriage had to go in file. The streets you know have no side walks, so the carriages kept one side, and the crowd on foot the other. We got out at the Coliseum, & the carriages all passed along behind the arc[h] of Constantine and the Palatine to the street which runs at the foot of the Palatine to the Forum. The street above which Cicero had lived & Augustus—and Cataline & many more less famous. The crowd filled the Arena and sat on the tiers of arches, & one had some notion of how it looked in the old days except that then the arena was clear for the gladiators and wild beasts, & the thousands sat on the thin marble benches that rose tier above tier to the sky with the great silk velarium[6] spread over to protect them from the sun's burning rays, except when Nero w[oul]d playfully

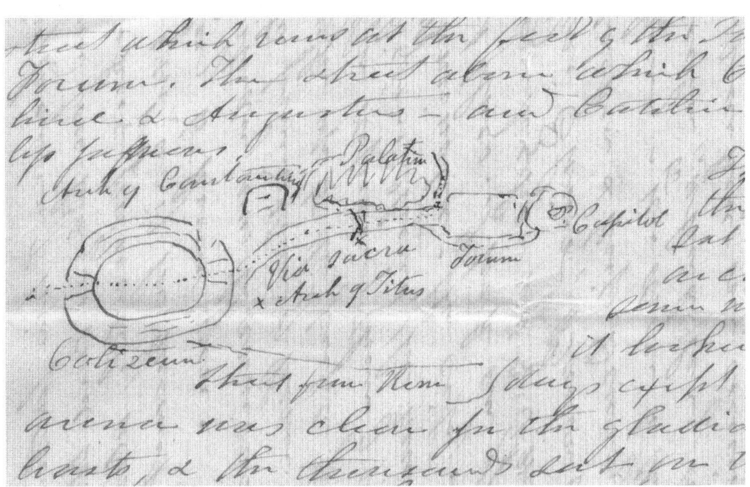

Map of ancient Rome sketched in letter of 22 April 1873.

have it drawn back half way and order the crowd to bake & die but not move from their seats till he chose to go. But to return to ourselves—We were in the midst of this immense crowd but they neither pushed nor swore nor spat—though they did smoke awfully. Presently the whole lower tier flamed out in red—then the next tier glowed a pale blue, then the third red again, & the fourth caught the blaze in blue. It was the most magnificent spectacle I ever beheld. The smoke from the Bengal lights[7] rose in all these hues high above gathered around the top and formed a glowing dome over the Coliseum as the velarium of silk must have done. I must confess that despite the immense size the air began to grow rather thick & we began to move out, & the crowd all seemed of the same mind & moved too. Posi was dreadfully afraid of some crushing as often takes place in such a crowd. But I have often been more pushed in a NY theatre door. Then we made our way too along the via sacra through the arch of Titus to see it & the Forum and the Capitol all flaming out, on top of the capitol was a blazing star, and that culminated the piece. We found our carriage with some trouble, owing to our dear Posi's giving the driver some stupid direction. But we got home safe & sound by 11½.

I got up this morning at 7 as usual had my breakfast & went to my drawing lesson. I am learning a great deal better way of buying all my colours, and I hope to send you some thing nice before long. . . . You ask for some sketches, I send you one not as a perfect specimen of beauty, but as an example of the style of painting I am adopting; to get rid of the miniature work that I hated so. This is a head I knocked off on a bit of paper I had been scribbling on as you see, & it is thought very fresh in colour—and much praised by Critics. By the way I have stumbled on a master the pendant to my dwarf Miller who taught me to paint photographs.[8] This little man Simoni[9] has lost a foot by accident. He is yet poor & little known to fame, but his painting is excellent & he will no doubt come to the height of fashionable prices. Meanwhile I am lucky in finding him out while he is obscure and can take some pains to teach me just what I have so long wanted to learn.

1. Benjamin Fordyce Barker (1818–91), a New York gynecologist and obstetrician and founder of the New York Medical College, had been CPC's physician in New York where he had pulled her through a near-fatal illness. Elizabeth Lee Dwight Barker was his wife. Both were part of the Astor social circle.

2. James Young Simpson (1811–70).
3. Not the brother of Louisa Crawford Terry but Samuel Gray Ward (1810–?), a Boston intellectual. CPC had sailed to England on the *Russia* in 1861.
4. English author (1822–88) and son of Thomas Arnold, headmaster of Rugby, a prestigious English public school.
5. Probably Mary Dewey, daughter of Unitarian clergyman Orville Dewey, who was a friend of CPC.
6. Awning.
7. Fireworks that give off a special blue light.
8. During the Civil War, CPC partially supported herself in New York by tinting photographs.
9. Gustavo Simoni (1846–1926).

May 8, 1873, Rome.

I went on Good Friday with Miss Goodridge to the Gesú. The grand central church of the Jesuits where a priest was to preach the three hours agony. It is very curious to us. The preaching is quite an occasional part of Catholic services, & is conducted in a singular way. A platform erected at one side against one of the great pillars of the church The platform covered with deep red cloth—a little table covered on one side and another little table on the steps at which sat an assistant old priest with his book. The people all huddled around sitting on rush bottomed chairs which you hire for 2 soldi[1] and plant where you can. The high altar & all the church draped in black for Good Friday.

The orator ascended the platform. He was dressed in the straight black flowing dress of the Jesuits with the red cross on the heart & string of beads a sort of raised scull cap on his head which he raised whenever he addressed God and put on in speaking to the people. His enunciation was very artificial and rhythmical very exact as you might imagine being brought up to studied & passionate declamation with an increase of precision. His face was just like a picture of abstinence. His office was to recall the passion of Christ during the three hours he was supposed to endure. He would pile up appeals to the people, and then fall on his knees and turn his discourse into a prayer accompanied by many sobs as the time went on. Then the quire struck in fully prepared for the last word of his ejaculations and sang beautiful misereres. Then the old priest on the step read out of his book a Latin Credo in which the people joined, and a few more words, which served as a text for the orator to proceed, which he putting on his cap did—again bringing himself up to the pitch of agony each time a little higher. Then again he fell on his knees, again the quire, and so round for seven times. When it was over, and he coolly walked down from off the platform & retired, without giving any blessing to the people—Who by the way whenever the preacher addressed God always slew round too dragging their chairs and then back again to the preacher. The crowd was quiet, but not much excited. Some peasant women only wept. Miss Goodridge says she has seen them with a more fiery preacher groan and prostrate themselves as in a Methodist camp meeting. The whole thing must interest the people just like the theatre. They may go and see beautiful gorgeous marbles, paintings & gilding and hear the most superb music for nothing, (but a few sous if they choose to give, & they always do).

Early one morning Easter week I heard a chanting & looked out supposing it was a funeral but it was a procession carrying the holy Sacrament to the sick, wh[ich] they do at Easter. Esterina my little maid said, if one must be sick it is a grand bella cosa[2] to be sick at Easter. About 20 boys in white carried lighted candles chanting priests following—then a canopy of gold & white under which walked the priest of eminence carrying the sacrament aloft and covered by his robe wrapped round his arm. Two other priests also bareheaded supported him, all clothed in stiff white silk embroidered in gold trailing in the dust, boys followed bearing their scull caps—and a little train of devout people joined singing the responses, & catching in little paper cornets the wax that drips from the candles, wh[ich] is sold and melted over. Also at Easter a Priest accompanied always by a boy to make the responses goes round to every house where the master does not refuse him entrance (which <u>now</u> some people do) and sprinkles each room and blesses it. He did not come while I was in but I left a lire for him with the charge to the Padrona[3] to have him especially bless your picture and Willie's. She assures me he fairly washed it in holy water and recited his very best prayers.

By the way I have taken your photo & Willie's and painted a sort of double framework for them of strawberry leaves which is greatly admired, along side your face is a Blossom.[4]

1. A soldo was then worth an English penny.
2. An excellent thing.
3. Landlady.
4. Like Jem, Blossom was a CPC nickname for James Carson.

June 2, 1873, Rome.

As I came in this afternoon from my walk I encountered a funeral, and as I have not described a Roman funeral for you I will do so now. A long train of Franciscans in brown gowns, barefoot & bareheaded tramp along taking up at regular intervals the chant of the priests in black who come behind preceding the Coffin which is borne on the shoulders of men. It is covered with a great trailing cloth of yellow ornamented with black in heavy bands and with grinning death's heads and cross bones in black. Along side are boys in stoles chanting in high voices bearing candles, and perhaps a dozen more dingy monks with lighted candles, by them run boys of the people with large sheets of grey paper twisted into cornucopias with which they catch the dripping wax of the candles. The old monks let them jog their candles about to get the wax without interrupting their chant or appearing to notice. The wax costs a great deal, and the priests regulate the required number of candles often ruining the poor family that has to pay for it all to get their relation buried out of the way.

Another funny thing is to see in the early morning the Peasants from the Campagna in their goatskin trousers, driving a company of goats to be milked at the doors of the houses. The creatures lie down and wait while one is being milked, and then the whole party trots off to an other customer's house. Only the poor people seem to take the goats' milk. There is excellent milk, cream and butter always at the numerous better stores. It is made fresh every day, and always sent you with fresh vine leaves on it and so it is put on the table. the cream (one cent's worth) is in a little bottle stopped so with a leaf folded up to make a stopper. There are plenty of strawberries now rather dearer than in NY and not near so good. The cherries however are plenty, cheap and good.

Perhaps you would enjoy the absence of ham. Not that the shops are not full of hams sausages & all sorts of porkeries, and Bologna the very birthplace of the sausage is a principal city of Italy. But the Italians have some such odd ways. Nobody boils a ham at home. You find it boiled in junks [*sic*] at the pizzacolo's [*sic*].[1] That is the grocer who has oil—candles, pickles, cheese and a most outrageous strong smell pervading his shop—so that in walking you hurry past the door. As for going inside one of them I would expect to be stifled if I ventured over the threshold. So that I have no wish to eat out of such an air a slice of pale half cooked ham. I have tried to get the Trattoria to boil me a ham. He replies that he buys his boiled from the pizzicololo [*sic*], and then cooks it over—to judge from the bits inserted in his messes, I concluded not to risk 20 francs on the ham which was to come through his hands after the pizzicarolo's. I am considering very much taking an apartment with a kitchen next winter. But it is hard to find what I should like, and the price would be double what I pay now! and that I could'nt compass. I am about to pack up for the summer move to Lucca, and I groan at the obligation, I do so hate to move.

1. Pizzicarolo, Roman usage for more usual *pizzicagnola,* a shop selling meat and cheese.

July 2, 1873, Bagni di Lucca, Italia.

All my life my great desire was to go to Rome—and here I am—and though a woman fifty years old I find myself full of enjoyment as any body I see, and more than most. . . . I left Rome 19th June by the night train, escorted to the station after my usual luck by a train of friends—Posi & Elinor[,] Simoni the painter & his brother Scipione, the Portiere[1] with my luggage and Posi's shopmen to prop up the weak places. Esterina & I were deposited in a railway carriage as they are called here—being really like large carriages on the rail. We breakfasted at the station at Florence and reached Lucca at 11 AM. There I found a note from Mrs Tilton who had kindly dispatched a carriage from the Bagni to bring me. It was in fact a comfortable stage which took all my luggage and us, the two hours journey for $2.60. I have got large comfortable rooms at Zanetta's hotel du Paix which is situated in a charming garden and a nightingale sings under my window all night long. I have a large parlour off my bedroom & a bath room to myself & then Esterina's room. I pay pretty high for it all about $24 a week. But when I consider what holes and corners I paid 30 for at Lenox![2] On the strength of your sending me $200 I have engaged a little barouche which holds two to drive three P.M's. a week. . . .

The country is a long narrow valley between beautiful mountains of the Appennines [*sic*]; with the Serchio running through it as fast as it can to join the Arno. It is fresh & cool and I am delighted with it. I paint all day. The ev[enin]gs I spend alone, and the air being quite exhilarating I don't drop to sleep as in Rome, but write my letters, and I hope to recover my reputation as a correspondent. I paint so much better since studying with Simoni, you can't think! By the way Simoni asked me if I had talked to my sons about him, and I really could'nt remember that I had. The poor little pittore[3] was very much mortified so lest he should ask me again I will tell you. It is really as hard to get a good master in Rome as in NY. Nobody who paints well wants to lose time teaching. After trying in vain, I saw one of Simoni's drawings in a shop window—inquired, found he was not an artist of repute—went after him and as he is very young (27) and poor he willingly took me at 100 lire a month—that is $20. I fell too [*sic*] like a beaver & went every morning at 10—staid till 1—ran home in the same street as my house, took a cup of tea & piece

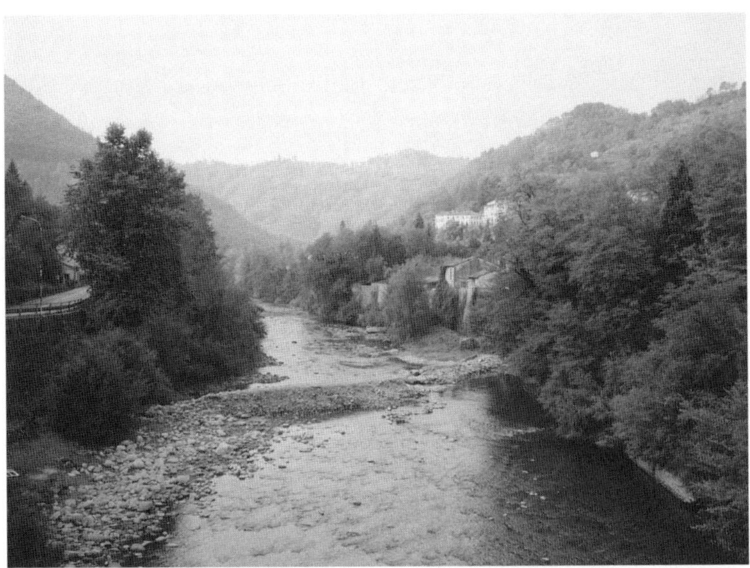

The Lima flowing through Bagni di Lucca. Photograph by William H. Pease, 1999.

of bread—returned to the studio till 3 or 4—for two months. My apartment was on the 3d floor up 75 steps. Simoni's was 116—made twice a day. You may "figure" them up. I got quite interested in my poor little master. He is 27 and he passed three years of his life from 14—in bed with a foot wh[ich] he injured in playing with some boys of his age. His father a barber was too poor to have it attended, and the end was an amputation of the foot, and the interruption of the studies he had begun at the free academy of drawing. When he got up with his wooden foot he had to work in the barber shop, and draw whenever he got a chance. He dwells with the utmost tenderness on his mother's devotion to him in his long sufferings—and then his happiness when he began to earn money by his brush and removed his mother & father along to a little house with a garden wh[ich] he made pretty for her—& then she died recommending to him his youngest brother Scipione now 19. The Father don't seem to do much good. Gustavo toils night and day to support himself & Scipione who has talent too as a painter but is as lazy as lazy can be. Gustavo is sure to make a name among the new men—but so far he is little known and gets trumpery prices from the dealers for his beautiful pictures. I hope to help him to get known.

1. Doorkeeper.
2. Town in the Massachusetts Berkshires where CPC had spent several summers while she lived in New York.
3. Painter.

July 30, 1873, Bagni di Lucca.

I expect to spend Oct[ober] in Florence it not being safe to go to Rome earlier. I want to go to Venice too, but Cholera is there. . . .

I continue to enjoy Lucca, tho' I am constrained to admit it is very hot all day. But the ev[enin]gs are deliciously cool. I enjoy the drives you procure me extremely.[1] Yesterday PM I went out on foot to sketch with Esterina carrying my apparatus. I scrambled down a path to the dry bed of the river Lima, which was running in a little stream under the banks, having all the middle dry clean stones. While I was painting the bank a small boy poked his head over my shoulder, and after a few questions & answers he ended by attaching himself to my party. His name is Pym, he is English, ten years old. He said I am the youngest & the pet of the family. I am to be a merchant, and so I am studying languages. I have three brothers. The eldest is a clergyman the second an Indian Judge and the third an engineer. At my door he said by the way this is the birth day of my eldest brother. I said how old is he? fifteen today. Also he is the clergyman. yes, he [who] is to be the Judge is 13 and the engineer 11—and I am ten. I will write to my brother and tell him I have met you on his birth day!

I went to take an ice, and took him along. Then he was going to the croquet ground, and asked me to come. No I said I am going home, "I will take you home he said, and return to the croquet ground." So we parted he having offered to come to see me and to introduce his parents to me. I never saw such a quizzy little old man. This morning he popped in before 12. He had been to morning service and wanted to know if I would come to the Croquet or the Casino evidently that there he might bring me & his mother together. I told him I never went, & if he would like me to know his father & mother he must bring them to see me. He said he told them he had made a friend and she had given him an ice, & they were much obliged to me. I went on with my drawing and he went round and poked into every box & book I have, presently I looked round & he was in my room diligently turning over everything in my brush basket. When he was gone I really went to see if every thing was there. So queer was the little imp. He examined your photo & Willie's in the strawberry leaf frame. He fixed upon Willie by name, but you he guessed to be George or Frederick, & gave it up. I told him I would write and tell you about him. . . . I must tell you about the Terrys and Tiltons and Storys that you may know the people I live with. But not tonight, for I must say good bye my darling.

1. James Carson had sent her $200 that made these drives possible.

August 9th, 1873, Bagni di Lucca.

It is so dreadfully hot this morning I can't open my window to see to paint, but through the Venetians filters enough light for me to write to you. Besides I feel like a long talk, and so I take a holiday from my incessant brushes. I am sorry for the beauty of the last specimen does'nt come up to the merit of the execution but I'll send you another before long. Meanwhile I enclose a slip which speaks volumes! It is from the pen of Miss Anna Brewster[1] to whom Dr Dewey gave me a letter. She is a wonderfully bright active little lady not at all like our "old maid" She has made herself a personage in Rome, has a "salon" receives all the lions and is a correspondent of several Am. newspapers. This notice you see was intended for Phila[delphia], but she sent me this copy that I might hear the blast she has given me. If she can make the travelling Americans think according to this I shall be very flourishing.

I send likewise a list of the company at the Baths of Lucca that you may see what grandees I move among. That is I drive out and see these princes & marquises pass if I only could distinguish them by their looks from the common herd. I am sorry to say however that except the Princess Russoli who is granddaughter of Lucien Buonaparte[2] Prince of Canino who is a superb looking creature, the rest are in no wise to be remarked. It is funny to see the immense number of American princesses one meets in Europe from the rage the Americans have to flourish in matrimonial alliances. There is not one of them who becomes her coronet as our Minna[3] does, and to think of her getting nothing better than Auschott.

Last ev[enin]g I went for the first time to the Casino Reale where there are billiards reading room and balls twice a week. By ill luck the Buonaparte Princess was not there, nor any of the real Italian swells except Malatesta[4] who is a stumpy young fellow with a head like a cannon ball with a blacking brush upon it. The field was left to an English Lady who had married one of the Chigi's.[5] She looked very stylish, but the belle of the ev[enin]g was the Marquise de Talleyrand, a Miss Curtis of Boston I believe,—but such a Curtis I never beheld. She looked like a very battered broom stick with all sorts of tinselled finery hung upon it, she managed to sit so as always to exhibit her legs up to the knees under pretense of showing her feet which were only pretty in comparison to the rest of her body. She has fine teeth, and so she grins incessantly, she flung about in the most extraordinary fashion, and altogether her whole appearance was the most vulgar and impudent I ever saw. Two or three men were always around her. I suppose she says anything and passes for a wit, at that cheap rate. It seems she was to have money of course, <u>but</u> her father failed and Talleyrand kept her all the same which is quite wonderful. He seemed pleased with her still. He is a little man somewhat like Crafts[6] only younger dark and very common looking.

With me went to the ball Mme Cortazzo who is another specimen of these marriages. She is no other than niece to our illustrious Gen Cullum.[7] Miss Huydekoper from Penn[sylvania] where her father is very rich. Nothing must serve her but to marry a Neapolitan of good enough family and a painter of considerable success now.[8] However he had nothing when she married and lived with him in rapture five years her father supplying the means. Then Cortazzo broke off took up with a woman old and evil at Paris, quit the apartment where they were living and took up his abode with the woman. Gen Cullum's niece could do nothing but wring her hands and wait for him to come back, but he would'nt come, so ill & broken hearted she has come to Italy, still lingering with the hope he will come to his senses and come back to her; for strange to say she loves him still. . . .

By the way I am one of the Commissioners on the Roman Board for nominating the Centennial at Phila[delphia]. Perhaps I may come over to that. If we gain the law suit[9] this winter I may need to go back before you will be free to come to me. I am more comfortable than I ever was here, but I don't think I can hold out to live away from you very long.

Tonight I am going with Mrs Tilton & Mme Cortazzo & Mr McLean (An old delightful Scotchman) to a concert at the Casino of Chev de Lyro, who is a brilliant man with an odd story. An Austrian officer of high family chose to marry a governess, & in the Aust. army the officers are required to have a certain income in marrying. So he had to retire on the reserved list & he gives lessons on the piano. The fair cause of the sacrifice is they say a very ordinary good woman who with the two children is in the Tyrol while de Lyro is plying his trade here; and the younger Miss [Mimoli] Crawford for want of another is flirting dreadfully with him, and making one awful talk.

1. Anna Hampton Brewster (1819–92), Roman correspondent for the *Philadelphia Bulletin* and *Public Ledger*, the *Boston Advertiser*, and various popular magazines.
2. Brother (1775–1840) or nephew (1803–57) of Napoleon Bonaparte.
3. Minna Detmold married a German count, Gaston Auschott.
4. Member of the family who had ruled Rimini from the thirteenth through the fifteenth centuries.
5. Prominent Roman family.

6. George W. Crafts, a Charleston lawyer.
7. George Washington Cullum (1809–92), West Point graduate with a pre-Civil War reputation as an engineer. During the war he served as chief of staff to General-in-chief Henry Wager Halleck (1815–72), whose wealthy widow he married in 1875. The Huydekopers made their home in Meadville, Pennsylvania.
8. Oreste Cortazzo.
9. In 1866 CPC began a legal battle to regain Dean Hall, the Carson plantation sold in 1858 on which CPC held a mortgage to be paid in United States currency. It had, however, been resold in 1863 when the mortgage was paid off in Confederate money. CPC's many legal actions to regain possession were still in the courts when she died in 1892.

August 24, 1873, Bagni di Lucca.

[Mme Cortazzo and I] set out to see a great spectacle at Siena, where for time immemorial they hold a race[1] on 15th Aug[ust] retaining the costumes and business of the middle ages! So it would have the effect of a real tournament. In this village of [Bagni di] Lucca we lie perched and cool like a cootah[2] in his shell, the minute we poke the head out it is pounced on by the sun like the cootah's head by the cook's fork, and plunged bodily we are in a boiling cauldron. By carriage & rail we roasted ten hours to Siena, and found the town full to overflowing every spot taken, and the race deferred till 17th to keep the strangers for more picking. As we could'nt stop three days with our chemise of change, we drove around from 6 P.M. to 8 ½ saw the beautiful Cathedral the Piazza for the race and the Park which is about as large as White Point Garden at Charleston. But instead of the sea it is on a high central plateau; with the most delicate air in Italy blowing over it. A band of music, a great crowd of people in holiday attire (but no middle age costumes) and a lot of Princes & Princesses driving in gorgeous equipages. One Lady dressed in a rose coloured gauze was alone in a carriage with servants in blue velvet liveries. Another lady & gentleman had a superb carriage two splendid footmen behind, and the horses driven by a postillion seated on the near horse. He was dressed like a jockey for a race, in a yellow satin jacket, white silk trousers, buff maroon boots, Blue velvet cap and a white curled wig. He was superlative.

I was quite satisfied to go off at 8 AM without any more costume. Mrs Cortazzo was ill all night and I had doubts whether she could move on, but she rallied like a hero's niece and was come back at our appointed time stopping three hours at Pisa. There I saw the famous leaning Tower, and the magnificent cathedral and the Campo Santo, so called because the crusaders filled their ships with holy earth from Jerusalem, and brought it to Pisa then a great sea port, tho' now five miles from the Mediterranean where Leghorn has grown up on the deposit of the Arno which has sent Pisa inland. In the holy earth only a few great personages have been buried, all round the four sides is a gallery open to the campo with exquisite light columns, against the walls are world famous frescoes—wonderfully preserved when one thinks of all the rain and storms that must have driven against them besides the wars and battles. Some of the beautiful sculptures have been injured by soldiers knocking off hands in sheer wantonness.

I have also been on a moon light pic nic up a mountain to which we went on donkeys. I contributed a plum cake or seed cake, and 2 doz little cakes which cost altogether $1.60. One observation I must make while thinking of it. It rains, and we had a hail storm the most tremendous I ever saw—the ground was white for two hours with the hail stones, and the vines corn & ches[t]nuts are greatly damaged. But for all that I have not been kept in a single afternoon all summer by rain. It clears up, and the ground becomes dry in a few minutes.

1. Il Palio.
2. Charleston pronunciation of cooter, aquatic turtle common to southern coastal waters.

September 7, 1873, Bagni di Lucca.

I gave you some insight into the people here. Now all the flirtations are winding up for the season. Baron Von Rabe[1] made a formal offer which Miss Annie Crawford accepted to the immense satisfaction of her step father Mr Terry no less than of the whole family. So cantankerous is the fair Annie that notwithstanding all her brilliant parts, they feel their house will be much more comfortable without her.[2] How the Baron's mother and sister in the chateau in Pomerania are going to enjoy themselves nobody knows yet. De Lyro had to tear himself from the feet of Mimolee the other

Crawford and go to his drill in Austria. The day after he left came a distracted letter from his wife in the Tyrol to Zanetta the hotel keeper to ask what had become of her husband who had ceased to write to her and she was afraid he had gone off with somebody. After all this the Terry party departed to Leghorn and those who were left behind discussed them. There are several more affairs of the same sort at hand but not quite so striking, so I pass them over. Gen Cullum's niece Mrs Cortazzo has gone to Paris to meet the Gen, and with a faint hope of reclaiming her recreant sicilian husband, who is not worth running after.

I rode Sunday P.M. on donkey with Mrs Tilton to the Bagni Caldi[3] to see Miss Brewster who is one of the notabilities I must introduce you to. Hers was the notice of Mrs Carson's studio wh[ich] I sent you. She is a bright little woman coquettish at 54 and has attached to her service a young sculptor Harnish[4] whom she pushes on, and in return he is devoted to her as son friend or lover according as one is malicious or not in viewing the connection. I suppose she has promised to leave him her little property; and mean while he is a domestic fellow who w[oul]d rather have a home than live scrambling in his studio. Mrs Tilton is my main stay in this society. . . . We w[oul]d have gone together to Venice but for the cholera. I shall stop two weeks longer and then go to Florence for a month. I w[oul]d take an apartment in Rome & furnish it & have my own kitchen if I had money enough. I dread returning to the trattoria dinners. I don't get enough to eat, and it is so unwholesome. I fear my digestion will be ruined and then what shall I do?

1. Erich von der Rabé, a Prussian army officer wounded in the Franco-Prussian War.
2. Annie bitterly resented her mother's marriage to Luther Terry to whom she attributed the severe reduction in Louisa's income that was, in fact, caused by disastrous speculations carried out by the New York cousin who managed the Ward family trust.
3. The warm springs, one of several spas at Bagni di Lucca.
4. Albert E. Harnisch (1843–?), American sculptor who shared Anna Brewster's fifteen-room apartment in Rome.

September 14, 1873, Bagni di Lucca.

It often comes over me that all the beauties of art and nature are as nothing to the company of my children, and it seems impossible to hold out on this side the Atlantic. Often times I am so hungry to see you that I have a great pain in my heart and go sighing all day. Never will you know how much I love you. Never understand the passionate sorrow I have for each word or look of sadness or pain of your childhood. You often laugh and run on about [your dog] Box and your schooling, and my own discipline of you. But you dont know how I bear in my heart every stroke ever laid upon you, and the pain it cost me then, now and always. I feel that never till we are both passed into the world of spirits will you know how dear you have ever been to me. You know how I did literally coin my blood for you to carry you through the mining school and at any minute I would lay down my life for you with joy. You remember that night in your room when I was so near death. I thought myself dying that time. You remember you sat by me holding my pulse and put the strong hartshorn I did smell to my nose. I felt the day would dawn and I should not be there. And then I said in my soul how will Jem get through his college and the fever seemed to stay my spirit on the eve of departure. This is all as real to me as any act of my life.

September 30, 1873, Bagni di Lucca.

What do you think has happened? I put your check away in happy security. Heard 8 days ago of Jay Cook's failure without a pang—and today went to draw my money—and—I dont know if you may get it back at Salt Lake[1]—or if by writing I ever shall get it from McCulloch. I hope at least you had'nt bought from them the 2nd £20 you promised me. I was awfully put up at it. Fortunately I had drawn the £10 but a week before so that is sound—at hand. . . .

Posi has engaged for me an apartment with a kitchen, so this winter I will not kill myself with eating messes out of a tin box, and topping off my dinner with hartshorn to digest the wretched stuff. Mrs Tilton & Mrs Crowninshield and the Newberys[2] have all been very kind in this attack of mine, standing around as the ladies used to do in N York. It is only in Charleston I used to be let to lie and die or get up as it chanced by myself. . . .

To lose my hundred dollars is heavy. But it was my fault for not drawing immediately. The Italian credit is so low I never care to have much of their paper on hand expecting the Italian Banks always to bust up. And I supposed a check on London better than gold, not considering it wasn't a Bank of England. One pays awfully for experience. This must profit both you and me in such matters.

1. James Carson was working in Utah at this time.
2. Helen S. Fairbanks Crowninshield, a wealthy Boston woman who, with her painter husband, Frederic Crowninshield (1845–1918), lived in Italy until 1878. The family of Walter Newbery was English.

October 2, 1873, Bagni di Lucca.

I add this letter to tell you the £20 are safe in my pocket. The day after the flurry of 30th Sep[tember] came the money changer to say he w[oul]d take it. So I took the money yesterday, losing on the transaction but 8 lire—about $1.60 which I thought better than to bother you to reclaim at the Salt Lake Bank, or on my part to risk holding it any longer. I believe McCulloch in London is supposed all sound. . . .

The Crowninshields went yesterday, & I have engaged their cook Mariano for the winter. A man in Rome costing very little more than a woman and being twice as useful. For the Italian women of all classes are kept very much like Turkish females in the matter of not being allowed to walk into the streets unguarded by a husband or father.

I can't send my maid for anything scarcely, and as for going out in the ev[enin]g and having her come for me it is out of the question. I had this summer a regular Contadina[1] come from the mountains to me as a model. She could'nt come along the great highroad at high noon without the escort of her father. Perhaps it comes of the terror of brigands who used to pick up every girl on the road in the old times. But why in the cities it is so, nobody can tell. One w[oul]d suppose the men were devouring beasts. But as far as I can see they are innocent beings enough.

The Newberys are devoted to me. I thought I had fallen on relations to your professor. But not at all. Mr N is an English merchant—who has had twenty years in America and left two sons there. There are two daughters very nice girls, and one son Walter who reminds me of you in his schemes. He has been in the merchant service in the US—and in

England—and has voyaged all over the world and had all sorts of adventures, and now he has set up a sawmill on the Tiber at Rome!

1. Country woman or peasant.

October 12, 1873, Florence.

I left the Bagni Monday 6th and am very comfortably lodged at Mme Bacbinse's pension (as boarding houses are called all over the continent). There are none but English and Americans in the house. Indeed it is funny to find how one is always immersed in a stream of the English speaking nations.

November 6, 1873, 155 Via delle Quattro Fontane, Rome.

This is my new address. I reached Rome four days ago. It was raining like the mischief when I arrived and I never saw such confusion as at the station. I had for compagnons de voyage a certain French of Texas his wife and daughter, whom you may have heard of there. . . . These Frenchs are rich, and when I found them travelling 2nd class I thought I ought to save money too, so I had a mighty uncomfortable seat all day, and in getting out found some one had stolen my English umbrella making my expense much more than the 1st class. So I am cured of that.

This apartment was occupied by the Youngs[1] four years ago, and always by people who were delighted with it, so I thought I had got a treasure. I engaged before hand a man to cook & to escort me about wh[ich] is very necessary in Rome where you can't send a young maid servant out alone on errands as with us. I have had four days hard work in trying to squeeze into my quarters. They are too nice. Full & blocked up with furniture so that I cant bring in my trunks nor establish my easel. It did finely for travellers with a single trunk no servant and trattoria fare. The cook has just told me he don't like it—so I shall let him go—and try something else. It rains incessantly and I can't go out . . . because the streets, all the principal ones are torn up for new sewers and no carriage can pass. Such is the Roman management, instead of mending the sewers

Caroline Carson, **Bagni di Lucca, 1874.** *Courtesy of Ashton and LaVonne Phillips.*

when the town was empty they wait till the strangers are coming and make the streets impassable. All the shop keepers are in despair at it.

1. Henry E. Young, a Charleston lawyer, handled CPC's South Carolina financial affairs.

December 2, 1873, Rome.

Nothing has turned up since I wrote but Dudley & Mrs Field[1] on their way to Australia. Doubtless you have seen in the papers notice of his success in the Italian Parliament in getting Mancini[2] to advocate the arbitration principle. There was a public dinner given to the English advocate Richard[3] and Dudley—at which DD delivered a speech in Italian! Who on earth but a Field would have undertaken a speech written or not in a tongue he don't speak! Mrs Dudley nearly gave out, and wanted to winter in Rome and meet DD in Geneva next summer. He was willing to let her stop, but wanted to take her along, and not only that but take that grandchild of hers too, and had provided her with an accomplished woman-courier-maid. She asked me to advise. I thought it over a night, and told her to go. She could but die of fatigue, but I did'nt think she would, and at all events it would never do to let Dudley go away from her to have some body or other tell him he had a wife too old to go about with him. She started you may be sure, and she was quite right to do so.

155 and 159 Via delle Quattro Fontane. Photograph by William H. Pease, 1992.

1. David Dudley Field (1805–94), an expert lawyer and legal reformer. His draft of an international code of law was translated into Italian and published in 1874. Mary E. Carr Field (?–1876), his third wife, had children by a previous marriage.
2. Pasquale Stanislao Mancini (1817–88), Neapolitan jurist and minister of justice in the left-leaning cabinet of Agostino Depretis. He taught law at the Universities of Turin and Rome.
3. Henry Richard (1812–88) had, in July 1873, carried the English House of Commons in support of his motion favoring arbitration to settle international disputes. Subsequently he traveled widely in Europe to promote his cause.

December 20, 1873, 155 Quattro Fontane.

I am to dine with the Story's Xmas day, & I have another invitation for same at Tilton's. Story's introduce me to all the big wigs—Lady this & Lady that, which is quite contrary to Mrs Story's custom as She has always been accused of suppressing the Americans. Either she thinks I do her credit or that I am harmless. I enjoy all the fine things and fine people.

Here I have been interrupted to receive the visit of the Duke of Sermoneta,[1] who is also Duke Caetani the oldest title of Roman nobility (equal with the Massimo who is descended from Fabius Maximus[)]. But the Sermoneta Duke is held from personal character as well as position as the head of all. He is however blind, for the past few years, but nevertheless most active in politics. My little maid Esterina is of a family of dependents, and last winter he came three times in his carriage to my door to settle something about her papers. You know all Continentals high to low must have papers. This winter I have thought of changing Esterina for a more useful sort of a maid if I could find one. And she ran off to the old Duke and asked him to come, and intercede with me to keep her. Monday he came, I was just at the door so he said he w[oul]d return next day. And sure enough Tuesday here he comes climbing up this breakneck stairs with his secretary, and under the guise of recommending Esterina he sat an hour discussing about everything, and asked leave to come again.

This is Sat[urday] and he has brought me his photograph and a photograph of a grand banquet he gave in the Theatre on his election to the Italian Parliament. All Rome is talking of his marriage with a Miss Seymour, English, which has been broken up by his not making the settlements she demanded. The old fellow has been twice married and says as he made no settlements before he won't begin now; and so his marriage is off.

Esterina has immediately made up her mind that an American would suit the Duke far better, and she could remain permanently in office! What do you say? He is blind he is near Seventy. But has one of the greatest positions in the world, and is one of the best and kindest of men according to all voices. I am sure you can't accuse me of not furnishing a scheme or two in my turn. While the Duke was here, Mrs Cortazzo called and also Dr Chotard head of the American College of the Priests. Esterina shut the door on them remorselessly. I shall have to get her nonsense out of her head somehow. I must write a note to Dr Chotard (not giving the reason for his exclusion of course) but apolegising [*sic*] that Est. did not know that all consignees must fall before one of his dignity. As an artist I am supposed to be at work, and "la Signora non riceve"[2] is accepted without offence.

1. Michelangelo Caetani, Duke of Sermoneta (1804–82), internationally known Dante scholar as well as a liberal who had once held political posts under Pope Pius IX but now served in King Victor Emmanuel's government. He was blinded in 1865.
2. Madame is not receiving [at this time].

1874

January 3, 1874, Rome.

I am very busy with the affairs of the season, visiting and making up my mind to take an apartment for three years time so as not to be so bothered as I am now. This one does not suit me nor last years neither. I want one where I can have a light for my painting and sun on my bed room—and a kitchen. I wish a one I have found next door to this in the quarter most pleasant to live in. I can have it for $400 a year, but I must furnish it myself and I am awfully perplexed what to do. I am so afraid of getting beyond my depth. . . . And if I let this apartment go, I'll not find another to suit me half so well in all Rome. My old Duke comes along in his visits and is very interesting, but there are many buts. . . .

Jan[uary] 6th

Annie Crawford was married 29th Dec. First at the Prussian Legation and after at the English Church. Then there was the reception, and in the ev[enin]g they went off to Albano where they now are. The whole party was magnificent—especially Von Rabe's brother in the white uniform of the Prussian Cuirassiers.

The wedding is made doubly notable by the conclusion of the great Story & Terry-Crawford war[1] which I told you has for 15 years desolated the American Colony at Rome. Edith Story who had never taken any part in the bitter words was asked to go to the wedding. And most flattering to me, instead of any of her life long associates has she asked me to escort her to the Church. I thought it so solemn an occasion that I threw over

Mrs Tilton [and] Mrs Cortazzo . . . and went with Edith. She was welcomed most affectionately by the Bride & all the family. Next day Mrs Story wrote a note to Mrs Terry to whom she has never spoken since she was Mrs Crawford, and now they are Louisa & Emelyn again, and are driving with each other. Everyone professes to be pleased; but I am inclined to think they will miss the excitement of watching the feud. . . .

Today is the Epiphany, a grand occasion of festivity in the churches and piazzas. All the people go about blaring fiery trumpets and buying dolls. I sent you last year a Bambino from Ara Coeli,[2] and I am going there this P.M. again, and tonight to the Marionettes which puppets are to exhibit the play of Joan of Arc. We have taken the whole theatre and are going in force for 20 cents apiece! wh[ich] is twice the fare because we have had the theatre cleaned for us. It's great fun, how I wish for you & Willie.

My friend Newbery has sent the enclosed from Naples "for Jem". . . . You see the cut. That is done by the Douane to fumigate the letters because there was cholera in Naples, and the Italians still believe in Fumigations. For two months all passengers arriving in Rome from any quarter were driven into a room & nearly stifled with some horrid fume before being allowed to proceed to their hotels.

1. Thomas Crawford and William Story had been friends from the mid-1840s until late in 1856. Yet Story was not among the 45 artists and others who met in Rome to commemorate Crawford's death in 1857. Their families' feuding probably originated in Story's apparently unwilling departure, early in 1857, from his studio at Crawford's Villa Negroni. Crawford, however, wrote his wife that Story had left his establishment because the work he was doing there was finished. At the time of his death Crawford was the best-known American sculptor working in Rome, while Story's only known work was a marble memorial to his father, United States Supreme Court Justice Joseph Story (1779–1845).
2. Santa Maria d'Aracoeli, the Church of the Altar of Heaven, whose Cappella del Santissimo Bambino holds a figure of the infant Christ believed to have been carved from the wood of an olive tree in the Garden of Gethsemane.

January 15, 1874, 155 Quattro Fontane.

Ever since I came to Rome this winter my eyes have been bothering me. For more than six weeks I have had to leave off painting, then reading, and finally to write was difficult. Besides my digestion was gone to the mischief. At last I said to Dr Aitken "there must be something behind all this,["] thereupon he looked about him and pounced upon the green paper of my salon, scraped off some, had it analysed and [it] proved to be Thiel's Green—arsenic.[1] I have had the mischief and all to make the Padrona take it down and put up another. I have recovered my digestion, but my eyes are still inflamed and swollen.

I shall be glad to have an apartment of my own, where whatever the worries I may have will be under my own control. These furnished rooms are full of furniture none of which suits. For instance my kitchen is full of superb copper vessels big enough for preparing dinners for a hotel, and nothing in which I can cook mine with less than a sack of charcoal to bake a potatoe. And when I go away they will most likely make me pay for retinning the whole array.

1. Arsenic compounds were frequently used as pigments in green and yellow paint.

February 2, 1874, 155 Quattro Fontane.

I have been very much afflicted by the effect of the arsenic green. . . . The paper was changed, the carpet taken up & shaken, and a general upset of the house for a week had to be endured. The Storys & Tiltons threw open their doors to me. Storys invited me to sleep there as well as to spend all the day. However that I did not do. My digestion & my head soon recovered—but the granulations having taken hold on the eyelids are harder to get rid of—and I suffer still. I can't read at all. . . .

Do you remember Gov Morgan[1] whom I had the passage at arms with in Washington when as Senator I thought he did'nt pay any attention to R. M's[2] letter of introduction? Well he and his wife have turned up as every one does in time at Rome, and he has under my guidance bought a picture of Simoni and ordered a drawing of me. Posi is the only person I don't seem to be able to push. the truth is it is vain to set up those who will not or cannot make themselves useful and agreeable. Dear Posi is too inert and dull in his manners and people <u>will not</u> take him for a teacher; the disappointment of his hopes scares and embitters him and he grows so morose I don't know how it will end. . . .Van Winkle[3] has departed for

Naples which is a great loss to me, as it was very convenient to have an agreeable young man to go out with me. The Duke of Sermoneta has not come for a week to see me. By the way he told me he had never thought of asking the English spinster to marry him, nor how could he blind and sad ask any lady. Still I fancy the notion may have come put in his head by the report if nothing else, and he may have gone off to make the proposition. She is an awful looking dragon of a woman whom if he could <u>see</u> he would fly from.

1. Edwin Denison Morgan (1811–83), Republican governor of New York 1859–62 and United States senator 1863–69.
2. Richard Milford Blatchford (1798–1865), New York lawyer, Republican activist, and an admirer of James L. Petigru. CPC had chaperoned his daughter's European tour in 1861.
3. A young New York clergyman.

March 10, 1874, 155 Quattro Fontane.

The labour and pain of poor Mrs Mott's[1] illness and death . . . is not yet ended. For very naturally her friends all write to ask details of her illness, so that I have had to go over it till I am nearly destroyed. And now begin to come the letters of her family full of thanks almost as overwhelming—and some requiring to be acknowledged. I feel that I am only in a small measure returning to them some of the kindnesses which good souls so long lavished on me. And would you think it dear Jem there are many persons here in Rome who rise up to comfort and to help me through all this in every way. Coming to drive me out—bringing me beef tea & medicines and flowers, and invitations to dinner, tea, lunch, every possible thing that one person can do to lift a burthen from another. Truly God is very good to me, and sends his servants to me always! I know very well that I am not so much more charming than other people, but that I simply try to do well and trust in God to bring me through—and He does. I look back through life and see so many evils turned into good that now I fear nothing. Nothing but disgrace. That may I be spared! In the horrid state of public morals it behooves each man of us to take heed lest he be drawn in by extravagance and speculation to do things which at the outset he would shrink from in disgust. . . .

I am very glad to have your consent to my marrying the Prince Caetani. It leaves my hands quite free. But he has'nt asked me yet,—and I don't think he has any idea of doing so. The story of the English Lady was made up of the whole cloth. And she encouraged the report. But he is really too much afflicted by his blindness and political disappointment in the way things are going in Italy to think of any thing else—besides the pleasure of coming to talk to me. Which he does steadily—and his servant who comes with him says he goes no where except to his son & daughter and to me, and three times to Mrs Story, where I have arranged the interviews. He is really a most eminent and original man, and every one tries to get him to their houses in vain. His blindness makes him very shy of general society. It is singular for an Italian Prince they say [of the] oldest & highest house in Rome to have chosen and followed the life he has had. Always in study and active effort to increase the education of the people and open their minds to [an]other sort of existence than the lazy ignorance they lay under. He has always been a liberal and he was foremost in bringing Victor Emmanuel to Rome. But like most reformers he lives to see his work either go far beyond him; or be turned aside from first intentions. And the latter is the Duke of Sermoneta's case. He sees the king instead of applying himself to consolidate Italy and give it a good & stable government, occupied only with the chase & wasting immense sums on building & enlarging Palaces already enormous and by a complicated system aggravating the taxes which are five times as much as they were under the Pope, with no corresponding increase in commerce or agriculture. So that the Duke is very sad and were it not for his wonderful use of his beautiful language, and the inexpressible wit of his discourse he would be but a dull companion. I am delighted to have his visits, but I should think many times, before undertaking anything else—I can tell you. So you have not disposed of your Ma you see!

1. Arabella Mott, wife of Alexander Mott, a New York physician.

April 2, 1874, 155 Quattro Fontane.

As I have not been able to paint all winter I have gained nothing, and I am rather frightened. . . .

Phoebe [Detmold] has at last had to get down from her high horse in her intercourse with me. I think the dig I gave her about Auschott[1] did her a great deal of good—and as I persevere in my lofty way & would not go to drive with her on short notice, she has come to writing in most flattering phrase to invite me—and having achieved that I am now quite affable to her. I am bound to confess however I don't think it altogether my tactics, but that I have for my friend so illustrious a Prince as the Caetani. He by the way was here this morning. His time is from 10 to 12—then he goes home to the unconsiderable Italian breakfast—& then to the Parliament. All winter that has been his proceeding except when he used to come at 5 P.M. after the Parliament on the cold & dark ev[enin]gs. The consequence is he has the coast clear, as nobody calls at those hours. Poor dear, I am very fond of him, and am very glad that in my society he finds some relief from the dreariness of his darkness. Now we are reading Dante—all of which he knows by heart, and I find him a professor very superior to our excellent Posi.

1. Gaston Auschott, though he was a count, was a penniless younger son.

April 13, [1874,] 155 Quattro Fontane.

I expect to move in two weeks. I have one carpet down & two mats, & my furniture was to have gone in today but it is pouring. I am attending sales and trying to get handsome old things for my drawing room. I bought a Cardinal Ambrogiani's throne chair the other day at a sale for $10. It is all red velvet and gilding, and when I took my seat upon it Mme Cortazzo said I looked very grand. Cardinal Bonnato head of the Jesuits died, and his things are to be sold at the Propaganda[1] Wed[nesday] & Friday, and I mean to put in for some choice pieces. I hope I'll not get swamped. But these old things are so much handsomer than modern upholstery that I can't endure to give the same money for the new things. But I get all the working chairs new for Roman chairs go down in the most awful way. Twelve in my salon this winter have collapsed thus. I shall have caned bottoms which are strong (as you know) and a few Cardinals to give dignity to the set out. I am awfully reluctant to begin the move. I haven't you nor anybody to hang pictures and help me. Posi has grown so lazey I never call him, tho he'd be ready enough to come.

1. The Office of the Congregation for the Propagation of the Faith was located in Rome rather than the Vatican.

May 17, 1874, 159 Quattro Fontane.

You must not suppose I have relinquished the search for your ring. But it is not easy to get the right thing, especially for a person ignorant of intaglios like me, but bent on not being taken in to get a poor thing. It would seem easy to find somebody who does know to help. But everybody gives a loose sort of opinion, and no one can be relied upon to follow up the matter to a good conclusion. I must end by informing myself about gems and learning to choose on my own taste. After hunting in every direction, I concluded to put myself in the hands of Castellani[1] the great jeweller and antiquarian. Not Augusto the jeweller, but Alessandro his brother the antiquarian who furnishes the most superior collections, & presents for all the great people of the earth. He told me he had nothing fit for me in his loose stores, and of course could not break a collection to give me one. But he was expecting a lot from Naples, and he would help me select one before putting them in his collection—if I w[oul]d wait ten days. I did—they had'nt come—and I wait two or three weeks more, it being too late to get it to you this spring by some returning American I thought it better to wait. Three days ago I went—Castellani had gone away for the summer! And everybody says he will keep promising to all eternity. The truth is a common place stone is to be had any where, and they cheat you into paying for modern things as if they were valuable antiques—and that is what makes me so cautious. The minute you want an extra fine thing the price trebles like that of diamonds on the size and water.[2] I went back to Depoliti[3] who is an esteemed antiquarian. He has plenty of things for 50 lire, 100—but when you want a fine one, the price jumps into the thousands at once. I took a head of Agrippina cut extremely well in red Carnelian[4] of the first century. I did it somewhat because so many persons here say I look like the statue of Agrippina in the Villa Albani. But tho that may have been the sister of Augustus—the most famous Agrippina is she who was the mother of Nero—famous for her beauty, her crimes, & her fate to be killed by the hand of her son. I can't say the face was really a portrait of myself. But the incision is good—and I bought it for 100 lire, and caused it to be set. But when I had slept upon it, I did not like to have you carry Agrippina on your finger as your tutelary genius. There was a fine head of Mars, a Pyrrhus dressed as Mars for l[ire] 200 in onyx—(and there is a good Minerva) in dark stone. I went back and got Depoliti to take back Agrippina that I could write to ask you about it. The only stone he has of a proper size shape & beautiful dark red carnelian is the head of Jupiter Pluvius. But he asked 600 lire—and came down to 500—that is $100. I have your 250 lire. If you concluded to give so much as a hundred for your ring £11 more would do it, for the rate of exchange on that w[oul]d give the money for the setting wh[ich] w[oul]d be about 70 lire. But this is a great deal to pay. But if you come out yourself—and if we go to Venice—we might find there what we want, for the things are not so much picked over as in Rome. An[d] at all events now we shall have to wait awhile.

The weather has been cold and rainy here like every where else this month, and there is no reason for thinking of moving yet. I am delighted with my house, and all my belongings, and feel quite like taking root. I only have my contract for three years, and I may be obliged to break it in two if the Padrone builds on to the back as he wants to do. But no need for me to worry about that yet. . . .

I am in one of my fits of discouragement just now, perhaps from the cold, and so many friends gone away. I have only the Storys and Tiltons left. And the Duca is all drawn up with the cold and looks awfully old!

1. Alessendro Castellani (1822–83), dealer in antique objets d'art.
2. A term defining the clarity and purity of a diamond.
3. Piere Depoliti, a Roman antiques dealer.
4. A variety of chalcedony, a form of quartz, characterized by a translucent or transparent red color.

June 2, 1874, 159 Via delle Quattro Fontane.

Pinches I do have, notwithstanding the great success of my Hegira to Rome. I have fits of despondency and loneliness, and feel there is no one here who cares for me except as I am agreeable and entertaining. I often however wonder that they find me so delightful when I think there are so many others fully [as] or more charming than myself. But let that pass.

I am perfectly comfortable here, and so far my means permit my living very much better than in N York, and enjoying society in the way that pleases me best.

At present all that is at an end. All the strangers have departed. The salons of the Storys and Terrys are empty. Miss Brewster's receptions have dwindled to nothing. The Romans don't go till much later, but they live in their great palaces dine with each other and drive out on the Pincio. The Princess Margherita and all her court are still here—and she drives with a black lace veil, & roses on her head and many ladies follow her fashion. But as I don't know any of the noblesse I only see them in passing. My Duca di Sermoneta is indeed the very top of the Roman nobility, but he lives a life apart shut up in his blindness, and only goes to one or two persons whom he likes, and where he runs no risk of meeting a crowd. Mrs Henry Field wrote me a long letter. She says you are rather jealous of a Duke or Count she don't know which—but someone you don't quite like having your Mamma devoted to. I assure you, you have no cause for jealousy. I am very fond of my Principé and he is of me, but I don't think either of us wants to go any further than friendship. So don't be alarmed. But he is a very grand personage. Prince Caetani & Prince of Teano, which title his son bears. The Duke is as witty a man as I ever met—and his noble character and terrible misfortune make him an object of veneration to all Italy—and indeed outside. If you will look into Murray's Guide book you will see him in the chapter of the Nobility and again his Palace under the head Palazzo Caserta. But I don't know Teano nor his wife who is a very handsome English woman—nor yet the Duke's daughter the Contessa Lovatelli. He is very fond of both his children—but his friendships I fancy he keeps to himself. He always comes led by his domestic Costantino a youth of 18 who is devoted to him, and punctual as a clock. You know I have always had some devoted admirer or other on hand besides you and Willie, and in your absence I really don't know what I should have done to fill up my leisure moments if this Duca had not stepped in. But I am not going to do a foolish thing be sure.

[June 17, 1874]

This is a capital season to visit the galleries, wh[ich] are so cold in winter that I never went into one. Last winter I tried three times and was made ill for a week each time. I passed this morning in the Borghese Gallery wh[ich] is one of the finest in the world—for its chef-d'oeuvres. Came home & painted on Willie's miniature wh[ich] I never have had a chance to finish before. It is nearly done and looks superb. Yours is greatly admired.

I hav'nt seen my friend the Caetani for six days. His daughter-in law the Princess Teano, is very ill with dip[h]theria—and he blind as he is passes hours sitting in her room, so kind is he—and he is afraid to bring the infection to me. So I don't know when I shall see him. Indeed I am very much afraid he may get the disease himself. But as I counted on his society to help through this month, I am particularly disappointed to lose him just now.

June 28, 1874, 159 Via delle Quattro Fontane.

I have been painting a great deal lately and hope to have a provision for sale against next winter. This is a very good time for visiting the galleries and I am making the rounds, now wh[ich] in winter I am afraid to do. People get those fevers from going out of the sun wh[ich] is always hot into the galleries which are like caves in winter. Now on the contrary they are a delightfully cool refuge from the heat outside. By the way talking of coolness, the Duke and I have had a falling out—so you need not vex your soul anymore about him. He is charming, witty, interesting, but too self willed to get on long with a person like me, who cannot yield my opinions to the fancies of others.

I don't think I ever happened to mention Joaquin Miller[1] who has been here all winter. You know the English took him up in the most wonderful way. He gave to Miss Brewster a note from Mrs Gladstone[2] inviting "dear Mr Miller to meet the Princess of Wales at a lunch party" And he had lots of such notes inviting him to great houses. I can't imagine what they were thinking of. People say "Harriet Gladstone" is a fool, but she is wife to the

Premier at the writing of her note, and one w[oul]d have thought if she asked Walkeen as a strange beast, she would have intimated that the Princess of Wales would honour the party with her presence. I am sure any American Lady (of my time) w[oul]d be surprised to be invited to meet a celebrity so questionable. Well here is Walkin, slap sided, lanky, with a twang addressing every one as "Lady" and dropping about with a sort of hangdog ease that you can imagine from having seen the thing in those people. Of course the Americans who never read a line of his poetry and would never have had a line in their houses, since he has been to all the great in England ask him too. He has something in him after all, and his ignorance makes that appear original in him because it is his, an acquisition of that which every educated person has learned with their A. B. C. Just as children seem so very smart because they produce the impression made directly on themselves for the first time. Walkin called on me, and I kept his card meaning to surprise you by putting it in one of my letters. But I always forgot it. He has written, Miss Brewster says a Tragedy a sort of happy go lucky affair I take it with neither plot nor personages, but some versifying. He has also written a book on Rome or in Rome I don't know which, which he has sent to his publisher in America and been paid for largely. And now Wurts (Sec of Am Legation, cousin of Mrs Robert Lenox Kennedy, and an immense swell) Wurts says Walkin has got into an intrigue with a half mad Mrs Godard from Phila[delphia]. So you perceive that changing skies he has not changed manners. Also came this winter Rhoda Broughton author of Red as a Rose [Is She] and all the rest ending with Nancy. She was at the Story's with a married sister who looked very nice. But all interest centered on Rhoda. She looks more like a clean cut, sharp pretty Yankee girl—than an English. She is restless, angular outspoken, predominant, but not vulgar nor noisy. She is less vulgar than her heroines—that is in an evening visit. What coarseness is in her mind we cannot doubt when we hear how she has her women to speak and think. But she is pretty, and dressed a good deal, tho' she had on her head a little cap several English girls affect! She said she wanted to stay longer but she had spent all the money she got for Nancy, and must go back to North Wales into a certain bare little room, in which only she could write; and when she had made some more money she would hasten back to Italy. "Is it true your Father bought Red as a Rose in a R[ail] way car, and when you took the book from the pocket of his travelling coat, he bid you put it down as a thing unfit for you to read?["] "She had never heard that among the stories told of her, and it could'nt be because her father was dead before she had written any thing." I wanted to say but if your father had been alive he w[oul]d have said so?—But somebody spoke and I kept my Dundrearyism for you.

1. Miller (1839?–1913) was an American writer whose first book of poems, *Specimens* (1868), was a great success in England. CPC delighted in spelling Joaquin phonetically.
2. Wife of Liberal British prime minister William Ewart Gladstone (1809–98).

July 7 [1874].

I found last Tuesday June 30th that Mr Terry is going to NY—and I decided to buy the Mars for the ring. It is a very handsome intaglio of the 1st or 2nd century and first & last pleases me better than all I have seen. The Jupiter Pluvius is rather large—& the stone w[oul]d run the risk of breaking in y[ou]r hard work. And in the battle of life we have to fight we had better put ourselves under the rule of the god of the "unconquered will." So I went to Depoliti. He had found nothing new at Naples—so the Mars valued at lire 200—I took— and carried it to Pieré the best setter and ordered a plain, solid ring as handsome as he could make it to be ready to send abroad. He would have it done Friday—Sure enough Friday morning it came, but tho' very elegant, not as solid as I wanted—I sent it back with notice it must go Monday ev[enin]g—yesterday morning hot as blazes I went at 10 AM to Piazza di Spagna drew my money and stopped in to make sure of the ring. He had'nt touched it—said it was just right and just as I had ordered—I said it was'nt & he should at once on Friday have sent to ask me to come down. He could make another in two days. No it was too late Mr Terry leaves Monday ev[enin]g. Take the stone out & give it back. Pieré said I was hard on him. I said he had put me out a great deal and I wished him to understand it so—and I w[oul]d wait for my stone—which I did & got. I was vexed indeed, and thought how put out you w[oul]d be to receive my little present and not y[ou]r ring. I drove to Palazzo Odescalchi—climbed up to Terry's found their departure was delayed till Wed[nesday]. Went back to P di Spagna to another Jeweller. He could not do the ring in that time.

Returned to Pieré, took a lofty air, said as the time had unexpectedly been lengthened he might yet be allowed to make the ring, agreed to pay a little more than the 150 for it; and now I wait for it tomorrow in good hope. Depoliti made a discount of 10 per cent on being paid cash, so your ring will come into your compass of £10. . . .

It is awful hot now, and I would pack up and be off to Switzerland in two days if I were not so cut up about paying this money.[1] I have some still in my letter of credit—but I hav't finished furnishing my house and expected to squeeze $500 out for that purpose without selling any of my little stock. It is thought necessary for foreigners to go every other year out of Italy and I had abandoned the idea of Lucca, and resolved to go and meet the Schuylers on some Alp. Perhaps I may renew my courage and start in a few days.

1. Unanticipated costs resulting from her suit to regain Dean Hall.

July 29, 1874, Bagni di Lucca.

I meant to run into Switzerland, but I gave it up—and tried to stick it out in Rome all July to save. But it grew so awfully hot that my eyes felt like balls of fire, and I was afraid of falling ill, wh[ich] w[oul]d have been more expensive than anything, so I packed my trunks, bid farewell to my Duca, and posted off to the Bagni by way of Leghorn this time. I stopped all night and half a day at Pisa to visit the Leaning Tower, Cathedral and Campo Santo, wh[ich] are the wonders of that City.

The Bagni are always cool and fresh. The objection is you meet the same people ones whom you have been with all winter in Rome—and are talked out. I have rooms even pleasanter than last year in a better Hotel than Zanettas. The table is excellent. I have a terrace off my salon, where you and Willie may sit and smoke in the moonlight.

September 12, 1874, Bagni di Lucca.[1]

Something disagreed with me at dinner and I had a regular bout. But Esterina got boiling hot water & rung out hot flannel and applied it to my stomach which stopped the vomiting, and today I have passed at a pic nic given to me by Mrs Lorimer Graham.[2] We drove in carriages ten miles to a most picturesque town Gallicano, and had our dinner on a flowery meadow and came back in good style by half past six.

1. CPC's two previous letters from Bagni di Lucca in July and August were monopolized by discussions of James's bad health and the homeopathic treatments that CPC recommended.
2. Lorimer Graham was the United States consul at Florence.

October 11, 1874, Rome, 159 Via delle Quattro Fontane.

I haven't told you I left the Bagni on 15th Sep[tember] stopped 12 days at Siena and saw the pictures and surrounding landscape—and made drawings of the Cathedral. Then a day at Orvieto to see the Cathedral—and there I was so delighted with the wine I brought a hamper at great expense with me to Rome, and it turns out not at all the wine I drank. Indeed it is execrable, and I nearly poisoned the Duke with it—fortunately he took a cup of tea instead. But he was accompanied by his Maestro di Casa the pivot of the house of Caetani and he took a glass to his great detriment.

Caroline Carson, Piazza del Campo and Palazzo Pubblico,* Siena, 1874. *Courtesy of Ashton and LaVonne Phillips.

1875

February 6, 1875, 159 Via delle Quattro Fontane.

The Carnival is going on—but it is a thing of the past, and there is no spirit in it as the people say who were in Rome long ago. It looks a little funny nevertheless to see people hanging about in Dominos and ugly masks. But they don't seem to have any idea of amusement beyond pelting each other with lime confetti—and now they have added flour & eggs—and really hurt people's eyes in spite of their masks by the handfuls of flour they throw in their faces. So they don't go into the Corso as they used to do. The balconies are all taken by foreigners who pelt each other in what they suppose is Roman fashion—and they might just as well do it in Broadway, for they are the same people whom they meet on that parade. The Storys have had theatricals, and I was called up and taken over in my rose coloured morning gown and enjoyed the first piece in which Edith Story acted in Faint Heart never won fair Lady. She was superbly dressed and acted well—but not as well as Marianna Porcher did the part—with any sort of dress, at Aunt Lou's.[1] Miss Hosmer[2] had furnished a dreary Burlesque to follow the play. It was an awful failure, wh[ich] she alone does not know—and she is having the thing printed, to the dismay of all such as fancy she may send them a copy.

1. Louise Petigru Porcher (1809–69), CPC's aunt and the mother of Mary Anna.
2. Harriet Goodhue Hosmer (1830–1908), American sculptor long resident in Rome whose masculine working garb and commercial success often provoked negative criticism.

April 8, 1875, 159 Via delle Quattro Fontane.

I have the prospect of a very nice summer. . . . Instead of going off by myself as before I am going with Mrs Alice Mason (formerly Sumner) to Venice in June. Thence to Coblenz on the Rhine where we will stop 6 weeks I to consult Meurer the oculist who promises to eradicate the cause of the inflammation of my eyes. After that Mrs Mason will go to France, and I return by the Alps into Italy. I shall take my maid this time, as I can never again face the solitary journey I made from London to Geneva. My friend Mrs Bigelow Lawrence[1] has today settled it all that I must make my journey comfortably and for it makes me a present of £100. It is wonderful how kind and loving people are to me; and I am a wretch not to feel more joyful. Take my word for it Jem, one can only be happy and respectable in their own home and their own family. And we who have lost our natural base must strive steadily to make another. . . .

Lou North has paid up the last installment on Badwell[2] which I hope is a token that she is prospering. . . . I asked Mr Bell to invest the money for me, as I am very desirous to increase my income before my pencil ceases to be a means of gain. For the success of painting is always a sort of chance. . . .

I am very much concerned now for Mrs John Ba[i]rd, sister of John Taylor Johnston.[3] She has been lying ill of the fever 46 days and her recovery is very doubtful. Her husband and her three daughters behave so well and so firmly. As soon as I have my tea & bread every morning I go to inquire after her, and sit an hour with the girls to wear away that much of the sad time at least. Then I come back and paint for two or three hours. Then lunch—and then I go out. There are always some visits to make. Most of the evenings I pass alone at home. Tho' I go pretty often to parties.

I have given two or three tea parties, and I have a reception every Sat[urday] P.M. from 3 to 6. There is a table set out with tea and little cakes, and people drop in, chat and go away quite contented. At ev[enin]g parties it is the same thing, tea little cakes, a glass of wine, talk, music. At dinners only do they bring out all the dishes with which we load down everything. It is much easier and pleasanter, and far more convenient.

Mrs Moulton[4] is here singing like an angel. In private only. The Moultons it is said don't want her to sing in public, and they educate the children, and give her some money, not a great deal however. She is very fascinating, and I dare say will make a good marriage.

There is a sad report of poor Mrs Hicks, that she has attempted to commit suicide, first by taking laudanum, and that being frustrated, that she drove to the bois de Boulogne and shot herself in the head with a pistol. She has gone into catholicism with redoubled ardour this winter, and in return has been pushed into the highest society in the Faubourg at St Germain together with Teresa Vielé, also a convert. The Priests (it is said Monsignor Cassel) projected marrying Mrs Hicks to Lord Courtney a bankrupt gambling catholic peer. And it is surmised that some hitch in the marriage has driven poor Annette to this desperate pass. Poor soul, it is a great pity. Grace[5] has gone into Papacy very strong, and I hear she had Charley baptized into the Church. Poor old Bristed. Johnny sells his books, and Grace makes his Babies a papist. Let us hope the dead do not know all that comes after them.

1. Katherine Bigelow Lawrence, widow of Abbott Lawrence (1792–1855), a merchant, textile manufacturing entrepreneur, and Massachusetts congressman.
2. CPC's cousin, Louise Gibert North (1833–96) had purchased Badwell, the Petigru family farm near Abbeville, South Carolina, which James L. Petigru had left to his daughters.
3. Johnston (1820–93) was a railroad executive, art collector, and first president of the Metropolitan Museum of Art.
4. Annie Lillie Greenough Moulton (1844–1928), the widow of Charles Raymond Moulton (1829–72), married Danish diplomat Johan Hegermann-Lindencrone (1813–1918) in 1875.
5. CPC's friendship with Grace Sedgwick Bristed, second wife of the writer and Astor heir Charles Astor Bristed (1820–70), began during her New York years. Charles was Grace's adolescent son. John Bristed, Grace's stepson, was mentally ill.

May 16, 1875, 159 Via delle Quattro Fontane.

Thursday last 13th I went with Mrs Mason to Tivoli.[1] At 3 PM she drove up in a comfortable barouche with her daughter Bel[2] on the front seat and off we went through the dust to Tivoli. The Campagna was lovely but for the clouds of dust in the road we travelled. As the carts approached we would first see only the ears of the mules so thick a cloud enveloped them. As we ascended the Alban mount however we left the dust and wound for an hour through a grove of fantastic old olive trees: which are the oddest things in nature. The leaves are a dusty gray and the trees many of them several hundred years old and all twisted in the most curious way, and seem to be dancing at each other in the most extravagant attitudes. We got our Rooms at the Regina, and hurried down to the garden of the Villa d'Esté to see the sun set far off on the Mediterranean. The Campagna in unutterable beauty lay before us with the Cupola of St Peter rising out of the distant line against the sky. Nearer two small pointed mountains crowned with villages and between them just as visible the point of Soracte[3] which lies beyond Rome standing alone among the Sabine hills.

This villa d'Este is one of the beauties of the world for its gardens. The Villa itself is no great thing though fine in its way. It belongs now to some German nobleman who has given Listz[4] a suite of apartments in it—on the door is Listz' name. The key is his—and here he is at home whenever

Caroline Carson, **Villa d'Esté, 14 May 1875.** ***Courtesy of Ashton and LaVonne Phillips.***

he chooses to go and take up his abode. They say he was there 8 months this year. He has his sec[re]t[ar]y—and receives visitors all the time, and comes into Rome to visit a favoured few. I have not had the luck ever to meet him. But not being musical it does not much signify to me. I don't know if you ever heard that he has been a great mangeur de coeurs,[5] and a famous and witty old Russian Princess Wittgenstein here was so pressing that Listz took to religion & became an abbé to save himself from her marrying him. But the gardens of the Villa are the great enchantment. They were made by the Cardinal Ippolite d'Este[6] brother of the Leonora d'Este whom poor Tasso[7] loved so unhappily, and whose gardens at Ferrara are the inspiration of his gardens of Armida in his Jerusalem Delivered. Such a marble terrace looking over the Campagna all bordered with roses in full bloom, such stately marble stairs winding down one terrace after another each with its fountains always playing. Hedges of box clipped square a grove of Ilex (Live oak) where the nightingales were singing all the day long. But the glory of all is the cypress. You remember those spindling little pyramidal cypresses at Dean Hall that in the clay would not send down their roots and were always tumbling over so wretchedly. Well that tree in its native soil grows as deep as high, a great shaft of dark verdure the most stately, solemn majestic of trees. An alley of them runs straight through the gardens, and clumps at intervals, and from the terraces this formal garden is so in harmony with the whole genius of the place that you feel delight.

We had dinner, and went to bed. Next morning I only went down to visit the famous waterfalls, and the lovely temple of Vesta[8] above them. Mrs Mason had seen them often so she spared herself fatigue and preceded me to the garden; where I joined her. I made a sketch of some of the cypresses—& the village of Tivoli—and we wandered there all the morning. At 2½ we had lunch. Then drove to the Villa of Hadrian[9] which once occupied miles, and which are still most inspiring after all the robberies it has suffered. From thence we continued our way back to Rome and having the wind in our faces the dust did not trouble us. We got back at 7 P.M. and I changed my dress & went over to dine with the Storys. Mrs Mason left the next morning for Perugia and will go on to Venice, where I shall join her the first of June.

May 23d

By the way I haven't told you of one of my occupations of late. Did I mention ever the Countess Gianotti? She was Miss Conny Kinney, & it was her brother you may remember at Stockbridge shot his lip & nose with his own gun. She was a mature and handsome Washington belle—and travelling four years ago fell in with a handsome Italian younger than herself & they were married & live in Rome, he being a major and on Prince Humbert's staff. So that the fair Contessa is in the highest court circle. She is an amiable soul however and fond of her country people. And some how throws herself on me for advice in difficult cases. A fortnight ago, just as I was at my dinner at 7 P.M. the Contessa Gianotti's maid was introduced, who had come to say I should come & encourage the Contessa who was in her pains & the Conte begged me to come. So as soon as I had dined off I went and found her to be sure in a fright. She had a baby 18 months ago in Florence. Mrs Kinney was with her, but she had been dreadfully ill, and was proportionately frightened this time. So they had two doctors Massori & Aitken. Gianotti the sage femme[10] myself and the maid all stood around her, and encouraged her as we could. And in one hour she was delivered of another little girl. I could'nt help laughing at the whole thing. Gianotti behaved like an angel he held her hand and kissed her and comforted her all he could, and seemed as if he would kiss us all in his joy when she was safely through. When the baby was dressed and handed up to him to inspect it was the prettiest thing to see this tall handsome fellow twirl his moustache and make little faces at it and say zou zou. So since that I have to trot over every day & go to see her and play the Grand maternal which I prefer to do vicariously remember! Annie Von Rabe is very funny with her baby which after all the fuss and waiting is only one little girl. We looked for a litter from the dimensions before hand. . . .

I have a new friend in Mme de Westenberg the wife of the Dutch Minister[11] to Italy. She was a Miss Jeanie Watson from Florida, was educated at Mme Dupre's in Charleston with Jane Porcher[12] & that set. She married Mr Birkhead of Balt[imore] who died leaving her with two children. She lived in NY—the daughter died of scarlet fever. She went to Linz 3 years ago with her handsome boy of 14 & he was drowned dragging down with him Kinzey Post the husband of poor Mary de Trobriand, as you may have heard. The handsome Mrs Birkhead in her grief captivated de Westenberg then Min. to Washington. They were married a year ago and he is transferred to Rome where they came this winter. She is large stout dark & amiable very—and he is a brisk little man very devoted to her—and both of them very kind to me. She too has been ill of a little fever, this week, and both of them flew to me. She is recovering however, so I should not be detained from seeing Venice. I felt if she were going to be seriously ill, I could scarcely desert my countrywoman among strangers. But I am very glad to have no such sacrifice to make. . . .

I can't stand this life much longer I pine for my children, and vainly do I try to fill my heart with the husks of society, tho' it's very gratifying that people seek me. But daily I feel more and more lonely and weary of it all. If I had married the Duke I should have had a great deal to contend with, and I dare say would have been more positively unhappy if he had turned out unmanageable. But it w[oul]d have been something to do at all events, and could have prevented my longing to get to you perhaps. But I dreaded too much the being without the freedom to go, wh[ich] at least I still have. I will stay out this next year. But after that I shall come to wherever you are, and move my tent around wherever it may be your fortune to go. I should be quite strong & well enough by that time I believe. You would scarcely know me so active as I have become and so light in figure.

1. Ancient city about fifteen miles east of Rome.
2. Isabel Hooper, daughter of Alice Mason and her first husband, William Sturgis Hooper.
3. A hill on the Tiber some twenty-four miles from Rome that was clearly visible from the city.
4. Franz Liszt (1811–86), pianist and composer.
5. Romantic exploiter, a Don Juan.
6. Ippolito II Cardinal d'Este (1509–72). The Este family once governed both Ferrara and Modena.
7. Torquato Tasso (1544–95), Italian epic poet.
8. Roman goddess of hearth and home.
9. Hadrian (76–138), the Roman emperor from 117 to 138.
10. Midwife.
11. B. O. T. H. de Westenberg.
12. Jane Porcher (1838–58) was CPC'c cousin.

June 6, 1875, Venice.

I left Rome June 1st with Miss Bartlett (niece she is by the way of Mr Sidney Bartlett[1] Mrs Willington's brother in law, and a devoted friend of Mrs Alice Mason). We stopped the first day at Terni[2] and drove out in the P.M. to see the falls which though artificially conducted to their present place of jumping do not look like it at all—and are said to be finer than the famous Swiss Pissevache.[3] Well it was a beautiful drive and we had to climb down to the bottom of the gorge, and mount up on donkeys for the best view, and it was awfully hot, and very fatiguing and the water though it fell in a fine volume was of a muddy colour and altogether we did'nt think we would do it ever again. At all events I hold myself discharged from any obligation to go to see any more falls unless they come under my nose.

Next day we started at 12 and after a hot steam we reached Bologna at 12 O['clock]. Next morning I sallied forth to the Gallery which is very fine. Bologna is built with the houses no more than three stories high perhaps for fear of earthquakes—but it is a city of colonnades, the pavements of the side walks are ten or twelve feet wide and the house is built out to the street with arches all along so that they walk always under cover from sun and rain. Some of the Palaces are magnificent especially the Bentivoglio, the cradle of the family from which Arturo Middleton[4] got his bride. There are two leaning towers almost as remarkable as that of Pisa. In the middle ages the nobles built themselves great square brick towers of a prodigious height from the loop holes of which they flung missiles at each other and mostly at the plebs beneath. In Florence, Siena &c—the people when they got strong compelled the nobles to pull down their towers, so there one sees only a few truncated harmless remnants of them. But at Bologna one still stands a monument of the insolence of those days. The tower of the Asinelli is 100 metres high, that is about 320 feet—and though some sinking of the foundation has made it incline a little from the perpendicular it is a fierce and savage looking structure still. Along side The Garisenda has lost half its height and is very much more slanted toward its rugged rival. I wished for you particularly at Bologna thinking how you w[oul]d be amused by the strange looking architecture; and it must have been prophetic that you were so in my mind for when I came to start on Friday for Venice I found my precious blue veil had disappeared. I wore it to the Gallery & I am sure the old fellow who took my parasol was not proof against the temptation of carrying it off. . . .

So now I am in Venice and it is all my fancy painted it. Mrs Mason has very fine rooms in the Grand Hotel and I am here as her guest, so I have nothing to do but enjoy it. The heat & dust gave me a horrid cough which is a draw back, but I hope to get over it soon. Lying off in a gondola is the very perfection of lazy enjoyment, and the whole city is one of palaces so wonderful in their colour and design that no extravagant praise goes beyond the reality. . . .

Monday. 15th . . .

Edith Story has just become engaged to Sig Peruzzi[5] of Florence who has nothing but high birth excellent manners and an irreproachable character. He is in the King's household, but his appointments are only enough for his own maintenance, & nevertheless the Storys are perfectly satisfied to give their only daughter, with a good portion to him because they esteem him so much. He is a great friend of mine:—and between ourselves, would never have carried his wooing to a successful end without my help. Both parties threw themselves upon me to negotiate. And both are so pleased that now I retire & will pretend I never had anything to do with it. You would be highly amused could I recite to you all the ins and outs of it. . . .

Venice is enchanting (tho' hot) Indeed it is a very hot June; and Rome was disagreeable before I came away. Last year June was lovely in Rome. I go out at 9 A.M and visit churches and galleries of most beautiful pictures, return for breakfast at 11. Then again often at 3 or 4 for another cruize returning in time to dress for dinner at 6—at 7½ invariably in the gondola to float free out on the smooth Adriatic with the city and the little islands sending long lines of light upon the waters which have colours of blue and purple unknown to our seas. Then about 10 to the Piazza of San Marco the most gorgeous in the world—exceeding the beauty of the Palais Royal of Paris. The church of San Marco which is a mass of coloured marbles and mosaics glows like a superb jewel. The architecture of the Ducal Palaces which surround the three other sides of the square is oriental and florid, the most exquisitely light and elegant. The ground floors are all shops brilliantly lit—and people sit on wooden chairs round little wooden tables and are served with delicious ices brought from Florian's by innumerable waiters who fly in and out and somehow find each group again to collect the very moderate sum charged for the refreshment. The streets are so narrow never I suppose more than twelve ft wide—and the shops are the gayest and most enticing I ever saw. Each house has some outlet on one of these little streets—but the main passage is always the canal, how the long gondolas push their way round the corners without running into each other is a mystery no unvenetian mind can fathom. The gondolier stands at the back of his boat 20 ft long; and with one oar which works in an oarlock about a foot & a half high with several notches in it, he moves, directs and altogether works his boat. You sit on a wide-cushioned seat with a high back, like the most comfortable of carriages, and are gently propelled wherever you wish to go. There is an awning in the day wh[ich] is lifted off in the ev[enin]g. Two persons generally make a load, but one more is often seated on a smaller seat at the side. You may hire a gondola by the day for 5 lire, and for that you have it all the time except for the necessary meals. Or you take one for a trip at the rate of a lire the first hour & ½ lira (10 cents) the other hours. If I were not going over the Alps to refresh myself with some brisk air I [would] wish to remain all summer at Venice. . . .

Oh I must give you a specimen of an inland Italian. Yesterday I gave Esterina leave to go out with some of the hotel servants—she came back delighted from the Lido wh[ich] you know is the farthest outlying Island, where people go to bathe & walk on the sand. She said Oh Signora it was so beautiful and we went by the Rail road. Why Esterina how could you go by a rail road, it is on an island. "I don't know she said but it was a rail road & it went through the water." "A steam boat you mean—a vapore" "Ah Signora you may call it a boat, but I saw the fire & the smoke." She had never seen a steam boat! There are some little piroscafi[6] in the Tiber but nobody ever sees them move off.

1. A Boston lawyer who at one time represented CPC in her litigation to regain Dean Hall.
2. Some forty-five miles northeast of Rome near the head of the Velino River.
3. Waterfall downstream from Vernayaz.
4. Arthur Middleton, the son of Gov. Henry Middleton (1770–1846) of South Carolina, married Paoline, Countess Bentivoglio in 1841.
5. Marquis Simone Peruzzi di Medici, a member of the Florentine nobility.
6. Steamboats.

June 20, [1875,] Venice.

I'll tell you the [typical] day. Tea & a roll in my room at 8—9½ sally forth in gondola with Miss Bartlett, or alone on foot to the piazza of San Marco where are all the shops—the cathedral & the Ducal Palaces. We go to visit the gallery or some churches till 11 AM. return for breakfast—by this time appears Mrs Mason with her daughter Bel Hooper. Then we repose, for the heat is oppressive—then sometimes at 3 gondola and more churches—dress for dinner at 6—7½ get in gondola and row up and down the harbour in the moonlight for two hours. Then to the piazza, meet every body, eat ices, and home to bed at 12.

The gondola is the most delightful motion in the world. The flatbottomed thing slides over the waters so smoothly and the lights dancing along the shores and long lines through the blue waters are glittering like gold & silver. There never was such light on the sea as here—and the glow of the sunset lingers in hues like an opal on the sky for hours—and are reflected in the waters in a wonderful glow of colours. Sometimes a distant point will remind me of light house island. But our boats, and our sea, and the old buildings of Charleston are far from the gorgeous beauty of Venice. By the way Prescott[1] describes one of the towns of the Incas (Mexico itself perhaps) as in some part resembling Venice built on islands with the river conducted in canals around it. If you can see it while you are in Mexico. Tho[ugh] judging by your descriptions of the travel, I sh[oul]d think one would not run about much on those roads.

I had an accident two days ago, stepping into the gondola my foot turned and I came down and strained all the veins in the other leg so they look as though they w[oul]d burst. However with arnica,[2] & keeping the leg straight on the sofa it is nearly well, and I shall go down to dinner today, & out in the gondola. If I had been a few years older my bones w[oul]d have snapped I suppose. I must take the warning to walk more circumspectly.

And by the way to talk likewise. I told you of the sad report about the fair Anette [Hicks] but I am glad to say it was not she at all, but some other unhappy woman who tried to destroy herself. Annette is flourishing on horse back in Rotten Row, [and] . . . lives at Claridges' hotel & entertains nobility.

Coblentz July 5th

I left Venice on 25th, parting with Mrs Mason at Verona. She going on to Château d'Oex of which I had enough two years ago. So with Esterina I began my adventurous journey to Germany without six words between us of German. ½ day at Verona to see the famous monuments of the Scaligers of whom the great Cane Grande was Dante's friend & protector.[3] Why he had the name of Cane (Dog) I never have learnt. It was no term of reproach but rather of respect to his valour.

At 5,50 AM I took the Brenner Route over the Alps which the railroad slowly climbs, at Innsbruck I stopped half a day and saw wonderful things in the monument of the first Maximilian Emp[eror] of Germany Grand father of Charles V.[4] It is the grandest structure of the kind I ever saw. It occupies the whole body of the church of St Francis. In the centre is an immense oblong square on the top of which is the kneeling Emperor in bronze with his regal robes & his diadem, all round the base are most exquisite reliefs in marble representing the scenes of his life, and along the pillars of the church are 28 colossal statues in bronze of distinguished kings & Princesses allied to Maximilian by blood or by grandeur of soul.

Sunday ev[enin]g I pushed on to Munich where I stopped three days visiting the splendid galleries and churches. How such a little kingdom as Bavaria could be rich enough to erect so many splendid churches monuments public buildings and gardens and buy so many pictures I can't imagine. Especially as the greater part has been done by Ludwig the patron of Lola Montez.[5] From Munich I took the night train to Mayence [Mainz] and thence boat down the Rhine to Coblenz where I arrived safe and sound Thursday July 1st.

Perhaps you remember my account of getting to Coblenz at midnight three years ago, and being in much trouble to find a lodgment. This time I wrote ahead and they had two rooms ready for me at the Géant—and it was midday, and everything was easy. I came out to see Dr Meürer who recommends my staying a fortnight now. So I moved to the Pension Ernan a mile out of Coblenz and just by the Oculist's house. I have comfortable rooms with a little parlor, and very poor fare. The garden touches the Rhine walk which is a beautiful shady promenade on the way into the town and far off beyond this house. It has ruins, and seats, & flowers, and every here and there a projecting balcony over the Rhine, where people

Caroline Carson, **Bridge over the Moselle at Coblentz, July 27, 1875.** *Courtesy of Ashton and LaVonne Phillips.*

sit & read or browse as they please. Interspersed along are restaurations where you may have coffee beer ices wine & cakes. . . .

July 18

My eyes are much better, and I hope Meürer will indeed make a cure of them. I am living in a stuffy boarding house with all the patients, but I live by myself in my pretty little salon. . . . Mrs Francis Fisher of Phila[delphia], formerly Miss [Eliza] Middleton of Ohio [plantation] whom I knew in my youth is here, an old lady with white hair the image of her brother Oliver. She has several of her grown up children & grandchildren with her, and all tinkering at eyes. I dined with her today, & she took me to drive along the Moselle. How beautiful it was—between the rain showers. But Europe is flooded & we are getting our portion here at Coblenz. Its vines will be destroyed, & general havock in crops. I have seen the Kaiser Wilhelm & the Kaiserin[6] whose favorite residence is at Coblenz. It is she who made the beautiful Rhine walk we enjoy. The Crown Prince[7] also passed two days with his mother, but I only caught a glimpse of his tall figure as he passed in the Rheinanlagen with the Empress on his arm. . . .

I send you the Lion of St Marks. This is the fellow which stands on the top of the Column before the Ducal Palace. It came originally from Greece, but where exactly is not known! But he is a grand old beast. I know you will be delighted with him.

1. William Hickling Prescott (1796–1859), American historian of Mexico and Peru.
2. A plant tincture specific for pains and bruises.
3. Cane Grande della Scala ruled Verona from 1311 to 1329.
4. Maximilian I was the first Hapsburg ruler of the Holy Roman Empire from 1493 to 1519. Charles V ruled both the Holy Roman Empire from 1519 to 1558 and Spain from 1516 to 1558.
5. British dancer (1818?–61), mistress of Ludwig I (1786–1868).
6. First emperor of a united Germany, who reigned from 1861 to 1888, and his wife Augusta of Weimar.
7. Frederick I, who reigned for only a few months in 1888.

August 16, 1875, Coblenz, Hotel Belle Vue.

I spent all July at the Pension Ernan following Meürer's practice and my eyes are so well that he has dismissed me with my phials to my own use. The Pension gave wretched food but my rooms were convenient & I paid $21 a week. The Rhine walk was the great attraction. But my rooms were engaged for a new married couple 30th July—& the Schuylers wrote at that juncture to ask me to come to meet them at Spa,[1] they coming from England to see me. This suited exactly so I went as their guest to the Hotel du Pays Bas Spa for ten days. . . . I returned 9th Aug[ust] to Coblenz & took up my abode at this Hotel. Phoebe & Detmold & Harriet came over from Ems to see me & invited me to go and spend a week with them at Ems.[2] Esterina is packing my trunks, & I will be off in one hour. I go to Schlangenbad[3] after Ems. . . . In Sep[tember] I go to Vevey[4] and over the Alps to Rome by October. I have enjoyed my summer. It has done me good. . . .

Tuesday 17th

Behold me the guest of Phoebe at the Kurhaus[5] Ems. I have a mighty comfortable room with Esterina opposite, and my friends as friendly as possible. We went yesterday P.M. to drive an hour after my arrival—high up through a beech forest to a mountain top whence we had a beautiful view of the Rhine hills as far as the Seven Mountains. Of course at the point to wh[ich] [we] ascended was a "restauration" and beer. And our enthusiastic young Hollander who travelled on foot with his map in his pocket to enjoy the scenery. Phoebe was awfully frightened at the steep road, but we met with no accident. We had tea on our return, and then Harriet & I strolled out in the moonlight to see the people and listen to the music. . . .

19th

The inauguration of a great statue of Arminius[6] at Detmold wh[ich] is supposed to be the place where he defeated Varius [*sic*] is the event of the day. [C. E.] Detmold of course intended going. But prudence prevailed not to expose himself to the crowd & the heat. The Artist Bandl[7] is you may be sure an old friend of the Detmold family at Harcom. The Kaiser has given him a handsome pension & all sorts of decorations. He was 40 years at work on the Statue forging it piece by piece with his own hands—the figure is 76 feet high, impossible to cast.

1. A Belgian resort some seventy miles west of Coblenz.
2. Bad Ems was barely five miles southeast of Coblenz.
3. Spa town just north of Wiesbaden, twenty-five miles southeast of Coblenz.
4. Swiss resort on Lake Leman.
5. Spa house.
6. Arminius (18 B.C.E.–19 C.E.), a German chieftain who had gained Roman citizenship, led a rebellion against Roman rule, and in 9 C.E. defeated the legions led by Quintilius Varus thereby driving the Romans from the regions north of present day Hanover and Brunswick. The Hanover town of Detmold is about sixty miles northeast of Bad Ems.
7. Ernst von Bandl (1800–1876).

September 5, 1875, Schlangenbad.

I have been here my two weeks bathing; my time is up and I move on tomorrow to Lake Leman. . . . Schlangenbad "the serpent's bath" is as pleasing a spot as ever I was on. The baths most beautifully arranged tho' I can't say the water is so sparkling and exhilarating as the Sweet spring Va.[1] But all the valley & hill sides is laid out in trim well kept walks winding about in the beech forest, which is the most cheerful wood I ever saw. The sun sifts between the light green leaves, and lies in golden patches on the soft moss, and brown fallen leaves, with a glimmer I never saw in any other kind of forest. When the rays slant through the tall pines they lie long and sharp on the thick firm straw which, indeed, sends out a very pleasant smell, but the moaning of the branches of the pines stirred by the wind is always sad, whereas those beeches wave their feathery branches and seem to draw in the light—and you at once understand all the German legends of wood sprites and little merry goblins. They spring up naturally here, and you expect them any minute to pop out from behind some tree or little hillock of moss.

You see all my companionship was with the forest—for not a creature here do I know; and I have passed my two weeks in solitude, broken only by a visit to Giesenheim. . . .

Sep[tember] 12th,[2] Clarens, Lake Leman.

I moved off from Schlangenbad Monday 6th & have done great things in the last week. I was to go to Basle the first night. But the spell that seems so strong to suck me into Frankfurt acted this time too. And the wicked conductor instead of the proper warning to change cars at Castel opposite Mayence, where I wanted to go, carried me off and it was only in the last station before Frankfurt that I managed to get off. I had to wait 2 hours pretty savage in humour, & <u>pay</u> to be taken back to Castel & over to Mayence losing of course my train for Basle. However next morning starting at 6½ I got to Basle at 3—and rested, then I strolled out and visited the Cathedral and, saw the drawings of the original Dance of Death falsely attributed to Holbein.[3] Sat a long time on the terrace watching the Rhine rushing clear and green between the houses with their high stone embankments. At 7 I went back to the Trois Rois, and had the best dinner I have eaten since Delmonico.[4] Off again at 6½ AM for Interlaken via Berne. Arrived about 2 P.M. at the Hotel des Alps, and got a room looking full at the Jung frau. I walked out in the afternoon and enjoyed the mountain views turning ever and anon to the incomparable Jung frau wrapped in her eternal snows with the Silber horn hung like an ornament upon her neck. I engaged a carriage & guide for the ascent of the Wengern Alp, and leaving Esterina at the hotel, took my venturous way Thurs[day] morning alone. Of all the excursionists that throng the mountains none seemed to be going exactly at my time and pace. I drove to Lauterbrunnen and had two hours looking at the Staubbach [waterfall] while the horse rested and the guide delectated himself with his friends. The way is to send the carriage back from Lauterbrunnen by men who convey it to Grindelwald to meet you and on the horse you mount the Alp the coachman being guide as well, and leading the horse all the way. The Staubbach is a thin stream falling straight down a prodigious rock which so breaks up the water that it comes all in a veil of spray swaying with the wind, and beautiful enough for all Byron has sung of it. I saw meantime many carriages pass farther up the road, & began to suspect something, so when I got out the guide I inquired for the valley of Lauterbrunnen and all its springs. I was still in the German Switzerland, but Nicolo spoke a sort of french. Oh he said the lilienthal—that was three miles farther up the road, and it w[oul]d be too far for me to go on horseback and then up the Wengel [*sic*] Alp. So he had cut me out of that, he had sent the carriage back two hours before; he ought to have driven me first to the valley & then returned to the Staubbach wh[ich] is just by the hotel in which his soul delighted. Of course after this I put no confidence in him, and was always on the look out for his cheating me again; which made some confusion in my mind with the extasy of the face of nature seen on the Alpine tops. I went winding up the mountain steeper & steeper at every step, and I met a good many travellers coming down on foot with their horses lead—and many travelling on foot up with their alp stocks in their hands and a bag carried for them by a guide. But they passed on and I was alone. I cannot tell you how grand it was at last when a turning brought me face to face with the Jungfrau and all her satellites. . . . On we went always higher and grander, till we came to a hotel of a simple construction but full before the grand show of the Jungfrau with the Eigger [*sic*] on her right and the Silber Horn on her left with the Mench [*sic*] dark in his naked rocks a little forward & below. About 4 P.M I reached the summit of the Wengern where was a very comfortable house called a hotel, and full of travellers as the evening drew on people came dropping in, some on foot & some on horseback. I sat out as late as possible to see the magnificent panorama spread out and hear the fall of the avalanches like thunder in the mountains. And very often I saw them pouring down through the clefts like a stream of snow, so fine in [is] the ice ground in its descent, and whenever it comes to an opening it shoots out in a fall of powdered ice, disappearing and coming out again till it disappears in the vast gorges of the mountain. I saw the sun rise on the Grindenwald [*sic*]—and at 8 AM set forth with my guide the descent on the other side the Wengern which was much worse than going up. Not only the motion of the horse makes it harder to keep one's seat, but the road down to Grindelwald was much worse than from Lauterbrunnen up. The fact was I had to walk most of the way—with all the morning the Schreckhorn & the Wetterhorn mountains right before me. At 12 I reached Grindelwald. Rested & dined out at 1,30 set off on horseback for the glacier. The road there was awful indeed. I stopped & drank a glass of beer. As for the guide he took so many petits verres[5] of cognac whenever we paused that I expected to see him reel—but he seemed used to it & did'nt alter his plod at the head of my beast. I saw the glacier indeed just like a frozen river tossed up in waves, it slips all the time gradually into the valley. . . . It is very fine to look at—and there is a cave dug into this about 50 yards I suppose and I walked into it to the end under the pale green ice on all sides. Came back to the inn at Grindelwald harnessed, and drove back to Interlaken wh[ich] I reached just in time to avoid a small tornado. All day the weather was superb. And the sun rose on the Jungfrau

Sat[urday] 11th perfectly beautiful.

I left at 6 A.M.! and reached Clarens where at 2 P.M I have come to stay instead of Vevey. My friend Clem Barclay has found out a mighty comfortable new hotel here. . . . I have two very nice rooms and pay for self & maid 10 francs a day. There are several persons in the house I know among them . . . a very nice Mrs Ten Broek who has gone this morning to Geneva to give her sister in marriage to an English clergyman. I am invited to the wedding but all this racketing about has stirred up the bile, and I have had so much giddiness that yesterday I had to take some very drastic physic and keep my bed. This morning I am better, but not equal to starting off at 8,30 with the rest— but I am going at 2 P.M. with one of Mr Barclay's sons, will get to Geneva at 6—tomorrow is the wedding, and on Wed[nesday] Mrs Graham Mrs Ten Broek and I start off for Chamouni [Chamonix][6] to see Mont Blanc. I am so roused up by my view of the high Alps, that I shall not rest without seeing Chamouni. . . . I return Sat[urday] 25th to Clarens, and will stop perhaps two weeks more here, and then via via[7] for Rome.

1. One of the Virginia springs CPC had visited for her health and amusement in the 1840s and 1850s.
2. Misdated, should read Friday, September 10.
3. Hans Holbein (1497–1543) made woodcuts of this painting.
4. New York restaurant famed for its European cuisine.
5. Little glasses.
6. On the French-Italian border.
7. By road.

October 23, 1875, 159 Via delle Quattro Fontane.

On the 13th I was . . . at Villa Colle Pistoja making a visit to the Lorimer Graham's. I meant to drop down leisurely to Rome stopping at Florence & Perugia. But I got a telegram from Posi that Dr Henry Field[1] & Clara were in Rome until 17th. I concluded that I must post on to see them, for this was my only opportunity of testifying my respect & affection for [his late wife] the lamented Harriette. So I travelled all night, and spent the Sunday with them. Next day they resumed their journey which is to take them round the world. I suppose every Field now feels bound to put a girdle round the earth since Cyrus[2] has bound the continents together. Henry was delighted to talk of his beloved companion. He has great solace in Clara who appears to great advantage. . . .

I have done nothing else but to get my apartment to rights. I have no Margaret here to have the carpets spread & the curtains hung as at 149 [West Twenty-Sixth Street, New York]. Mrs Posi comes ahead and has my rooms swept out, & she & Posi always meet me at the station. Posi by the way has got into a small banking house just started. I am very glad for him, & hope it may succeed. But I do not feel inclined to give up Hooker who has treated me very well, & been most kind and attentive always. I fear Posi will be hurt—but it is a risky thing to put your little money into a feeble bank. I haven't enough to profit Posi, but enough to embarrass me dreadfully if Demarq & Co came to grief. . . .

1. Henry Martin Field (1822–1907), Presbyterian cleric and writer. Clara was his niece, later Mme Carra.
2. Cyrus West Field (1819–1907), merchant and the entrepreneur responsible for laying the first transatlantic cable in 1867.

November 16, 1875, 159 Via delle Quattro Fontane.

How I wish you could drop in & spend the evening with me! My salon is so bright & pretty, and we would have such a talk. I don't think I ever described my salon to you. The carpet is red the wall paper bunches of flowers & ceiling gayly frescoed. Two beautiful gold corner stands a perfect gold & marble pier table with tall gilt branches on it—a Venetian marble top centre table upheld by three carved nigs[1]—blue & gold. A mirror over the mantle piece set in black & gold and a glass chandelier. My writing table is covered by my old Mexican blanket! which with its cream coloured ground corresponds with the curtains and sofa of chintz covered with birds and foliage. It is altogether the brightest looking room in Rome. I aimed to make it gay that I might mope as little as possible when sitting here all my evenings alone.

1. This term for African Americans was quite common in the usage of Southern white people after the Civil War.

December 10, 1875, 159 Via delle Quattro Fontane.

Mrs [Alice] Mason has just come. I have seen her but once, so I have had no opportunity to present your homage to her nor to Bel [Hooper], who is very pretty, very nice, and so rich! Mrs Mason has brought me a bonnet from Paris and a pillow wh[ich] I sent for with two p[ai]r boots. I am very fine this winter. I have a black velvet jacket, and a complete suit of brown merino [wool] trimmed with brown silk and I have a pale lilac silk evening dress making, wh[ich] I shall wear whenever Edith Story's marriage obtains the Pope's permission to be effected. . . .

I look very fine indeed and I must contrive to make a sketch of myself in the brown dress for you. I am as slim—let me see as slim, nearly, as Charlotte Hamilton[1] in it! You w[oul]dn't know me, if that's any recommendation. I have painted a big piece for the Centennial,[2] and now I am busy on two portraits wh[ich] is what I always long to do, but have always been interrupted by illness whenever I tried before. If I succeed now I shall be interested and pleased always. Flower painting I find very monotonous, and I like having faces to do.

Sunday AM, [December] 26th [1875].

I had to post off to church yesterday, where indeed I had been half of Friday helping to decorate with green & flowers. I never have been well enough before to lend a helping hand on such festivals, and I thought it my duty to go now. After service stopped to lunch with Mrs Mason & Bel Hooper & Ellen Tappan now Mrs Dixey.[3] After stopped to wish a merry Xmas to Mme De Westenberg, and then home, where I found my tables covered with notes and presents. I had barely time to look over them, when I had to get ready to go back to church to assist at the christening of Contessa Gianotti's baby. The same at whose birth I presided last April, as I wrote you. I took Esterina and almost ran it is a walk of half an hour one way to the Am Chapel from my house. We christened the baby in the presence of the smallest congregation I have seen since the off Sundays at Strawberry Chapel.[4] I had an hour to rest and then dressed for the Xmas & baptismal dinner at the Gianottis' at 7 PM. Now I am profiting by half an hour to add a few words.

1. A New York friend.
2. Celebration of the hundredth anniversary of the American Revolution that Philadelphia hosted in 1876.
3. A wealthy young American who had married her impoverished piano teacher.
4. An Episcopal chapel of ease near Dean Hall, the Carsons' Cooper River plantation.

Caroline Carson, **Ehrenbreitstein, July 1875.** *Courtesy of Ashton and LaVonne Phillips.*

1876

March 10, 1876, 159 Via delle Quattro Fontane.

I am very busy painting diligently, for no particular purpose, as nobody buys anything this year—so it is a good time to study, and I am taking lessons in landscape with Corlandi.[1] I told you Simoni has grown famous & beyond giving lessons. There is a Soc[iety] of Water Colourists just established in Rome, & I have joined it. The only lady and only foreigner the rest all eminent Italian artists. The Exhibition was visited by the Princess Margherita,[2] and the "Libertá" had an article about it, and mentioned the things praised by her R H among wh[ich] conspicuous were the Fiori[3] di Madame Carson. The Story's have had private theatricals this week, "School" well acted.

1. Onorato Carlandi (1848–1939) Landscape painter and watercolorist.
2. Cousin and wife of Prince Humbert, the heir to the Italian throne.
3. Flowers.

May 8, 1876, Castagneto, Cava near Naples.

You will be quite surprised at my booming off to Naples. But I will tell you how it came about. You remember the first winter I came to Rome the fair Annette [Hicks] invited me for a week to Naples, and I have pined ever since to see Naples more thoroughly; for that time I had one day at Naples in the Museum—one at Pompei, three at Sorrento—and the other two days for the journey back and forth Rome. But Naples has such an awful

Caroline Carson, "Pomegranate Branch." Courtesy of Ashton and LaVonne Phillips.

name for fever that people who live in Rome dread it worse than the pest; just as Columbia [South Carolina] people used to fear Charleston. The drainage is awful and some of the hotels are sure fever traps. However I have some friends, the Newberys, you remember whom I met at the Baths of Lucca; and my friend Walter sent you some greetings. He has been hanging on at Naples these three years waiting for some good business opening, and meanwhile figuring down the matter of living to the ground he says. Papa & Mamma Newbery & one daughter stopped in Rome this winter two weeks mainly to see me—and they proposed I sh[oul]d come & join them & make the excursions around Naples. So at last I came—leaving Esterina in the apartment in Rome as costing less than to bring her along; besides that ladie's maids don't care for scenery, and make themselves a nuisance on such occasions.

I stopped two days in Rome to attend a fête of Lady Paget's to be given on their advancement from minister to ambassador to V Emmanuel.[1] Hitherto the great powers have accredited only ministers to United Italy, but now all are advanced to full ambassadors, Italy being considered surely settled in its government. On this occasion the King & Princess of Piedmont were to be present, & the fête was from 3 to 7 PM—in the garden. Behold it rained, and was put off—for two days more—so I concluded to wait no more, but came on 27th to Naples, where I found my Newbery's just ready to leave for Cava,[2] wh[ich] we had agreed upon as our headquarters, from whence to make the excursions. So I stopped three days to visit the

Museum where are the most beautiful of the antique marbles—as well as all the remnants rescued from Pompei. When they make the excavations, they remove all valuable things to the Museum. There you see the utensils jewels household furniture, and even the charred bread and nuts & spices wh[ich] have been dug out. I drove about and enjoyed the beautiful views and visited the Royal Palace, a very desirable residence indeed.

Monday 1st I took the rail to Cava wh[ich] owing to slow rate of moving & much stopping takes two hours journey. Mr Newbery met me at the station, and took me to a funny old villa, kept by three very funny old sisters, who strange to say have their house as neat as wax, and we have it all to ourselves. The fare is very good and I pay 6 lire a day—(lira 20 cents) Mrs Newbery started off excursioning with me, and took a cold which has laid her up ever since, & Mr N stays by her. So George, Bertha and I go on donkeys, and sketch rocks mountains and churches—and the last two days, being now at 11th May we went to Amalfi—which is on the coast the most wonderful piles of mountain, villages stretching from the sea to the mountain tops. The Mediterranean glittering with an immortal blue. The people rugged picturesque, strong and happy, the little ones all but naked screaming for bajocci[3]—which they don't seem to expect to get, but merely keep up the habit of asking for the fun of the thing, and the possible chance of somebody's giving one.

Caroline Carson, "Flowers of an Unidentified Leguminous Plant." Courtesy of Ashton and LaVonne Phillips.

We slept at Amalfi & by 8½ were in our saddles to climb up through a village the streets of which run through the houses, half of which are occupied by makers of maccaroni. after climbing in this way an hour we came out on a level space over hanging the town & the sea where an Englishman Mr Reid has bought an old villa and made it his residence. It was originally built by the Saracens[4] who came from the neighbouring coast of Tunis as [*sic*] took possession of this part of the country building as was their wont beautiful fortified houses and making gardens—till they were driven out by the Normans[5] who of all people made their way in their ships to these enchanting shores—& held on till in their turn expelled by the Spanish & sometimes the French.[6] Nothing can be more lovely than Mr Reid's garden and such part of the seascape as he liberally lets strangers visit—built upon restored parts of the saracenic buildings with their beautiful arches & delicate little double columns & elaborate carvings. The Nightingales sang in the woods, and not a thing was wanting to complete the enchantment of the scene.

Sat[urday] 13th

Yesterday I spent at Paestum. All the Newberys were broken down with colds & headaches except George, so we two went alone. It is an expensive trip because you send a carriage on to take you up from Battipaglia wh[ich] is an hour & half by rail—thence in the carriage two hours on a level plain infested by malaria, but at this season blooming with flowers and superb crops of wheat. The inhabitants however have fevers like in our swamps and fly to the surrounding Abruzzi Mountains in the summer. At length you reach Paestum the most perfect remains of three Grecian temples are here. It was a colony of the Sybarites who built a city of which one gate still remains & three temples.[7] The finest of which is the Temple of Neptune which I send you. Nothing could surpass the beauty & grandeur of this temple of travertine stone grown a rich brownish yellow with age, looking out on a flat campagna to the glittering blue sea. It has grown up thick around with sweet scented clover, the crows flew in and out of the columns, the air was perfectly delicious, and one could scarcely believe that at sunset it became so deadly as to make the place deserted. Something must have happened to change the character of the exhalations since the time the Greek colony chose it for a favourite residence & built these splendid temples. We could stay but three hours to enjoy it all. But both George & I made sketches, mine I hope some day to show you. On returning to Battipaglia we had to wait for the train, & I sketched an old man in the waiting room to the great interest & delight of the bystanders, who all offered their criticism & approval. I return to Rome tomorrow—and will write you thence.

1. Wife of Sir Augustus Berkeley Paget (1823–96), who had been the British minister to Italy since 1867. Victor Emmanuel (1820–78), first king of Italy (1861–78).
2. Cava di Tirenni, some thirty-five miles south of Naples.
3. The baiocco, a papal coin, was of minimal value worth about as much as a British half penny.
4. In the ninth and tenth centuries.
5. In the twelfth century.
6. From the thirteenth to the eighteenth century.
7. Ca. 600–400 B.C.E.

July 5, 1876. 159 Via delle Quattro Fontane.

When I came to Europe after Willie[1] I sailed 2d July & returned 10th of Nov[ember]. I had $1000. I went to Dresden had a maid, paid Willie's expenses for six weeks—staid six weeks in Paris at a first class hotel—Had a carriage every day—went often to Theatres & Opera—and I had 200 over when I got to N York. Last summer, I went from here and cruised around in Germany was gone four months & spent $800—had my maid along—costs nearly double as in rail ways I pay the same for her. I travel 2nd class—and my baggage costs a great deal. One trunk w[oul]d cost nothing scarcely.

1. In 1861 CPC had gone to Europe ostensibly to check up on her older son's business education in Switzerland and Germany.

[September 1876?]

I send the Photo of the "Muse of Cortona."[1] The only Greek painting extant. You must hold it very precious. It represents the Muse Polihymnia[2] one of the Muses of Poetry. It was dug up in a field near Cortona having lain buried for centuries. It was first set up as an image of the Blessed Virgin & adored as such by the peasants. Some priest noticing the Lyre exploded that belief, and she fell into contempt, and a peasant took her to make the door of his oven. [It] is painted in Encaustic[3] an art which is lost—and judging by this specimen is as far beyond all oil & wate[r] colours as

Caroline Carson, **Perugia, 14 July 1876.** *Courtesy of Ashton and LaVonne Phillips.*

Greek statues excel all that the Moderns strain for. It is painted on slate, & the peasant with a hatchet rudely hacked it in the pointed shape you see to fit his oven. At last a gentleman spied it all smoky & battered, bought and washed it—and dying left it to the Town of Cortona on condition it should never be parted with. Cortona is so out of the way few visit it—but nevertheless great sums have been offered, of course in vain. Even in the Photo, the longer you look at it the more you will grow to admire her. Leaving Perugia I made a trip at Mrs Hooker's invitation to Cortona to visit this enchanting picture.

1. A Tuscan town about twenty-six miles northwest of Perugia.
2. Polyhymnia, the muse of the sublime hymn.
3. An especially durable mixture of pigment and wax or resin rarely used in modern times.

November 6, 1876, 159 Via delle Quattro Fontane.

I don't see my way to making anything of Phil's[1] photo, but I'll try, if I ever have any leisure. Shillaber, partner of Jas Lick[2] of S[an] Francisco is here with his wife. She came to visit my studio yesterday, but instead of buying some of the handsome things already done, she ordered a pitiful little piece to be painted on silk for a screen—Mortifying! but useless to fret about it. By the way—I bequeathed my three pieces at the Phil[adelphia] Centennial to Mr Schuyler not knowing what to do with them—but I do wish you w[oul]d talk with him about getting my table and trying to have it patented. It is a good thing the things were consigned by "Dumaresq & Co Rome["] to John Sartain[3] chief of Art Bureau—Women's Dept—and the Number here was 74—what it may be at the Centennial I dont know.

1. Philip J. Porcher Jr. (1835–64), CPC's cousin, lost at sea during the Civil War.
2. James Lick (1796–1876), California real estate baron and philanthropist.
3. Sartain (1808–97) was an engraver and publisher who was the chief of the entire Art Bureau for the 1876 Philadelphia Centennial Exhibition.

December 28, 1876, 159 Via delle Quattro Fontane.

Every body is so poor this winter I thought there w[oul]d be no presents but behold I had a good many. Here is the list. Miss Bartlett a package of au la Rue's note paper & envelopes—Miss Sarah Freeman Clarke a wooden paper holder—Miss Brewster a little china jar. Mrs Bristed, photograph from Bunzino (a beauty), China jar & Note Book. Mr & Mrs Posi, a silver spadina[1] for the hair. Mrs Story a Silver amulet bracelet. Mr Hooker a little trunk of Chocolates. Misses Guild, bouquet of fresh flowers. Mme de Westenberg a beautiful Minton china dish. Mrs Hooker a cake. Contesse Gianotti a big Japanese lacquered egg full of bonbons. I dined with the Gianottis & was invited to Mme de Westenberg & by Mrs Tilton besides. On my saint's day San Carlino the Marchesa Longhi, Sermoneta's sister had brought me a beautiful bonbonniere full of confetti. So I sent her at Xmas seven pots of growing plants for her loggia. I also sent Miss Brewster two pots, and I painted a bunch of flowers for Mrs Hooker. That was all I did—in the way of presents except some toys to Co[n]t[e]ss[e] Gianotti's children & Chocolates to Charley [Bristed]. I have been with Grace [Bristed] to the theatre several times lately.

1. Sword shaped hairpin.

1877

March 4, 1877, 159 Via delle Quattro Fontane.

Here is the 4th & tomorrow will be a field day with the Republic. May the lesson we have had and the dangers so narrowly escaped teach the people wisdom and make them put down corruption and jobbery. We need an entirely new party—neither of the old ones is to be trusted. Would that the young men of this generation, to whom indeed the work of the time, belongs[,] organize a new system, and compel the old vagrants and tricksters to get out of the way. It is a solemn turning point in our history, and it beho[o]ves each man to do his own share in pressing reform, honesty & good faith. If Hay[e]s be a great and a good man, he may be a second Washington. But he will need the wisdom and the unshirking justice of Washington to effect the reformation needed. But neither he nor Washington could do it unless every right thinking man in the country set his energy to the work.[1]

Last Sunday I was at Orvieto to meet Mrs Young![2] She & the girls have come to Florence for a "little trip," and having decided not to come to Rome, we agreed each to go half way to meet. It was like a lovers' tryst. She left the girls & came alone on Sat[urday] 24th Feb[ruary]. I started on my side alone and at 2 PM we met at the Station at Orvieto, spent all the afternoon, Sunday & till 1,30 Monday talking, even while visiting the grand old Cathedral of Orvieto. We enjoyed our meeting extremely—and it did us good to renew all the old topics. She looks much the same, but she is not so strong. I am twice as strong as she. If it were not for a kind of heat [rash] this Roman climate produces on my skin I should be as well and brisk as I was at 18.

I am sorry the table[3] makes so poor an appearance and is too shacklety to prove its merits. The wood here is not seasoned, and consequently does not stand changes of temperature. All the new furniture I bought has from time to time expanded with a report like a pistol, and remains with great seams gaping. Sometimes they fill them in with putty! and assure you your furniture is as handsome as ever! Blessed Italians! They have so many ways like the nigs. . . .

Mrs Hooker & Miss Bartlett go to America middle of April that is leave here then, and want me to go along. But how can I manage it. It w[oul]d take $1000 and I have $400 a year to pay for my house rent—and this year my income is $1700—so if I spent in 4 months one thousand & some for house there w[oul]d be but three hundred for the rest of the year to live & buy my clothes—of wh[ich] I have got nothing new this winter at all, & I will have to have two new dresses next winter.

1. Because Republican Rutherford B. Hayes's election depended on electoral college votes cast by corrupt Reconstruction governments in Florida, Louisiana, and South Carolina and was salvaged from Democratic challenges only by the last minute compromise of a special election commission on March 2, his peaceful inauguration was uncertain until March 4 when it occurred without any renewal of sectional conflict.
2. Probably the wife of CPC's Charleston lawyer, Henry E. Young.
3. CPC had devised a drawing table and had sent a version of it to her son to see if he could get it patented.

March 29, 1877, 159 Via delle Quattro Fontane.

Hayes seems to be the needful man for the times however lame the election was—and we may begin to hope the people have had such an exhibition of the pass to which the Republic has come in its working gear, that they will now seriously set themselves to mend their ways. One thing in all this gives me most satisfaction, and that is that Mr Evarts[1] comes to the highest place by sheer force of his own value. The proper rewards of an honourable ambition are so miserably frustrated by the baseness of elections, that men almost cease to try for anything but money. Mr Evarts has tried again & again to go to the Senate, & for other things in the gift of the people, but never could get himself elected. But holding fast to his purpose you see the time at last accords him his hour.[2]

1. William Maxwell Evarts (1818–1901) served as Hayes's secretary of state. He was finally elected senator from New York in 1885.
2. This excerpt is from the last known letter of substance that CPC wrote James Carson from Europe in 1877. On April 11 she left Rome to go to the United States on business connected with her legal efforts to regain Dean Hall and to visit her sons. She returned to Rome the following winter.

Part II

Settling into Permanent Residence, 1878–1882

1878

January 18, 1878, 159 Via delle Quattro Fontane.

I shall send you illustrations of the King's death & funeral as soon as there are enough of them out. It has been the most wonderful excitement. 200000 persons they say have come into Rome for the funeral, and the hum of the multitudes in the street night and day is something most strange in this quiet city. I went Sat[urday] with Esterina to see the Chapelle ardente[1] with Victor Emanuele lying in state. It was at 1 PM the earliest hour—and already the crowd was so great that we were nearly crushed. She was forced past me in the rush as the Bersaglieri[2] made way, and I was driven up against the wall & I thought my last moment had come—for there is nothing more perilous than the rush of a crowd. I screamed with all my might, and a guard laid hold of me & dragged me within the Quirinal gate where I found Esterina crying. We recovered ourselves and the crowd being barred out till this batch had passed through, we did make our way still much thronged, into the immense room hung with <u>red</u> according to the etiquette of the House of Savoy—a great catafalque was raised covered with red with a great crown overhead and large curtains of ermine[.] Innumerable wax candles in great golden candelabra ten feet high were dispersed on the platform and step leading up to the estrade where lay the body of the King in his military dress with all his orders and a great purple mantle of the order of the Amionciadie[3] around him, around stood his chamberlains in full dress, and certain cuirassiers in superb uniform standing immobile as statues, a row of capuchine friars mumbled prayers, and the King's almoner sat at the foot in his religious attire & his book of devotions. The King was awful to be hold it was a grand spectacle—but I w[oul]d'nt care to see another dead King. This little photo must have been taken before he was settled—for they had to try several times before they got him set up right. He was lifted up much higher, and the mantle is not wrapped round him, and the great candelabra like trees do not appear.

Yesterday was a tremendous time with the funeral. You will read in the papers of all the royal persons sent to do him honour. But I'll try to tell you what I saw. The cortège was to pass down the Quattro Fontane to go to the Pantheon. The Quirinal is just behind my house[4]—by 8 oclock the troops began to take position in a line on the edge of the pavement the whole way—so that tho' there was such an immense concourse of military only very few companies marched past—only the veriest elite, the rest were echelonné[5] the whole way through the way of the procession. Banners were planted all along. Houses all hung with black & flags in mourning of course. (By the way I wish you w[oul]d send me a flag some time. I borrowed a ragged old one) At 9 Oclock the ladies to whom I had given places came, for it was impossible to pass after. The crowd took every inch of space climbing up every projection and hanging on to the heads & noses of all the big statues & the gratings of the windows. Precisely at 11 the procession filed into sight. Nothing could be more imposing only a few officers on horseback—all followed on foot. Even the general officers who made a splendid flashing squad themselves. The Senate & all the Parliament in citizens clothes, every one who had a decoration wearing it. The Colleges in Black gowns with such ruffs & jabots of white[.] The banners and the wreathes and the bands of music all passed under a dull gray sky, the sun shone out when the catafalque reached the Pantheon. The most splendid show of all were the law Courts. The judges had the most gorgeous dresses of scarlet velvet, with great chains of gold, and trimmings of ermine & sashes of satin, and they were such tremendous men so grand and magnificent they looked like Titians Doges, marching down. Then came the Ambassadors in full fig then the Royal Princes. Amadeus in the midst with his nephew the heir of Portugal at his right hand & with him the Crown Prince of Germany—& lots more who had been sent for the occasion. Then the great chevaliers of the Amionciadie among whom most conspicuous of all was the blind Duke of Sermoneta with the splendid collar of the order leaning on the arm of his tall son Prince Teano.[6] Next was the catafalque drawn by six horses covered with crepe tossing & fretting in their golden harness[.] The catafalque most imposing of course. Then the crown of Lombardy[7] carried on a cushion by Correnti[8] who I thought would fall on his nose very soon—but I did'nt hear he did so. The sword was carried by Gen. di Medici[9]—the mace & sceptre by various persons. Then the Deputations of all the towns of Italy each with their banner. Then the guilds of the different trades with their banners—then a company of soldiers, and all was over. It took one hour and a half to pass.

Today I went to see the Pantheon and the decorations there, & tomorrow I will see the new King & Queen[10] go to the Parliament to take the oath.

1. Massed lights surrounding a coffin.
2. The Bersaglieri were a troop of light infantry skilled in special formations and kept in Rome to participate in special ceremonies. They moved at double time and were often followed by exuberant crowds for whom they opened the way.
3. The Order of the Amionciadie or Order of the Most Holy Annunciation was the most important honor the House of Savoy could bestow for it made the recipient a "cousin of the king." The purple mantle was worn only by the "Great Master" who was always the king.
4. About one-fifth of a mile from the rear of her apartment.
5. Arrayed in formations by grade.
6. Onorato Caetani, destined to be the next Duke of Sermoneta.
7. Sixth-century iron cross believed to be made from the nails of the true cross. It was used to crown the rulers of Lombardy from Charlemagne to Napoleon I and, after Italian unification, the kings of Italy.
8. Cesare Correnti, a parliamentary leader from Lombardy.
9. Marquis Giacomo di Medici, who, although he had supported uniting Italy as a republic, had become a loyal supporter of the royal family.
10. Humbert I and Margherita.

February 10, 1878, 159 Via delle Quattro Fontane.

You see we have just buried the King, when the Pope has followed on his heels. It is a very important crisis for the whole Catholic church, and a great deal depends on the character of the man who shall be elected Pope.

I for one heartily hope the Conclave may be united in wisdom and animated by true religion to make a good choice. We may then hope to see the Church purify itself of its gross errors which grew out of the interests of the temporal power, and returning to the true object of religion to induce men to follow after Christ; not after this or that dogma.

The Pope is lying in state now at St Peters'. But I'll not go till tomorrow, as I had enough of pushing through the crowds to view Victor Emmanuel. There is yet to be a grand mass in the Pantheon (which has long been converted into a church) for the repose of the soul of V E. But the crowd will be very great, & had I a ticket I w[oul]d not go, for they have introduced gas for the occasion to light the dome, and I look for nothing less than some dreadful catastrophe from the decorations taking fire, or a panic at least.

I have been busy all winter painting fans—some I have done on Parchment very distinguished! I have been getting my things ready for the Water Colour exhibition wh[ich] takes place next week. I am the only lady member of the Society.[1] I have been a member three years, and they treat me with a great deal of deference.

1. La Societá Degli Acquarellisti in Roma or the Roman Society of Watercolorists.

February 23, [1878,] 159 Via delle Quattro Fontane.

The Silver Bill breaks my back.[1] My heart broke when the first shot was fired at the U S flag—but if after all we have suffered the Republic plunges into repudiation and such foolish dishonesty it is vain to have lived and endured so much. I look for nothing less than to see a separation between the west & the eastern states. But no separation will ever take place peaceably.

I sent you pictures of the King's death & funeral. Now we have lost Pio IX and now a new Pope. The obsequies of Pio nono were extremely simple and true to their system of shutting out the uninitiated they closed the doors of St Peter's after the lying in state (wh[ich] was very little state indeed) and all the funeral services the public were excluded from. I did not attempt to get in. Grace [Bristed] was admitted once into the Sistine chapel. The new man has yet to show what he is. The 20th when the news of the election ran round the city every one hurried to the piazza of St Peters, hoping to see Leo XIII come out into the balcony & give the Apostolic blessing ab urbis ed Orbis.[2] But he passed along the gallery leading from the Vatican to St Peters' & when he came to the balcony he hesitated,—and then turned and entering the Tribune that looks down into the church, he gave the blessing inside over the heads of those who had made their way within. Had he turned outside and blessed the people according to ancient custom, it w[oul]d have been received as an earnest of accepting the Bishopric shorn of the Temporal power. Whether or not he will come forth and officiate here often, or constitute himself a "prisoner" in the Vatican, is what nobody yet knows. He is said to be very intelligent and moderate in his views. He only came to Rome after the death of Antonelli who was his enemy—so it is expected he will not act as Antonelli[3] had influenced Pius IX to do. Meanwhile he seems to be making a clean sweep at the Vatican—cutting down expenses, and dismissing all useless retainers. Among the first was a plain intimation to the Gen[eral] of the Papal troops that he did'nt need him till he should think of going to war—and all the Swiss guard are trembling in their middle age costumes lest they be all dismissed. Yesterday his dinner being served after soup & boulli[4] they brought in a roast. Take it away says the Pope. I will have a little more soup—and that was his whole regale.[5] His friends say he nourishes himself only on a little soup & boulli—and Italian soups & lesso[6] are mighty thin fare.

1. The Bland-Allison Act, pressed by Western farmers and silver miners and intended as an inflationary stimulus to a depressed economy, obliged the secretary of treasury to purchase at least two million dollars worth of silver each month. In fact, the silver went uncoined and therefore had no significant effect on the economy
2. Gioacchino Pecci, archbishop of Perugia (1846–77), served as Pope Leo XIII from 1878 to 1903. Rumor had it that Vatican officials had blocked the hall leading to the balcony to keep the new pope from using it.
3. Giacomo Antonelli (1806–76) became a cardinal in 1846. As papal secretary of state after 1849 he influenced Pius IX's resolute opposition to Italian unification.
4. Boiled food.
5. Old fashioned expression for the delicacies of the table.
6. Boiled meat.

March 2, 1878, 159 Via delle Quattro Fontane.

I will send you Leo XIII photograph as soon as it is struck. He was to have come into St Peters' tomorrow after his incoronation in the Sistine chapel—but he has given it up on some ridiculous pretense. Last ev[enin]g Grace [Bristed] gave such a stupid party that I am sick today, and could not go to lunch at Mme de Westenbergs, wh[ich] I regret she always has such good grub, and Mrs Turnbull[1] & Mrs Story were going.

1. New York socialite Kitty Screven (Mrs. Robert) Turnbull.

March 31, [1878,] 159 Via delle Quattro Fontane.

Gen & Mrs Grant are here.[1] They receive attention but not such a fuss &c [as] was made over them in England. The court being in mourning makes any demonstration & festivity impossible. They appear extremely well. Very self-possessed, simple and quite unspoiled by all the attentions they have rec[eive]d. They seemed really pleased to see me. Master Jesse is a conceited cub, and quite carries out the reputation he has made for himself in other places. Mrs Grant says when she passed by Tenedos[2] she thought within herself that she was much wiser than Penelope, for she stuck to her Ulysses and did not let him roam the world without her. I went last ev[enin]g to a reception of the Marquise de Noailles[3] at the Farnese palace given to the Grants. The Ministers give them dinners & parties, & McMillan[4] the Consul Gen threw open his house in their honour, and we had to go—tho' McMillan is a bore and one likes to keep out of the way of his entertainments.

I have done nothing but paint fans all winter and I have been as busy as possible. Tho' it does'nt pay a great deal, no other artist has sold anything scarcely. I don't mean the price paid for my fans is not high, but it takes me a long time to do them as I do them.

1. President (1869–77) Ulysses Simpson Grant (1822–85) and Julia Dent Grant (1826–1902).
2. Now Bozca, an island off the Turkish coast that was the base for Greek naval operations during the Trojan War.

3. Wife of the vicomte who served as the French minister to Italy, 1876–80.
4. Charles McMillan, American consul general appointed in 1877.

July 11, [1878,] Ischia.[1]

Here I am on this most beautiful Island, wh[ich] is not at all like Sullivan's[2] —having no beach, but a rocky shore, a volcanic mountain long since extinct in the centre of it, forming all sorts of beautiful accidents of landscape—and wherever the lava has crumbled enough to become earth, the growth is prodigious. Such profusion of grapes on the vines I never before beheld even in Italy, and among them grow all sorts of vegetables, under the very vines, the sun seeming to penetrate sufficiently to [shine] upon every thing. There are peaches and apricots and pears, melons[,] great big plums of all colours and flavours, figs and green almonds wh[ich] they serve you on the half shell like oysters! Fish in plenty tho' very inferior in taste to ours. There are plenty of donkeys and little horses and little carriages, to climb up the mountain, or to drive from one rocky village to another. But never a cow on the Island. Only goats' milk. It is hot but the breeze seems always to blow enough to freshen every body. I think I shall enjoy my sojourn . . . there are very distinguished people only in the house, and most strange to say a great preponderance of men! In every other watering place I ever was at except Saratoga in the old old times, there has been more or less deficiency of men. Here they are three to one to the women. Diplomats who have to stay at their post in Italy, but send their families over the Alps in summer, and a number of young English officers from Malta, who have come here for a short leave and to stretch their legs; after being shut up in Malta Ischia offers great variety. I expect to move on to Capri after a while, and then to la Cava[3] where my friends the Newberys have a villa.

1. CPC's letters to her son from February to July 1878 deal almost exclusively with her attempts to organize James's love life and get him prosperously married. He never did marry.
2. Sullivan's Island lies across the Cooper River from Charleston.
3. Corpo di Cava, a mountain village southwest of Cava di Tirreni, about thirty miles from Naples.

July 15, [1878,] Ischia.

In Italy & France and indeed in the east, the raising of the silk is only a part of the farming operations. The whole crop is made & done in six weeks, and then they sell the cocoons to those who have establishments for winding They bake the cocoons before selling. At Lucca & at Perugia I saw the cocoons piled up in heaps like threshed corn—but I never was in the country in May & June the season for the worms. . . .

Ischia is pretty hot, but I am getting on very well. My sketches however so far have not pleased me at all. I am not in the vein. My heart is away with you my Blossom, not in my work.

August 18, [1878,] Corpo di Cava.

There came to Ischia four young English officers from Malta, and one of them Lt Chapman who had immediately scraped an acquaintance with me, fell ill two days after. As there did not seem much the matter, his companions went on their tour expecting him to overtake them, but he, instead, continued to get worse till it was clear he was in for intermittant fever.[1] His room was near mine and I went in to see him, and I was filled with compassion for him. And I thought of you and how you lay ill of the same fever with no help or comfort—and so in this stranger I nursed you for three weeks—and when he could move I brought him away to this place high up in the Calabrian mountains. I feel it my duty to return to the sick a little of the kindness that was so long & profusely bestowed upon me. The father & brother of Chapman traveled post haste from England when they heard how ill he was, and arrived here yesterday. The father who is over 60 was quite upset by the journey, and I had to begin forthwith to prescribe for him. He is better this morning, & I hope to escape having another sick man on my hands. The first one is getting on quite well, tho' he is still weak.

This Corpo di Cava is the most retired spot in Italy I do believe. You who have been in upland Spanish towns may have some idea of the hap hazard way every thing goes. Cava proper is quite a place with two very good hotels, but this is an hour's drive up the mountain where the air is much finer. So we take this in preference. The "Hotel" was so awful I could'nt stand it, so we moved to the Villa Guariglia, wh[ich] is a large stone mansion (tho all the villages are stone & mortar only) with a garden & fountains & plenty of excellent water. Very large rooms wh[ere] for three days I was following the women as if they had been July[2] in petticoats, to constrain them to clean thoroughly—and now we are quite at home and very fine. The cook is a tailor for women's dresses! who kindly lends a hand when Guariglia rents his rooms. You may suppose what his cooking is. But with resolution & praising his intelligence, I have brought him to make very good soup already and to do the meat in wholesome fashion. Sweet things he does by nature being a Neapolitan. And fruit we have in plenty. Here I shall camp for a month. Chapman's leave expires in ten days from this, and he'll have to go. But my dear Newberys, whom I have often mentioned to you, have a villa & live here, it was through them I knew of the place.

1. Malaria.
2. A servant at Dean Hall.

Caroline Carson*, Corpo di Cava looking to Mt Postiglione from Villa Guariglia 6 AM, Sep 8th/78. *In the editors' possession.

Abbazio delle SS Trinitá above Torrente Bonea. Photograph by William H. Pease, 1999.

September 9, 1878, Corpo di Cava, Villa Guariglia.

Lt Chapman has returned to Malta, and I have had a quiet comfortable time here—sketching and painting flowers. I send you a photo of the Monastery, which is a famous one, and very extensive as you see. Corpo di Cava is perched still higher up—you can see one of the houses in the right hand top corner. That is the next house to Villa Guariglia wh[ich] is <u>not</u> seen.

September 22, 1878, Corpo di Cava.

I meant to leave today for Naples, so as to take the boat to Capri Monday morning. The boats running but twice a week. Posi had written he w[oul]d come and join me, as he has been waiting all summer for an outing. But when I got all packed up yesterday, I rec[eive]d a letter from him that he could'nt come. The truth is the poor man is really out of health and more heavy to move than ever. I did not count on a gay companion in him, but at least it w[oul]d have been somebody to go about the Island of Capri with me. One must be always on the move there, and coast around in little boats. I know myself too well to undertake it alone. Beautiful as Capri is, and much as I desire to see it I know that I hate scrambling about by myself—and with half savage guides. Not that I am afraid of them, but I myself get dull and cross in strange places, if I have to go around. When I settle down for some time in a place I can enjoy it perfectly, quite alone. But travelling in search of the picturesque alone I do not enjoy. So I have changed my plan, and being under no necessity to catch the Capri boat, I will not travel on Sunday—but go tomorrow and proceed at once to Rome. Thus ends my summer which on the whole has gone very well.

Caroline Carson, **Grotto of Bonea Cava, May 3, 1876.** ***Courtesy of Ashton and LaVonne Phillips.***

107B Via delle Quattro Fontane. Photograph by William H. Pease, 1992.

October 7, 1878, 159 Via delle Quattro Fontane.

I have to change my apartment, and in the new one I will require a good many more things. I have taken to painting in oil, and my present studio is too small. . . .

I shall have a great deal of trouble & expense in moving, and I quake at it. But I hope it will turn out well. . . . I have just come back from Florence. I had just returned to Rome on 24th when I got a letter from Mr Schuyler asking me to go and pay a visit to him and Georgy at Florence, and I set right off that night. I enjoyed it very much, tho[ugh] it was sad too to remark the changes of time and sorrow. Mr Schuyler has become an old man, and I suppose I am getting old too, for when I got back Sat[urday] 5th I was tired to death, and scarcely feel rested yet. I went without Esterina, for as I went as Mr S's guest I could not increase the expense.

November 17, 1878, 107B Via delle Quattro Fontane.

I have made my flitting, but I have a great deal to do to settle myself in my new quarters. I have a good deal more room. That is my rooms are larger—and I c[oul]d contrive a bed for a friend.

December 15, 1878, 107B Via delle Quattro Fontane.

There is talk of superseding the Consul Gen[eral] at Rome, so I wrote to the powers that be to put in a claim for our William. It is a forlorn hope, and it cost me an effort to appear again as a solicitor. But I did it. McMillan however was put in through Sherman's[1] interest, and very likely will be backed up strongly. He has been picked up drunk it is true, but on the whole he has discharged his function very fairly well. And he does'nt drink any thing compared to his predecessor Dahlgren who was allowed to die of delirium tremens in peace, as also did Lorimer Graham consul at Florence for many years. But McMillan gets pulled up for drinking when perhaps he looked upon it as one of the qualifications expected of an American consul. . . .

I like my new apartment except that it is very cold. The rooms are twice as large as the old ones, and as it is a story higher it comes under the roof which makes it colder than the other. Moreover we have had a long rainy spell, and when the sun does'nt shine in Rome it gets very cold and very miserable. Today at last the sun was out clear, and I hope the season now will be fine.

1. Ohio senator John Sherman (1823–1900) became secretary of the treasury in 1877.

December 31, 1878, 107B Quattro Fontane.

Xmas day was very odd, I meant to write to you on coming back from church. I had no engagement for the only time in all these years, and I had laid out to eat my plum pudding & beef alone, and write to you. But when I came in there lay the name of Miss Screven,[1] Hotel de Russie.

So off I went to inspect Mary and I found she had been here a fortnight, and had never till that time found out that her courier might discover my address. She looked very well, really pretty, and seemed pleased to see me. I proposed she sh[oul]d come to dine with me, wh[ich] she readily accepted. Miss Secunda[2] did not show herself—and Mary did not seem to consider it at all necessary to take her along.

So I went off and ordered an extra dish & got some flowers for the table, and at 6 she came. We had a snug dinner and a good deal of talk. I would'nt write thus till I had seen more of her. Sat[urday] she was to come but she sent me a bouquet & did not appear. Sunday I went to drive with her in the Pincio,[3] and she said how disappointed she had been not to come, but Miss Secunda could'nt be induced to appear when she thought to meet people. Mary confesses Miss Secunda is a failure and very dull company. She can speak no language but her own, and thinks nothing like Charleston. But she wants to travel every where—and Mary proposes leaving in a few days for Sicily Malta Egypt Greece, Vienna Norway Sweden—!! But she says by spring she will be tired of Miss Secunda and go home. However she w[oul]d like a year in France to improve her French, and she may get somebody else and come back. I offered to make a party for her for Tuesday but that she declined on account of her sick headaches. However she wanted to hear the new Organ at the Am[erican] Church[4] yesterday afternoon at a grand exhibition of it. I had two tickets, so Mary was pleased to come & lunch with me. I then took her to Mr Story's studio, and thence to the prova[5] at the church. The Organ is magnificent. Mary has a maid whom she quotes very much as indeed she sees nobody else, and the most miserable looking courier I ever beheld, who has got her the meanest turn out for her money you ever saw. Nevertheless Mary felt herself very fine, and enjoys her liberty and freedom to go where she pleases and do as she likes.

1. Mary Screven, a debutante from Charleston and New York whom James Carson had been courting with little success.
2. Secunda Grimké, an older Charlestonian acting as Screven's companion and chaperone.
3. Hilltop park overlooking the Piazza del Populo, noted for both its views and its fashionable promenades and carriage drives.
4. St Paul's Episcopal Church, built on the modern Via Nazionale between 1872 and 1876.
5. A test or trial.

1879

January 26, 1879, 107B Via delle Quattro Fontane.

I wrote . . . [Mary Screven] to urge upon her prudence in going about in Naples, and that when she comes away to go clear out of Italy, not to come up by Rome & Florence. Fever contracted in Naples seems to have an awful proclivity for developing in the other Italian cities. I was kept in alarm all the time M. S. was here. The weather was dreadful, incessant rain, and she went about all the time, & without overshoes. She drove it is true, but one gets out & walks through awful damp. And she had put herself in rooms in the Hotel de Russie just under the Pincian Hill, wh[ich] we Romans look upon as stepping into a fever trap. I tried to make her move but every day she said she was going away and it was'nt worth while. . . .

I have been taken up for the last fortnight with Georgy & Lou Schuyler. They came up from Naples, & Georgy fell ill of the fever. I have been with them all the time, and I have cooked all her beef tea & jellies, for such things can never be done tolerably in hotels. I go the first thing in the morning & see how the night has passed, then I come home & see Lorenzo[1] get on with the Beef tea—and I paint (on order) for two hours at 2½ I go back and stay three or four hours with Georgy while Louisa goes out & refreshes a little. . . . Today the fever broke, and I hope & trust Georgy will get safely through, and Louisa not break down when it is over.

1. Lorenzo Pizzuti, whom CPC had hired as cook and courier in November when she took the apartment at 107B Via delle Quattro Fontane.

Feb 4th, 1879, 107B Via delle Quattro Fontane.

I have just sold two pictures for 500 lire, which is about 90 dollars. I hasten to send to you a check on Appleton[1] for $100—Which I hope will put you through.

1. Thomas Gold Appleton (1812–84) managed the trust fund that "Several Boston Gentlemen" had established for CPC in her father's honor after he died in 1863. CPC frequently lent or gave sums from the trust income to her sons and occasionally withdrew capital.

February 23, 1879, 107B Via delle Quattro Fontane.

As for Esterina and Lorenzo,[1] I admit it is a risk; but I put all the consequences before her—and she declared herself ready to take them. Very likely she counts I will relent, but sh[oul]d I not see the way to do so, I shall not relent, and I am not bound to do any more. So far they have done beautifully. Lorenzo turns out a very good cook, and if it can go on I shall only have to applaud my courage in undertaking it. There is so far no prospect of my being called for as Godmother. After all we had the nigs married and still do their service. These poor people get thro' their confinement and put the child out in their own village where they always have grandmothers and aunts. I hope we may go on indefinitely without recurring to them.

1. They had asked CPC's consent to their marrying and still remaining in her service. She had apparently agreed but stipulated that if they had children she might well dismiss her long-time maid.

February 25, 1879, 107B Via delle Quattro Fontane.

Carnival ends today in a rain storm. I haven't been over to the Corso. My rheumatic head was not to be ventured at an open window.

March 16, [1879,] 107B Via delle Quattro Fontane.

I have heard that Mrs Harry Brevoort[1] is in Paris trying to get a situation as companion to some lady! That Alfred Schermerhorn has died leaving very little & she is penniless! Whether the law let Harry go scott free or not, he sh[oul]d in common decency make a provision for her. What an unfortunate being she has been; and what a set they are all round. . . . I admit it was a risk to let Esterina & Lorenzo marry but it has done extremely well so far, and no breakers ahead yet.

1. Bessie Schermerhorn Brevoort had divorced CPC's grandnephew Henry (Harry) Brevoort.

April 3, 1879, 107B Via delle Quattro Fontane.

I've just accepted to give some lessons in order to be able (with justice) to send you some money—and I enclose 2 checks for $50, each that you may use one or both according to your extremity.

May 18, 1879, 107B Via delle Quattro Fontane.

The winter here has ended at last. The incessant rain, Georgy's illness, and my anxiety about you have made it seem four years long to me. Tho' I have done pretty well in my trade. I have been paid $500. . . .

I expect to go up into the Alps this summer, as a set off to the last at Ischia. . . . I have been very busy painting a picture for the Munich Exhibition the Roman Soc[iety] of Acquarellisti decided to send in a body, so I had to put in an appearance. I painted an Etruscan Vase full of Poppies, wild mignonnette & grasses. It was very effective, but I hated to do it when I had other things to paint for which I am to be paid more money—$300 more of orders. And at these exhibitions one sells nothing and has the expense for praise. I have also copied in the Villa Ludivisi[1] two beautiful frescos of Guircino,[2] in water Colours. The Notte and the Sera.[3] They have never been copied to my knowledge. The <u>Piombini</u>[4] being

Caroline Carson, "Still Life, Decorated Vase against Yellow Damask." Courtesy of Ashton and LaVonne Phillips.

excessively jealous of their possessions. The old Prince is immensely rich and has lands and palaces all about in Italy. This Villa Ludovisi is a garden of many acres in the midst of Rome. It has groves of Ilex and pine trees—walks & drives—flower gardens. Statues [and] three beautiful Villas on the grounds inhabited in the Spring by the Princess, and her son the Duke of Sora & daughter Princess Teano.[5] There are horses and a cow establishment, and about 50 persons in all with their families on the place to keep it in order. It is impossible to get permission to copy! but my carpenter Pippo set me to ask the Maestro di Casa,[6] and after dancing attendance at the Pal[azzo] Piombino in the Corso for a week I did at last obtain the boon—and to the envy of everybody I have been enjoying my freedom there at pleasure for two months. It has rained however so awfully I could not avail myself largely of the privilege. My dance is up now for the Princess moves into her Casino[7] where I was painting, tomorrow.

1. A grand old villa destroyed in the building boom of the 1880s and 1890s that produced modern Rome.
2. Giovanni Francesco Barbieri Guercino (1591–1666).
3. The Night and the Evening.
4. The prominent Roman family to whom the Villa Ludovisi belonged.
5. Daughter-in-law of the Duke of Sermoneta.
6. Major domo.
7. Country house.

June 1, 1879, 107B Via delle Quattro Fontane.

The little man [de Westenberg] is very cantankerous, and he chose to abuse Mrs Mason[1] awfully to me every time I saw him, so that when she was coming this winter I felt bound to tell Mme de Westenberg that I sh[oul]d tell Mrs Mason not to call on her, since her husband declared his intention to insult her. Thereupon de Westenberg turned about, and made war upon me—so now we don't speak at all. The provoking part is that Mme de W. for two years has been talking it over with me, professing her admiration for Mrs Mason & her pleasure in her society, and her intense regret that her husband disliked her & was prejudiced against her—and then when the little villain ran about town abusing the lady so outrageously that two gentlemen came to me as Mrs Mason's friend to ask what was the meaning of it, and I did the only thing left, namely to protect Mrs Mason from going to his house to be treated with insult, they both turn upon me and say I have slandered him. It is too ridiculous and silly. . . .

We have had such rains since December that the crops are carried away, and disasters by flood and field are numerous: besides both Vesuvius & Etna in eruption. This adverse combination of the planets seems a serious thing! The sun has come out at last however, and if he can hold his own against the still returning clouds for a few days, he may put them to flight altogether.

June 6th

Nothing has transpired in these intervening days except that I have finished a fan for Georgina Schuyler on parchment, the Parnassus of Raphael.[2] I never did anything that gave me so much trouble. I did it last year & sold to an Englishman for £20. Georgy saw it and wanted one. But whereas I did the first one in 14 days, I tried to do this in a better way, and it took 27 days and is not as good I think as the first was—or perhaps it is that I am so tired of it, and moreover my eyes are a year older and the miniature painting more painful. However it is done and I am glad to be quit of it.

I had yesterday a tea at 5 PM for the Marchesa Longhi—(sister of the Duke of Sermoneta) and her daughters, one of whom was lately married. There were only 8 persons, one was a young Waldstein—a NewYorker of german parents, who has got as much in his head as Johnston Pettigrew[3] had at his years—except that the part J. gave to Law he has devoted to science, and he is as frank and ready for society as Johnston was reserved. My tea went off very well. I gave them strawberries, and waffles made in the iron I brought in my trunk from America.

1. Perhaps because of her divorce from Sen. Charles Sumner.
2. Raphael Santi or Sanzio (1483–1520), Renaissance painter. His Parnassus is a lunette painted above a window in the Vatican's Stanza della Segnatura (Tribunal of the Holy See).
3. CPC's second cousin, James Johnston Pettigrew (1828–63), a Civil War general with a reputation for brilliance in several fields, had studied law with James L. Petigru.

June 19, 1879, 107B Via delle Quattro Fontane.

The weather is so delightful in Rome now that I hate to leave, but I know I must be off 1st July on penalty of losing my whole winter, as I did once before by staying two summers consecutively in Italy. My eyes & my digestion both gave out. I might escape to be sure—but the risk is too great to run. So I will take up my march and go over the St Gothard to lake Lucerne in Switzerland. . . . I am going with Mrs [Annie Fitch] Hyde who will meet her sister Mrs Robert Gracie at Lucerne. So I shall be among old friends as it were. As I have known Mrs Robert off and on since I was 15. Mr Hyde is the father of our Sec of Legation G W. Wurts—& Mrs Hyde is very agreeable & cultivated.[1] I met her at Como three years ago. . . .

I am trying to make a likeness of Phil [Porcher] in oil out of that horrid little photograph. I don't know yet how it will succeed, but at all events I have tried to do what you ask.

1. Henry Baldwin Hyde (1834–99), founder of the Equitable Life Insurance Company. His daughter by an earlier marriage was the wife of George Washington Wurts, therefore Hyde was Wurts' father-in-law, not his father.

July 7, 1879, Pension Felsberg, Lucerne, Suisse.

Here am I having travelled over the St Gothard in a snow-storm, and arriving at Lucerne for my summering to find it as cold as november. . . .

I left Rome July 1st with Esterina at 2.30 P.M. Posi & Elena seeing me off. . . . I went all that night reaching Genoa at 4 AM & keeping right on to Arona at the bottom of Lake Maggiore where I found Mr & Mrs Hyde with whom I had agreed to travel. The lake was so rough that we stopped till next morning & then had a beautiful sail up in the Steamer to Locarno—thence by rail to Biasca—and next morning we were to take the Diligence in wh[ich] we had best seats to cross the St Gothard.[1] But we allowed ourselves to be persuaded by the Innkeeper to take a carriage instead wh[ich] cost no more, & where we were to take our own time! Soon we repented when too late—for it came on to rain and we often had to shut up the carriage & then it was no better for seeing out than the diligence,

Caroline Carson, Andermatt 1874. *Courtesy of Ashton and LaVonne Phillips.*

indeed not half so good as the coupé seats we had abandoned. Of course the mail must go through and has plenty of relay horses. We got on well enough however to Airolo when it began to be very cold, & I bought a flannel petticoat and put it on. We had most inadequate wraps, for I have so often lugged them along never using them, that this time I left them all, just when the season turns out most cold. We soon came to ice & snow and a cutting wind, and going on we passed into a really terrific region—for two hours up to the top of the St Gothard we passed between walls of hard packed snow through which the road had been cut out, for the most part it was 20 feet high on each hand and once 30—and one time a gallery cut under the snow. And finally towards the top the clouds came down in snow around us. There was every fear the horses w[oul]d break down, tho' they had put on two extra strong horses at Airolo. But they pulled through, as on the descent we left the snow walls in about a half an hour; it was not however till 10 PM that we reached Andermatt; and were glad to get to bed safe. You see at Biasca nobody hinted the St Gothard pass was in such a condition, We w[oul]d have stuck to the diligence.

Next morning we left & came through superb scenery but awfully cold, & wet down to Alt[d]orf where William Tell shot the apple off his son's head—but we could'nt stop to see his statue with his bow & arrows, except in passing. [G]ot to Fluelen on Lake Lucerne and took the boat for the town of Lucerne which is at the extreme further end—and the sail ought to have been beautiful, but it was so cold we had to keep in the cabin, or venturing out go and sit on the boiler, which was a great square comfortable box somewhere forward. We arrived alive & well however and taking a carriage in 15 min drove to this Pension above the town. I am quite comfortable here, or rather will be so when the sun returns to warm the place. Last week they say it was very hot.

Mrs Hyde's two sisters Mrs Robert & Mrs Wm Gracie[2] are here wh[ich] was Mrs Hyde's attraction making her give up the Dolomites & Venice, to which I had fondly hoped to go. But I am so tired of going off alone of summers, that I decided to adhere to Mrs Hyde and see how the balance will be at the end of the season. Mrs Wm Gracie you may remember was the Lady who had charge of Gabrielle Nottlech whom I was to have superceded. I haven't yet had any talk with her on that subject, and I don't think I'll ever let on that I had any dealings about those girls.

But the oddest meeting is with Bessie Schermerhorn![3] Mrs Schermerhorn she is called! Alfred [Schermerhorn][4] her father is dead & has left her very little & wanted her to live with her step mother, which she will not do. A Miss Alden friend of her own mother gave her $1000 after the divorce to come away & refresh herself. She proceeded to Paris and at Miss Ellis's boarding house fell in with Mrs Gracie (Robt) who has taken her in tow. Mrs Hyde told me last winter how that she was trying to get a place as governess or lady's companion, for neither of which she is fit in any way, of course. I was very much shocked that she sh[oul]d be in this destitute condition & mentioned it to Phoebe last winter in Rome. Phoebe said she had heard of her from a lady who had made the passage out in the same ship & she said her manners & behaviour were very flirting & improper. She sits opposite me at table & immediately introduced herself—and seems quite unconcerned. She is very pretty. All these ladies are very sorry for her don't see any harm in her, but say she is luxuriously fond of amusement and eager for pleasure. Poor thing! What will become of her! I shall observe her curiously you may be sure and try to find out what is the truth about her. Her friends say the divorce was obtained by Harry on the ground of <u>her</u> desertion as she went back to her father on her own demand. That is sheer nonsense, as she & her family we know wanted her to be taken back. They also admit that at first the Brevoorts offered her $5000 a year to agree to the divorce, but her father would'nt take it holding out for more, & now she has got nothing. It is very ugly. Though some method of law may have freed Harry, he & his people ought to feel they should in common decency make a provision for her. Such selfishness & greed cannot prosper in the day when the great accounts of life are to be made up.

1. A pass some seven thousand feet above sea level.
2. Mrs. Robert Gracie was a New York socialite. Less fortunate, Mrs. William Gracie had, at some time, been a governess.
3. She had resumed her maiden name after she divorced Harry Brevoort.
4. A member of the Astors' social circle in New York with whom CPC also had connections.

July 27, 1879, Lucerne.

It has rained all this month as if we were in the tropics in the rainy season, only ours is a cold rain. We had two good days, and I went on a cruize on the Lake yesterday PM. It was very lovely Today is a straight down pour.

Bessie Schermerhorn has told Mrs Gracie that she it was who at last sued for the divorce, and went into Connecticut to get it; and Harry's lawyers demanded the surrender of all her claims on his estate, and her friends advised her to give up every thing to obtain her freedom. So she signed any paper they presented, and so has got her divorce but no alimony Her lawyer must have been of no account, and her friends very silly all the way through. For as Harry was manifestly crazy to be free, they should have bargained with him for a good sum as the condition for her bringing her demand for his desertion. As it is she is no better, but worse off for the divorce. Without any money she will find no one to marry her as her friend Miss Colman fondly hopes—and to say she is divorced without alimony at once puts her before the world in the wrong. She is very pretty attractive and gay—just the sort of person to suit Harry—no sensibility, but lively & full of go. There is in this Pension a young German who has fallen in love with her so they all say. He is very nice, manly, simple outspoken. He plays the piano like a German & sings, and dances, and is good humoured and friendly, and very good manners. His story is touching. He is only 32. Has been married to an Englis[h] girl, who died in a year, and as he told me, he put her baby in her arms in the same coffiin, and took them back & buried them in England. He has a photograph of her that looks like Bessie Schermerhorn. Then he has a photo of a charming house & gardens wh[ich] he says was his, but soon after the death of his wife in these German failures[1] he lost all his property in business, & it was sold up. Now he is going to Russia as agent to some great estate, where he says in ten years he will make a fortune, but meanwhile it is a life entirely solitary no neighbours within 20 miles—and he must bind himself to leave only once in three years for an excursion to see his mother. He can't be very hard hit in three weeks, but I shall feel sorry if he carry this additional thorn into his exile.

1. Probably a reference to losses sustained in the financial panic of 1873 and the depression that followed.

September 17, 1879, Stresa, Lago Maggiori.

Stresa is a lovely place & I enjoy it and I make sketches, one of which I will send you when you get back if you are ever stationary any where long enough. . . . I long to get back to Rome, and I hope in two weeks to be there.

October 2, [1879,] Rome, 107B Via delle Quattro Fontane.

I rec[eive]d No 43[1] just as I was leaving Stresa. I set out at 2,43 Tuesday and arrived at 1,30 Oct[ober] 1st at Rome doing the journey without stopping in about 24 hours. I found Mrs Posi and Lorenzo waiting at the station and very glad am I to be at home again. It has been a tolerable summer but not one I w[oul]d wish to repeat. Luzern is a depressing climate.

1. The Carsons numbered as well as dated their letters so that they would know when one went astray.

December 14, 1879, 107B Via delle Quattro Fontane.

You have no idea how cold it is here this winter. I was fairly frozen out of my bedroom, which was an end one projecting to the south; & ought to have been warm, but it is alone on three sides, and under the roof (I live up 84 steps) At night I had a little fire to go to bed by, and I wound up & got quite warm all my body; but I was woke up all the time by my eyes paining with cold. I tied a h[an]dk[erchief] over them in vain. So at last I moved my bed into a middle room. . . . I have shut the door of the far room, and I am only half frozen now. I havn't felt anything like it since the old Carolina days when we used to terminate our letters saying our fingers were too cold to write any more.

1880

February 11, 1880, Ash Wesnesday, 107B Via delle Quattro Fontane.

I haven't been to church since New Year's day because I have had such a cold and rheumatism in my right leg. I can go out but not walk enough for health. I have been to but three evening parties all winter, and I achieve a few dinners. But the church is heated when we go in, and after creeps up a chill that goes to my marrow. I got this pain in my leg there any way.

Well we have done the carnival and as I was all the PM yesterday on the Corso with Grace throwing bouquets & holding nuvoletti [?][1] I thought I must be up to the rail on Ash Wed[nesday]—so I went—it is a damp day after the beautiful carnival weather we have had. I was not seated 15 min before I felt the chill & the pain so strong that I got up and came away. . . .

Clarence Seward writes I may be summoned home.[2] I hope I will not have to get up and go before the spring. I am sure it would fix this rheumatism on me, and if it be possible I wish to avoid it. Also I w[oul]d have to arrange a great deal about my apartment, and provide for my two servants—and whether to bring clothes for a year or less. It would be more convenient to me to go in June (If go I must) and even stay over the winter & the next summer than to go now. My lease runs till Nov[ember] 1881 and I'd have to arrange a great deal before I could settle how to renew or what to do. . . . My apartment has to undergo repairs this summer

Caroline Carson,* Colle Savelli, 2 Maggio 1880. *Courtesy of Ashton and LaVonne Phillips.

wh[ich] the Padrone has to put, & I shall have to keep Lorenzo in it, as I could'nt leave all my furniture open to the workmen. . . .

I never mentioned the Calhoun Mon[ument].[3] because I was always so busy talking with you about other things. I have inherited too much from you to have made a profit out of my recommendation of the artist whose merits I desired to set forth. But I did it with all my heart & took a great deal of pains and trouble, hoping that by the system of compensation some friend would be raised up for my sons in time, and with trust in God that he will not desert us.

1. Lime-covered confetti.
2. New York lawyer Clarence Seward, although he was not then taking an active role in CPC's legal efforts to regain Dean Hall, advised her to change her legal residence to some state other than New York to escape the jurisdiction of its state courts.
3. Charleston mayor William A. Courtenay had asked CPC to suggest an American sculptor living in Italy to design and execute a monument that would memorialize South Carolina senator and political theorist John Caldwell Calhoun (1782–1850). The commission was given to Albert E. Harnisch apparently at her recommendation.

July 10, 1880, 107B Via delle Quattro Fontane.

[Grace Bristed] has taken a villa [at Castel Gondolfo][1] in the Alban hills, and invited me out for a month. I shall go 13th to stop two weeks. Return and start for the hot baths of Acqui [Terme] near Genoa, where I hope to get rid of the rheumatism which has got hold of my right elbow now. In Sep[tember] I'll go to Venice. D[eo] V[olente].[2]

1. About twelve miles southeast of Rome.
2. God willing.

July 25, 1880, St James's Day, Castel Gondolfo.

It is awful hot here, never again will I be caught at this season near Rome. Grace's Villa is large & lofty, but the hot air wraps one as in a mantle, like at Badwell. But when evening comes and the cool creeps up, unlike Badwell, we must shut our windows from the night air before going to bed. The vapours from the Campagna being more deadly than the Rice fields.

August 22, [1880,] Pension Suisse, Venice.

I took my 12 mud baths at Acqui, & five others. But it soon appeared I could not take the 2nd hot bath a day—so these were left off. They were very unpleasant as you may imagine. Called up at 6 AM—scramble on coverings & cloak, go down where a girl received me in a little steaming room with two baths, one with a long sack filled with straw, and covered by a large coarse linen sheet, a large basket of hot sulphur mud quite black when wet—she lays a course of this down one side the sheet, and I lie down on the affected side in it—she packs the hot mud from my foot up to the shoulder pinning down my right arm—then she tucks the sheet over me leaving only my head out. In 15 min. she returns and asks me how I am, wipes my reeking face & administers a glass of the hot sulphur water, and saying "bene" departs. 20 min more and she returns, the other bath has been filled with warm water, she scrapes off the mud & helps me

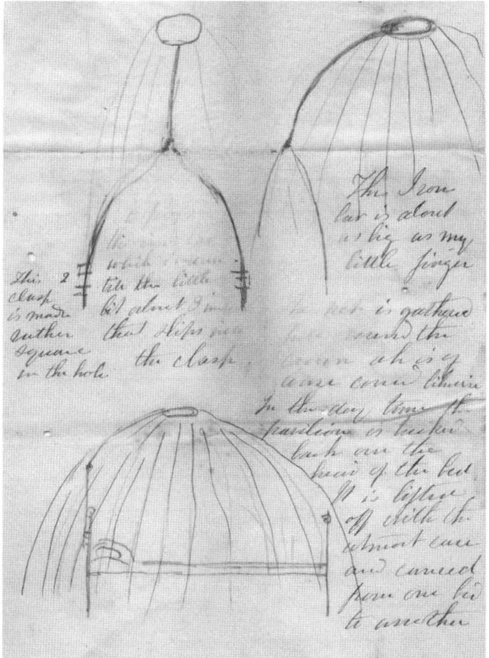

Enclosure in letter from Caroline Carson to James Carson, 22 August 1880. "(This clasp is made rather square in the hole to press the iron bar which is round till the little bit about 3 inches that slips into the clasp. The Iron bar is about as big as my little finger The net is gathered full round the crown wh[ich] is of course covered likewise. In the day time the pavilion is tucked back over the head of the bed. It is lifted off with the utmost ease and carried from one bed to another.) All the Italians use iron bedsteads by the way but the clasp might be secured on any sort of bed. It is for hanging mosquito nets—& far more simple & less costly than the patent apparatus used in N York."

into the water. Fetches a large drum full of hot cloths and goes off to order my bed heated with a warming pan (in August!) I scurry up tumble into bed & <u>sweat</u> two hours. Esterina makes me a cup of tea (which the establishment does not give) and I get up. Acqui was cool & pleasant enough with shady walks & nice drives. But it was awfully expensive. Altogether baths [illegible] it cost me $5 a day. Fortunately in 15 days the cure was pronounced complete and I could come away. Most part of the time I had a horrid cough; taken from not putting on enough cloaks & shawls coming up from the first bath. . . .

By the way you may take out a patent for an excellent invention I find here in Venice. (This clasp is made rather square in the hole to press the iron bar which is round till the little bit about 3 inches that slips into the clasp. The Iron bar is about as big as my little finger The net is gathered full round the crown wh[ich] is of course covered likewise. In the day time the pavilion is tucked back over the head of the bed. It is lifted off with the utmost ease and carried from one bed to another.) All the Italians use iron bedsteads by the way but the clasp might be secured on any sort of bed. It is for hanging mosquito nets—& far more simple & less costly than the patent apparatus used in N York.

September 5, 1880, Venice.

I am sorry Phil's picture stuck, but I don't believe cleaning will do any good—for if the paint was too fresh, it would only get more blurred by rubbing. You see I am not experienced in oils, and the picture bothered me a great deal. I was never satisfied with it, and kept on painting on it till the last minute before Go[u]v[ernor] Wilkins left—and I did not put any turpentine. . . .

I send you three drawings of the view from my window. Stick them down on large Bristol board—a little gum Arabic at the four corners does it—and you can tack up the card board in your room to enliven it.

October 3, 1880, Venice.

I note what you say about voting for Hancock,[1] and I don't object, because you say you are in no ways a Democrat. I can't help thinking the Republicans have been long enough in power, and the good they have done is too long past, and the evil too present. It is time to cut and make a new deal. But there is no occasion to enrol oneself with the democrats who from Jefferson down have been the bane of the republic. I read Sen Bayard's[2] speech at Columbia, which is extremely good as far as it goes in promise; but I should trust more to the democrats if there were a majority among them of men like Bayard, and more to Bayard himself if in praising the democratic party as the upholders of a sound currency he did not ignore all the democratic howling for inflation which we have heard with our ears. . . .

I wish indeed I might come to see you next year. Sometimes I feel as if I can hold out no longer. But when I set myself to "figure it out" I cannot see the way [unless] you were really settled somewhere. But to go and come back I have not the money for that last time, (which I am most thankful to have had with you) we had but five weeks after all—and the rest of the time I was billeted on friends who might not invite me another time—and besides I sh[oul]d not wish to go and be so little with you; and I could'nt pay the board all summer. And my house rent goes on here, & I could not keep my two servants without paying them. And dismissing them I might never get the same comfortable arrangement again. My lease runs out a year from Nov[ember]. While things go pretty well with me as it is, I had best make no changes. But if some break happens then I may pull up and come away. . . .

I should have been in Rome yesterday according to custom. But I have been copying a very important picture in the Gallery (not ordered alas!) and it is not finished. However I make an end of it tomorrow, and leave Tuesday for Florence where I must stop to see Mrs Huntington, who is in great affliction: her son Henry who is a great friend & favourite of mine has had an access of insanity and has to be put in the asylum of Pistoja.

1. Winfield Scott Hancock (1824–80), Democratic nominee for president in 1880.
2. Thomas Francis Bayard (1828–98), Democratic United States senator from Delaware, 1869–81.

December 5, 1880, 107B Via delle Quattro Fontane.

I'll give you the benefit of my experience. After finishing my solitary dinner, if I drop into a chair with a book to digest—intending after a while to rouse up and write letters (to do which I never have time in the day) I find the letters seldom get written. I doze off and there is the end of my evening. So that with a resolute effort I have learned to sit down immediately after dinner to write, and after a while I brighten up & get through the letters very well. But it requires a pressure on myself each time. . . .

We are all gathered pretty much in Rome now. . . . Mrs Strong[1] has returned with her dame de compagnie & her courier. The former a promoted Irish servant and the latter an anomely. A good looking Italian who treats her with strange familiarity. Maria Roosevelt's husband Scovell—is to come out as tenor in the Sonnambula slightly veiled as Edouardo Scovello. His voice is lovely. It remains to be seen if it is strong enough to fill a large house. It is very spirited of him and of her that he follows his art instead of fattening in idleness. He speaks with gratitude of all she has done for him, and he is very attentive to her. She seems quite happy and is far less hideous than she used to be. She had with her last winter a lovely little girl, and she has now given birth to a boy and gone to Nice, there to await the experiment of Scovello's voice. I saw Mme de Westenberg in church this morning. She has turned quite grey and very stout and looks like an old woman. . . .

Dec[ember] 7th

[T]he universal Lorenzo, who cooks waits on me in society, papers screws puts the well[?] in order—plants & tends flowers in pots, paints, hammers and is in fact man of all work. Esterina has even got him at the sewing machine, he rips up my dresses when she has to alter them, and does every thing but stops short at the leather wedge. . . .

I have been thinking of taking the agency for Count Neutter's remedies. Those little febbrifuge pillules I sent you to Nevada. He is a man of rank & immense fortune who has devoted his life to chemical explorations of medicine, and he has found some wonderful secrets of Electro Homeopathy he calls it. He has remedies for every ill of the human body. Rheumatism & even cancer. If I took the agency it w[oul]d be transferred to you. But whether we could make anything of it. Much advertising w[oul]d have to be done, & w[oul]d you have time any way to see to it?[2]

1. Eleanor Burrill Fearing Strong (Mrs. Charles Edward), a New York socialite who lived mostly in Europe where her husband visited her periodically.

2. CPC here looked to both her need to garner a greater income and her personal reliance on homeopathic medicine, the benefits of which she constantly commended to her son.

1881

January 26, [1881,] 107B Via delle Quattro Fontane.

I had a letter yesterday from Mary March[1] at Naples. She has been frightened to death by all the reports the rival cities & hotels put about the pestilential condition of Rome. Which has been perfectly healthy all winter. Mary scurried through to Naples tho' I had written to her at Paris, to warn her against going first to Naples & then coming to Rome, which we do not think well for unacclimated people. Stop first as long as one wants in Rome, then go to Naples, and coming back pass on without much stoppage at Rome. But now she writes she wants to stop at Rome—and she is going back to Paris to be more in reach of getting at Charles who would not come with her but went off to Dresden. Both her sons are poorly & Clem needed a warmer climate, but by this plan the poor woman is torn to tatters and neither son benefitted. . . .

I have been to a ball on 18th at Lady Pagets'—Ambassadress of England. It was very elegant. Tuesday ev[enin]g I was to go to a dancing party at an English house—but when I went to dress, I crept into bed instead. But tonight I am going to a party at Mrs Huyland's—she is the daughter of the Jessup[2] who bought Mrs Blodgett's place at Newport & turned 100000 upon it in a year! Hard on Mrs Blodgett.

1. Mary Livingston Lowndes (Mrs John Payne) March was the daughter of Rawlin Lowndes, whose South Carolina property James L. Petigru defended against Confederate confiscation during the Civil War when his family, like CPC, was exiled in New York.

2. Probably Morris Ketchum Jessup (1830–1908), banker, railroad capitalist, and, after his retirement, a philanthropist who gave millions to natural history and religious institutions.

April 3, [1881,] 107B Via delle Quattro Fontane.

I am doing very well in my art. I paint with more ease & skill and I have done very well, sold for $600-worth so far—this is the harvest season of art, but I may pick up some gleaning later on—and I work without ceasing all the year round to make this.

April 17, [1881,] Easter morning, 107B Via delle Quattro Fontane.

I am glad Miss Datté has resumed her sway at Dean Hall, and I hope the hours she marks, will be happier than those I spent there. And yet perhaps the seed I sowed there in tears may cause me to come in joy bringing my sheaves with me. There I learned to bear disappointment and humiliation,[1] and when my just expectations were laid low—I bent myself to bear my mistake with patience and to do the best I could with mind, heart & conscience, waiting for God's time of deliverance. I have had much to suffer but if my sons thereby are better and higher men I have my reward, even if Dean Hall come to naught, and we have to go on to the end of the chapter as day labourers. After all life is not long, and if we stand up manfully and cheerfully to duty there is great satisfaction in the sense of inward power.

1. The reference is to her disastrous marriage.

June 25, 1881, 107B Via delle Quattro Fontane.

I was enjoying June very much, every body is gone but two or three old stayers, and I could paint all day without interruption and no visits to make. But the comet rushed in a few days ago, and it has become boiling hot. I shall not be able to stand it till middle of July as I intended, but I must hurry up and get off to some high perch in Switzerland. There is such demand for panel flower pieces that I have to go in for doing them in oils. I must paint my flowers first in water colours, and then copy them more leisurely into oils. Double work—and I don't know if it will pay. But I have always made Æsop's wild boar my model who in time of peace sharpened his tusks for the enemy.

July 30, 1881, Gavignano Pistojese.

I was so dismayed by the news from Dean Hall that I abandoned the journey to Switzerland, tho' to cross the Alps every other year is very necessary to my health. Italy is so dry in summer I get parched up like the fields, and I feel my skin shrivel and my head full. I came up to San Marcello[1] a little beyond Florence to a pension full of extremely pleasant people, but I had no settled room not having engaged one before—and Esterina was poked into a place over the kitchen without the means to wash or sleep scarcely—and I had to pay 13 fr[anc]s a day. I cast about and found in a village up the mountain a clean little country inn, where the Padrone, an old courier of Mrs Alice Mason, instantly recognizing me—and putting his house at my disposal. So to the amazement of all the fine company at Villa Margherita,[2] I quit and came up here three days ago. There is not a creature in the house but myself and a young Egyptian! Italian from Alessandria who for bronchitis has been ordered to mountain air. I suppose he has caught one of the bronchite Europeans are sent to Egypt to get rid of. I have here plenty of space which is the thing I require most for comfort—and I pay 10 fr[anc]s a day for me & Esterina. She is delighted for the padrone's family are company for her and <u>we</u> are great personages in Gavignano instead of the tail end of Villa Margherita.

I walked down the mountain there last ev[enin]g with a stout staff a contadino[3] cut for me—and I was received with great applause and a party escorted me half way back—Paul Tilton[4] coming quite up home with me. I shall do very well for a month, and if I don't hear some more bad news I will go to Venice in September for refreshment. There will be assembled the Geographical Congress, and I hope to meet Judge & Mrs Daly[5]—and Grace [Bristed] is to meet me there.

But Grace is "such an uncertain devil" that I dont count on her. She has done the queerest thing about Charley. She put him to a Jesuit College for the Spring at Frascati[6]—that was well enough as she thought he needed to be more with boys of his age—and she was busy furnishing her apartment; which this time is a very delightful one in the Piazza del Popolo. But when she was to go to Kissengen last week she consigns Charles to a priest to take down the Naples road and up into the Abruzzi[7] to stay with his family a month—& then the priest is to bring him to her! She says she can't afford to take Charles to Kissengen! Having $8,000 a year for his maintenance. Besides she is sure to have to pay the priest more than Charles going with her could have cost. And a priest's family are just as likely as not to be the veriest peasants.—Grace is incomprehensible. She has got an odour of the sacristy about her which is suffocating to all natural growth. And she has got into such a poor, low set of bigots. . . .[8]

The President's case occupies much of my interest.[9] These horrid envoys of glycerine to England[10] and the wide spread rage for destruction and murder in cold blood is enough to make us think we are coming to the end of the world. It is a sort of disintegration of society, and return to worse than savage ferocity. It is an awful problem the worst I suppose that has been presented to mankind to deal with. You have fallen upon evil times in your generation my dear James. Hold fast to faith in God I beseech you my son in this sceptical age which denies all faith and with it as the corollary comes the denial of justice and morality. The masses are fast falling below the standard of heathens—and of the old Greeks and Romans—and the worst is that it is not the ignorant who have engendered this, but the so-called wise and progressive. To what it will bring society who shall say? But let us not let go the only stay; the hope & trust in another world where the crooked will be straight & we shall be rewarded as we have borne ourselves in this life of trial.

1. San Marcello Pistojese and Gavignano Pistojese are Tuscan resorts in the Apennines.
2. The pension at San Marcello.
3. Peasant.
4. Paul Henry Tilton was, like his father, John Rollin Tilton, a painter.
5. Charles Patrick Daly (1816–99) and his wife, Maria Lydig Daly, were among CPC's closest friends in New York where Judge Daly served as chief justice of the municipal

court for twenty-seven years. He was also actively involved in the Geographical Society and thus a participant in the geographical conference held in Venice in 1881.

6. Town about eighteen miles southeast of Rome.
7. A generally impoverished region northeast of Rome bordering on the Adriatic Sea.
8. Like many Americans, including three of Louisa Ward Crawford Terry's children, Grace Bristed converted to Catholicism in Rome. This pattern much disturbed CPC—as it did Mrs Terry.
9. On July 2, Charles Guiteau, a disappointed office seeker, had shot President James Garfield, who died of the wounds on September 19.
10. In 1881, in response to a new English Land Act and coercive measures to enforce it, Irish nationalists responded violently as part of Charles Parnell's campaign to gain home rule for Ireland.

August 14, 1881, Gavignano, Hotel Ferrucci.

I might have staid in this village till October to save a few dollars—but this news[1] drives me to keeping the point of going in Sep[tember] to Venice. The entire solitude here is too much with these dreary thoughts pursuing me. I have to keep busy day & night to drive them off, and my eyes will not hold out. So I'll go to Venice, see my friends the Dalys—and Grace—and return Oct[ober] to Rome to await with fortitude whatever trial it please God to send. This life is not the end of man—and we may well spend it in bearing bravely the discipline we cannot escape.

1. The Supreme Court of South Carolina had ruled that a new plaintiff, not included in previous decisions favoring CPC, had a legitimate claim on Dean Hall.

September 16, 1881, Venice, Hotel di Roma.

The [Geographical] Congress has brought lots of people to Venice, and last night there was a splendid illumination of the Piazza of San Marco, and San Giorgio out in the water. Judge & Mrs Daly are here, & Osten Sacken, & Gen & Mrs Cullum. . . . [Y]esterday I went round all the afternoon in a gondola with Mrs Daly & O. S.

September 25, 1881, 107B Via delle Quattro Fontane.

I had a delightful time [in Venice]. . . . The Illuminations were splendid, and the rigatta, but the arrangements for the Congressional delegates were not well managed—consequently there was much discontent. Judge Daly as President of his Geog[raphical] society rec[eive]d his honours & was invited to the King's dinner party—but the Vice pres[idents] & delegates of Societies had no particular attentions paid them. Delegates from Governments were recognized. Now our gov[ernment] as usual made no account of the thing & sent no delegates. But a certain Wheeler[1] who was travelling was acute enough to ask the War Dep[artmen]t for a letter, and so he was recognized as a Government agent from US and received all the honours invitations boxes at the Opera—&c to the intense disgust of the other Americans. [One delegate] took himself off in two days. Our illus[tri]ous Cullum staid there in a rage & declares he will complain of the Italians far and near. Even Botta[2] (who I hear) was there was furious. Wheeler accepted every thing for himself & wife instead of sharing the Opera boxes &c with the American Societies as the other head[s] were understood to do.

[Maria Daly] had her niece fraulein Otto with her, an extremely nice & handsome girl whom she & the Judge are quite in love with. We parted with great regret. Mrs Daly took a lot of my fans to see if she can open a trade for me with Tiffany,[3] and she insisted on paying for them ahead. I had painted one for her in anticipation of our meeting. . . .

I sent Esterina back to Rome from Gavignano for economy. But the consequence was I was tired to death every day, and if my friends had not been there, I could not have gone out painting. I wanted to stop a week in Florence, but I could not endure two packings—so I pushed on from Venice to Rome in 18 hours—and tho' I had the carriage to myself half the night, and stretched off & slept, I was so tired all day yesterday after arriving I could not budge. I am afraid I am growing older. Any way the experiment shows me once more, that there are certain things that conserve my strength—and that I cannot do without a maid, if I am to do any sort of work besides. I am so glad to get home, and my apartment looks so nice and spacious.

1. George Wheeler (1842–1905), a topographical engineer with the United States Geographical Survey, was the official U. S. Commissioner at the congress.

Caroline Carson, portrait of James Louis Petigru [1881?]. Courtesy of the University of South Carolina School of Law.

Caroline Carson, copy of Thomas Sully's 1842 portrait of James Louis Petigru, 1881. Courtesy of the South Carolina Historical Society.

2. Vicenzo Botta (1818–94), Italian-born Dante scholar who taught Italian at New York University.
3. A fashionable New York store featuring jewelry and other expensive wares.

October 16, 1881, 107B Via delle Quattro Fontane.

[Our cousin Thomas Lesesne's recent death] added to the painful feeling left by the President's death. How wonderful the tide of sympathy for him is. Even here the English church opened its doors, and a sermon was preached—the clergyman beginning—"We are met to do honour to the President" Just as he might have said "the Queen" without limitation of United States. . . .

I have painted in oils two portraits of Mr Petigru[1] one a copy of Sully's & the other from the Photo an original of my own. I have had two very handsome frames made and I intend to send them to [James] Lowndes (the Sully) & to Judge Magrath. They really look very fine. I painted them in June—but I would not send them till some months of absence enabled me to judge them with a fresh eye. I have some finishing to put upon them before starting them off. I paint a great deal better than I did and in another 50 years I shall come to be a very superior artist with steady work!

1. CPC frequently referred thus to her father, James Louis Petigru (1789–1863).

October 30, 1881, 107B Via delle Quattro Fontane.

[I]f my eyes hold out I shall conquer yet at my original purpose, which was to paint likenesses when I began those miniatures so long ago. I have stuck to my favourite maxim, which at school at Miss Susan Robertson's[1] I printed on the border of my slate, arithmetic being my great stumbling block—Patience and Perseverance overcome many obstacles. You see my motto was very moderate. It did not promise to prevail against every thing, sickness, war, accident for instance, but it exhorted to continuous and persistent push in the direction one would go. You may draw the inference. Believe me there is no use in being in too great a hurry to enjoy the fruits of life. They hang all along the road, and tho' some have to wait late for the harvest, while others have spring & summer crops, each one gets his basket full if he will go on contentedly & hopefully. . . .

My own plan [for personal behavior] is not complicate.[2] It is to concern myself to act as well as I can up to my own standard, without regard to the language or behaviour of the other person. It is a recipe that has brought me through many rubs—and I recommend you to try it. And especially I would press upon you the experience of the disgust of all beginnings, and how one must work them smooth by a good deal of patience, time and hope.

Ne'er think the victory won,
Nor lay thine armour down;
The arduous task is but begun,
Till thou obtain the crown. . . .

I am very disappointed that Charles March does not come to Rome this winter. He wanted to, and it would have been a great thing for me to have had an elegant clever young man at my disposal. But his Mother who is better in health, is nevertheless so nervous and terrified about the climate of Rome! that he has had to yield, & go to Florence instead. The idea has got fixed in the American brain that it is death to tarry in Rome, so that many are deterred by their own fears or that of their friends; and those who venture are under such pressure of apprehension, that they think only of glancing at the ruins and getting away. It is a bad look out for artists to sell their works. . . .

Henry Young has sent me a number of photographs to have painted on ivory. I should like to do them for him, but my eyes will not do miniature work any more. By the way Staigg gave up miniatures for portraiture in oil to save his eyes. Now the poor fellow has finished all his labours together. He had had a lawsuit with Buck Lawrence[3] for 20 years, over a lot of land at Newport Staigg had bought at public auction, & Lawrence wanted to take back because it had gone cheap. At the end of 20 years the suit was settled in Staigg's favour, but Lawrence was so near his death his last moments were not disturbed by the telling him of it. Neither did Staigg live to enjoy his victory. So I suppose it will be with me & Dean Hall. It has gone on seventeen years, and they say it will take four more—and by that time where shall I be? Nevertheless I am fitting myself to pass the last days there in silk raising and the like, when my eyes fail for painting.

1. One of two Scottish-born sisters who ran the girls school in Charleston that CPC attended until she was fourteen.
2. This follows extensive advice to her son that he mend his ways and bearing toward others according to the motto "Suaviter in modo, fortiter in re."
3. Probably William Beach Lawrence (1800–1881), lawyer and legal scholar, longtime resident of Newport, and onetime lieutenant governor of Rhode Island.

November 20, 1881, 107B Via delle Quattro Fontane.

I am intent now to paint portraits in oils. My flowers have come pretty nigh perfection, and so I may move on I think. I painted a vast number of flowers in the spring, for winter trade—and in July began the two portraits of J L P[etigru] which I finished on my return to Rome in October. I painted a lot of fans, likewise for winter provision, but I sold them all in Venice—my dear kind Mrs Daly taking those which were left to N York for sale—& insisting on depositing nearly as much money as she expects to get for them. She is most kind. Her niece has sent me her photograph and I must try to make a picture from it for Mrs Daly. I have made a beautiful picture of the Countess Gianotti but I am keeping it for a Xmas present. Oils however cost me much outlay, and the framing is a heavy item when I give away.

I shaved so close however last summer, and having made $1000, I am able [to meet my obligations] . . . without disturbing any investment, which I am very glad of. It may have been bad economy not to go out of Italy this summer—for tho' I am quite well I do not feel brisk as usual. Then as to art, it is so uncertain. I never can count on selling. Some years I sold only for $300—and the panic of the climate of Rome is so great the visitors are diminished, and those who do come are in such terror of their lives, and in such haste to see the antiquities and be off, that they have little time or inclination for modern art. However let us hope I shall not vainly spread my nets.

I wish you would get Mallock's[1] "Is Life worth living" I think his Romance of XIXth Century, so far from an immoral book, that it is an electric light shed on the sloughs of mud & misery into which mankind is hurrying by the denial of faith and the modern scientific question whether there be a God at all, and if there be that individuals are nothing to him. There has always been wickedness and wrong—but the sort of negation of the present day is a new thing under the sun, and leads to worse than all the rest. Like the devils to believe and tremble is a fortunate condition in comparison with those who have no belief, neither love nor fear to direct this life. People must soon fall into a horrid sensuality according to their opportunities, or sink into a dull indifference and despair. This is all that is offered in exchange for the hopes that animate us to take this life as God wills; that make small things as great honourable for being borne in his service, which ennobles every trial and gives a generous patience to endure; secure that as we have stood to our post here, so shall be our reward here after, when the crooked is made straight, and all the confusions of this world will be made clear to our understandings. I have not read Mallock's "Is Life Worth living" but from what he has written before I see how it will go, and I would be glad you would read what a layman says, which comes home the more that it is not his function to preach; but he is one struggling with the questions of the day from which no one can escape. St Paul says "we should be prepared to give a reason for the faith that is in us" and never was it more necessary than now that every thing is questioned.

1. William Hurrell Mallock (1849–1923), British satirist and essayist on social and economic issues.

1882

January 30, 1882, 107B Via delle Quattro Fontane.

Mr Harnisch was to sail today from Messina with his models for the Calhoun monument.[1] I sent by him a worsted cap for you which you can draw quite over your ears in the cold. . . . I also sent the portraits handsomely framed of Mr Petigru. The copy of Sully for Jas Lowndes and an original Carson from the photograph, for Judge Magrath. I painted them last summer. . . .

Rome is very full but people buy nothing. I shall starve. By this time I scarcely sell enough to maintain me for several months. This year only for 195 lire—that is $39. I wonder if the time will come when I may go and sit down near you, and not have to work for my daily bread & butter.

1. The statue designed for Charleston's Marion Square.

February 26, 1882, 107B Via delle Quattro Fontane.

I have been reading an excellent book of Freeman Clarke,[1] Thomas Didymus. I wish you would get & read it. No one can accuse F C of not knowing all modern science, and yet you see what a good stroke he gives for the faith we live by. The modern materialistic assertions which depriving us of all hope for another life would leave us to grope despairing in this, driven only by necessity or by sensual pleasures is the most horrid phase the human mind has had to traverse. In the meanest religions there was always something beyond to hope or fear. But your complacent Huxleys[2] et al having themselves by inheritance a good share of this world's goods, and an ineffible conceit of their own powers, denounce as base & idle superstition all that lifts the human mind into a spiritual atmosphere—and gives to the unfortunate & disappointed no remedy—but suicide. "Then farewell hope, and with hope farewell fear! Evil be thou my god," says the fallen angel of Milton.[3] We might suppose that Evil will indeed triumph over all in the present development of doubt, negation, dynamite, no rent, and all the rest which grows from this root of materialism as naturally as the prickles on the thorn. What sorrow would be like ours could the whole world be orphaned under the Heaven in which were no God the Father. . . .

Art is at a low ebb this year Rome is full, but the people buy all their things from the picture shops, who for the most part have their own painters whom they keep at starvation prices, and put all the money in their own pockets. Last year I made $1200—the year before $1000—But this year I have not yet made $300—and this is the harvest time! Mrs Samuel Colt came along and bought a flower piece for $100 which makes the third of this sum. If I make out $500 this year it will be as much as I can hope for—and it would just pull me through. This summer I must cross the Alps indeed.[4]

1. James Freeman Clarke (1810–88), American Unitarian clergyman and reformer.
2. Thomas H. Huxley (1825–95) and his son Leonard (1860–1933) were prominent exponents of Darwinism.
3. John Milton, *Paradise Lost*, line 108.
4. In Rome, as in Naples, the hot, humid summer months were thought to be dangerous to health. Many foreigners therefore believed that they must spend at least every third summer in a climate more northerly than Italy's.

March 26, 1882, 107B Via delle Quattro Fontane.

We are very much exercised by Mrs Strong who persists in coming back with her favourite companions the Irish housemaid & the Courier "the descendant of two Doges." She has been put in coventry in every salon where she has presented herself. She had not been to mine yet, but I had declined her invitation to drive. Phil Sherwood came back from Sorrento this week, & he came here yesterday, and seized a moment to tell me he had driven with Mrs Strong on Friday, and he had told her of all that had been said of her, and how that I & Mrs Van Rensselaer[1] had said we should not receive her! (Just imagine Phil's going & telling her this) I had no time nor chance to put in a word, for he had seized me away from my other guests, as he was following the lady he came with. But he added that Mrs Strong had said she should come to call on me all the same at my reception. Soon enough later she sailed in with perfect self possession, talked to Mrs Haseltine and other ladies present—and outsat them all. Now I thought when the others left, she will open upon me. But not a bit—she sat half an hour later, conversed with perfect complacency on every subject—very well too, for she is clever, and took herself off asking me to come to her on Wednesdays. She stumbled down the long stairs as best she could. Of course I sent no one with her, when she keeps that Courier not to assist her up & down stairs as his duty is to do. I suppose we will send our cards to her and let her make of it what she will. But I never could have imagined such assurance, carried out in such way.

Sara Bernhardt[2] has been here, but I did not see her, not feeling like giving 30 fr[anc]s for the entertainment—and I have come to the pass I don't want to see tragedies acted any more. I w[oul]d rather go to the theatre to be amused. There are too many tragedies in real life.

1. A New York socialite.
2. Sarah Bernhardt (1844–1923), the famous French actress, who had begun to tour Europe in 1880.

April 7, 1882, Good Friday, 107B Via delle Quattro Fontane.

There has come a telegram from Mr Harnisch that he has signed his contract with the Calhoun Monumentalists. . . . I have more success for others than for myself, and Mr Harnisch having got his contract does not encourage me to hope for more personal good fortune. But we will doggedly plod on and as Washington Irving said some where "It will be strange if some ray of sunshine do not at last shine on the particular spot where we are posted". . . .

Easter . . .

Since I began this letter three days ago I have rec[eive]d besides Willie's one from Henry Young, praising amply the two portraits of my Father which I sent to Judge Magrath & James Lowndes. . . . I am very glad they are so highly approved. I hope you will some time see them. It was a wrench to me to part with the one I painted for Judge Magrath. It was so like, and often while painting I had to stop to recover myself as the eyes so long unseen looked out on me from the canvas. But I began another from the photograph and it promises to be as good. But I have had to put aside oil painting for four months to paint the things of the moment to sell. In June & July I will take the oils again.

April 27, 1882, 107B Via delle Quattro Fontane.

By the way . . . do you remember those Miss Parnells[1] at the New York Hotel in 1877. And their flirtation with Joaquin Miller? And my coming upon one of them with Walkin in the corridor, & her telling him to "put out the light" And his trying to explain it away to me next day. And I pretended not to understand what he was saying, being determined he should not talk to me about such a thing? Well those are the very same hussys who are making such mischief now in Ireland as Land Leaguers. I wish they were all hanged along with Guiteau.

1. Sisters of Charles Stuart Parnell (1846–91), the Irish nationalist leader.

May 14, 1882, 107B Via delle Quattro Fontane.

I wonder how you will like the little portrait I sent to Willie. I have an enthusiastic letter from Lowndes in acknowledgment of the copy of the Sully, and I nearly forgive him all the disappointments he has procured me for the way in which he speaks of Papa. Judge Magrath also wrote warmly thanking me for the portrait I made from the photograph, and declaring each picture perfect especially the eyes. It was hard for me to part with that one. But I immediately began another which I mean for you. I had to leave off however in Jan[uary] to paint fans & flowers, and I have not yet been able to get out the oils again. I am so impatient to get my provision of flowers done that I cant bear to look at them; and painting against the grain I never went so slow—just when I want to go fastest. . . .

Last Wed[nesday] I was invited to three dinners a garden party and the Opera. I went only to the last. The wind being high I shirked the garden which was however a grand affair at Princess Brancaccio's & her mother Mrs Hickson Field.[1] Yesterday I had three more invitations—and today I breakfasted after church with Mrs Heywood & drove with her in the afternoon in Villa Borghese where was all the world. Likewise Mrs Strong in a one horse carriage & Mrs Riley—looking very forlorn.

1. Mrs. Field was a New York socialite whose daughter had married a Neapolitan prince.

June 4, 1882, 107B Via delle Quattro Fontane.

Last ev[enin]g Mr Harnisch arrived by the Naples train at 10. Miss Brewster who is his patron saint, and who lives on the floor below me, and is moreover the sister of the illustrious Benjamin Att Gen.[1] had an assembly of Harnisch's most intimate friends to welcome him back, the triumphant competitor for the Calhoun Monument.

1. Benjamin Harris Brewster (1816–88), United States attorney general from 1881 to 1884.

June 25, [1882,] 107B Via delle Quattro Fontane.

You may be sure I am disgusted with the howls of the Herald and the World on Lowell.[1] Those naturalized Irish Americans are a nuisance intolerable, and if a minister is to be pulled up for acting & speaking squarely about them, we might at once confess that the Great Republic is merely an Irish colony to be ruled by Patrick and Bridget. I hate the Irish—and I consider the whole Parnell family a blister. . . .

I suppose you do not take much interest in the Egyptian Affairs. I who am by instinct conservative, hate to see England put to the wall. The Sultan has outgeneraled them all so far, and Arabi Bey[2] snapping his fingers at the European Conference[3] is a picture for Punch, but a melancholy exhibition of the imbecility of the means taken to restrain him. England seems to have got into a dreadful tangle in the hands of Gladstone, and all his enemies are coming down upon him. We have witnessed the decay & degradation of France. I for one, don't want to see that of England.

1. James Russell Lowell (1819–91), as United States minister to Great Britain, had demanded that the British government release unconditionally the Irish-born American citizens currently being held in a British jail and denied the right of *habeas corpus* for having taken part in violent actions designed to bring about home rule in Ireland. But privately Lowell suggested that their release be made conditional on their leaving Ireland. Reports of that and his known disapproval of the violent actions attributed to

Caroline Carson, **Saarnen. July 21, 1882.** *Courtesy of Ashton and LaVonne Phillips.*

the Irish Land League made him a target for hostile criticism from American politicians and from the pro-Democratic New York newspapers, the *Herald* and the *World*.

2. In 1881 Ahmed Arabi had led an uprising of Egyptian officers, the first overt expression of a new nationalist, Muslim-inspired movement. In the nationalist ministry under Mahmud Sami that followed, Arabi became war minister. In April 1882 an uprising of Circassian officers led the khedive to appeal to Great Britain and France for support. Their naval squadrons appeared in Alexandria on May 20. On May 25 an ultimatum from both powers forced the nationalist government to resign but, unable to form a new ministry, the khedive had to recall Arabi and the nationalists. On June 12 riots broke out in Alexandria in which 50 Europeans were killed—perhaps at the instigation of the khedive to force more extensive foreign intervention on his behalf.
3. An ambassadorial conference convened June 23 at Constantinople to consider how Turkish intervention could supplement French and British action in Egypt.

July 16, [1882,] Near Vevey, Hotel Chemenin.

This is a most lovely spot—but I fear it will be to[o] hot, and that I shall have to move up the mountains somewhere. Yesterday I took a little trip to Bex[1] to see Mrs Huntington. I had a pleasant three hours with her, but getting back at 6 PM I walked up here from the station thro' the vineyards & a rough cobblestone road, and today I am so tired I can't budge. Clement March[2] says he will come to Vevey to stay with me, and we have a plan to go to Spain in October. He to catch the Florio[3] boat at Gibraltar, and I to get a return one from thence to Italy. I have long desired to see the pictures in Spain, and to visit Grenada, and if I can carry it through this time I'll spend the Summerville lot[4] in the expedition. I always try to save those windfalls, and then I find myself chanced out of them. This time I think I will take a spree.

1. Bex is about twenty miles from Vevey in the Alpine foothills south of Lake Leman.
2. The son of CPC's close friend Mary Lowndes March.
3. While retaining its distinctive name, the Florio line merged with the Rubattino line in 1881 in a single government-sponsored shipping company that carried both freight and passengers on irregular schedules and at reduced rates.
4. A lot in Summerville, South Carolina, that CPC had inherited from her father had recently been sold.

August 13, [1882,] Hotel Mooser, Chemenin, prés Vevey.

As things turn out it is well . . . that I had given up the project of going to Spain; for I have a letter from Henry Young showing that Mr Burney had not paid the taxes for the last years of his possession, and Dean Hall is to be sold up for the State tax of $500. So my Summerville money will be used up for that. I never get a little windfall and think I will give myself a fling, but that something does not come up to carry it off. . . .

What a good time I had going to Interlaken with Clarence Seward as his guest. He was most magnificent and so kind! Dr & Mrs B[arker] had gone visiting in Scotland, so Clarence was alone & my company was a gain to him he said. Last week I was really ill from drinking a glass of lemonade which does not agree with me—and I begin to think I am not as strong as I used to be, for things upset me. However Friday ev[enin]g there was a ball, and all the boys insisted I should dance! And so I took refuge with Major Dresser an old West Pointer, and actually went through the German![1] coming off with more favors than any other lady—especially two beautiful Jap[anese] umbrellas which I shall set up in Rome as trophies.

1. An elaborate social dance resembling a cotillion.

August 27, 1882, Hotel Mooser.

On the whole I have had the pleasantest summer since being separated from you. The boys[1] were devoted to me. They insisted on my taking part in all their sports. They sat around me while I painted, and one or the other was in attendance to walk with me always—and they would have me dance! I was the greatest belle in the cotillion, and had the most favours which I shall take to ornament the studio in Rome, where you shall see them, along with my Alpen stock. Major Dresser & family have gone. She is a lovely woman—but a sufferer and the Major is a good soul though rough. . . .

We are delighted with Willie Astor's nomination to Rome.[2] It will make a revolution in the American Legation. Poor old Mr Marsh was so heavy and half dead these 8 years past.

Mr & Mrs Elizabeth Murray[3] are come to Vevey, she is so changed! She looks like a corpse already, and I sh[oul]d think she has not long to live, but she talks much the same, and she told me how Schuyler Crosby[4] was a scoundrel to [at?] Florence, not so much for his intrigues with women, for people were accustomed to that in Florence—but for his introducing doubtful ladies into society, which is not permitted—& still more that he traded on the credulity of his countrymen in art—recommending them to buy certain things and getting a percentage from the artists—and finally that a gentleman preparing to buy a picture and confessing he knew nothing of art, Crosby offered his services. The picture was bought for $700 and the Gentleman found out that Crosby paid the artist, 300 and put 400, in his own pocket. This passes permission. Mrs Murray told it with great gusto.

1. Clement March and his brother, Charles.
2. William Waldorf Astor (1848–1919), an amateur sculptor, had just been appointed to replace George Perkins Marsh (1801–82), who served as the American minister to Italy from 1860 to 1881.
3. Elizabeth Heaphy Murray (1815–82), American landscape painter and cousin of Louisa Ward Crawford Terry. Her husband was John M. Murray.
4. John Schuyler Crosby (1839–1914), American consul in Florence, 1876–82.

September 10, 1882, Hotel Mooser, Chemenin.

I have had the pleasantest summer I ever had since parting with you and Willie. Neilson Potter is like all the Potters, most correct friendly & ready for any fun in a quiet way. His wife is as ugly as a woman can be, and yet so pleasant & genial one w[oul]d not swap her for a beauty, and they have two very nice little girls, & one awful plain one. Mrs Edward Jones & her daughter, (mother & sister of Mrs Potter) are the very kindest cheerful people. Robert Cushing[1] is most elegant and refined—his wife Miss Dulany is a beauty now over blown—it is true, but in English eyes the most superb American ever seen. Grafton is 6 ft 3 and in proportion as easy as Gen Scott.[2] He is handsome, joyous, and as gay as a kitten. Louisa 16 is rather heavy—Howard at 13 is slender and taller than most men, he is not a boy in anything but sweetness & docility: but he is courtly as a chevalier of the olden time—and he has a wonderful talent for drawing.

We have interminable art talks. Olivia the baby is as big & handsome as a Newfoundland pup. They are really delightful people. Then we have Mr & Mrs Thomas Dehon. She was a Miss Hoffmann a friend of Dolly's [Brevoort], and she remembers you very well at Bedford.

We all make one family, and we are always getting up some frolic or other. Occasionally letting in a few outsiders. Clem March is always saying sharp things—and moreover professing the most extravagant admiration for me. Indeed, they all make a great deal of me—and as there is no very taking young lady, I am the belle of the house! The Dressers are gone, and we hear poor Mrs Dresser is not doing well. Grafton leaves tomorrow to return to Harvard college—and I have just come from a meeting summoned in Mrs Cushing's parlour, where I made a neat & appropriate speech, and read them some verses composed for the occasion which of course were received with great applause and the whole party appended their names. It seems hard I should be flourishing around the favourite playmate of all these boys, while my own are far away. But in some sort these boys hanging about me cheat me into a kind of feeling of having you near me. They are all very nice boys. They have a friend with them besides, one Wheatland who was in love with Miss Dresser twice as tall as he. He is a dull little fellow but very gentlemanly.

Our fun is nearly over however. We all break up this week.

1. Robert Cushing, his wife, and their four children were probably a Boston family.
2. Gen. Winfield Scott (1786–1866) was six feet, five inches tall and so bulky in his mature years that he had to be hoisted onto his horse by a sling.

September 27, 1882, Hotel Chemenin.

Our gay party here is dissolving into its elements. . . . [Tomorrow I go] to Lausanne & branch off to Geneva. At 9 PM I shall take the train for Mt Cenis & D[eo] V[olente] will be in Florence Tuesday 19th at 9 PM. Every body troops over the new St Gothard, wherefore I go by the Mt Cenis as being less crowded, and the competition has made them wondrous civil. At the frontier at Modane I used to be so hustled about, that I dreaded that part of the journey more than all the rest. But when I passed in July they were changed in the most amiable way.

I shall paint in the Pitti the pendant to the Medici Prince[1] in swaddling clothes you saw in my portfolio. I always have wanted to paint the fellow. I was in terror for a long time lest some one should buy that Bambino. But I have never had an offer for it, and I consider my possession now permanent. I have done very well this summer having sold f1060—of water colours—that is $212—which brings up my gains this year to 750. Last year I made 1200. I wish I could make pounds instead of francs like Mrs Eliz. Murray: who by the way looks like a corpse. She has been in this house four days, & I have devoted myself to her. She seems quite grateful. Her energy is as great as ever, but her strength is quite gone—and she is awfully frightened at illness. Mr Elizabeth is as careful & tender of her as ever he can be, and she has spirit enough to scold him all the same. . . .

It has been so chilly all summer we have never sat out of doors of an ev[enin]g but twice—and now we have had a heavy fall of snow on the mountains all around. A thing not seen for 30 years. It is cold and wretched. The grapes are ruined, there will be no harvest at all. I will be glad to see the sun and Italy; and get something good to eat cooked by Lorenzo. Esterina has applied herself to learning French, and it is very funny to hear her: she is going to bore me to death to speak to her in French.

We are delighted at the English advance to Cairo,[2] and I hope England will put Ireland down and "establish truth & justice for all generations"[3]

1. Probably the bas-relief bust of Cosimo III as an infant, executed by Pietro da Cortona in his design for the walls and ceiling of the Venus room in the Galleria of the Pitti Palace, whose art collection was second only to that of the Uffizi Museum.
2. Following the British defeat of Egypt at the battle of Tel-el-Kebir (13 September 1882), the British occupied Cairo.
3. The struggle for Irish home rule had turned increasingly violent following the assassination of Lord Frederick Cavendish, newly chosen chief secretary for Ireland, in May 1882.

October 22, 1882, 107B Via delle Quattro Fontane.

I got to Florence on the 28th Sep[tember] and stopped 24 days, of which 3 were Sundays, one I took to get my permit to copy in the Pitti, & stretch my paper for the work—19 in the Pitti from 10 to 4. PM—and one day I gave to my kind friend Mrs [Annie Fitch] Hyde, coming away at night to reach Rome Oct[ober] 15th. I painted two pictures, which I may say are chef d'oeuvres! I stopped the first ten days at the boarding house of the Miss Godkins sisters of the Nation,[1] whom I had met last summer at Gavi[g]nano. One is literary and awful ugly. The other who runs the house, is a cheerful bright woman whom I like. There is a very clumsy old mother whom they are devoted to. I wonder if the Nation helps them? They seem very poor.

I was a fortnight with the Hydes, who hospitably urged me to stay longer. It was most kind of them to have me, for I really almost made their house a convenience. Going off at 9½ and coming back at 4½. So thus I only dined & spent the evening with them.

I think I will write your name on the back of this last picture the Princess Eleonora Gonzaga of Mantua, afterwards married to the Emperor Ferdinand II [S]he must have been betrothed when a child, for she is in the most gorgeous apparel all of which I have got most amazingly. My copies I do not want to sell. I do them for my own pleasure & instruction. You remember the Baby swathed in jewels in my portfolio you saw in 77. I have now done the pendant to him, another Medici prince afterwards a cardinal. . . .

I am glad to get home tho' I had one of the pleasantest summers of my life. I have a table covered with the presents each one gave me on parting, as tokens of their good will. They all said I was the life of the house, and made it pleasant for them. I wish you could see Clem March & get his account of things. Poor Mrs Eliz Murray I told you is so ill, but she roused up to exhibit her pictures to me and I took all my friends in with me, and we were delighted she paints better than me. I told her Mrs Cushing w[oul]d like to buy one, & she immediately told me she w[oul]d pay me 10% if I got it sold! (Thus carrying out what you say of her business capacity.) I had done all I could without any arrière pensée[2]—and the result is Mrs Cushing wrote for the picture, & it is gone to Dresden. Mrs Murray wrote to propose sending me a postal order to Rome. I am bound to say no such order has come to hand! Since it comes to that I have turned myself about, and I have just written to San Remo to say I am in Rome, & orders can safely be sent. It w[oul]d indeed be a good thing for me to have such a reciprocity treaty with her—and with other artists.

Suppose I were to have a per centage on the Calhoun Mon[ument]? But then after all the public would pay no more heed to the commendation of one artist for another, if it was known to be interested. It would indeed be well if artists praised each other more. I am sorry to say the contrary is the rule. The praise is the exception.

1. Irish-born Edwin Lawrence Godkin (1831–1902) edited the *Nation* from its founding in 1865 until 1882.
2. Mental reservations.

November 2, 1882, 107B Via delle Quattro Fontane.

I have just felt bound to give all I could to the inondati.[1] When one lives in a country, I think one is bound to bear a hand in the help for the calamities that come upon it. My neighbour Miss Brewster who went summering to Innsbrück has been shut up there by the floods for six weeks, and there seems no present prospect of her getting away. We have some sunshine in Rome. But the wretched people drowned out in Northern Italy must come more or less upon all the others. And the price of provisions rises at once.

The preparations for the International artistic exhibition[2] goes on—and I am busy getting my pictures ready, and the framing will be a heavy item of expense. All the world is mad now about exhibitions, one has to go under the yoke. I shall send your Princess Eleonora of Mantua, and four flower pieces. . . .

By the way the day after I wrote you No 39, I had a letter from Mrs Eliz. Murray sending the order for 75 francs. The transaction to be strictly secret—mind you don't tell any body whatsoever. Poor Mrs Eliz wrote with the most shaky hand. I fear she can never be better.

1. Flood victims.
2. *Esposizione di belle arti a Roma* in 1883.

Part III

The Gradual Disintegration of a Dream World, 1883–1892

1883

May 20th, 1883, 107B Via delle Quattro Fontane.

I have . . . letters from Clem March & Dr & Mrs Barker asking me to go to Schwalbach this summer to stay by May[1] in the cure Dr Barker thinks most important for her. They dared not even propose her coming abroad which she hates, unless I will consent to spend the summer with her (as her guest)—and Clem begged me to telegraph, and on my answer would depend their persuasions to her. Of course I must consent. It upsets all my plans of Corpo di Cava, & practice in portrait painting—but my success in that department of art depends on so many other things—and my duty to my friends is unquestionable. It is by no means certain May will consent to come even with the inducement of my delightful society. I have not yet an answer to my telegram which was sent three days ago. . . .

I have been having a time with that wretch Anne.[2] Her malice envy & jealousy are beyond belief, and she has frightened Harnisch so that he does not speak to me in her presence and he has never been into my apartment since the day he dined with you here. Tho[ugh] I told him plainly, meeting him at the Storys, that he was the only person who had not called on me to condole at your departure. Nonetheless he has never come. Anne has been complaining of me far and near because it seems it came back to her that she called Mrs Terry an ass! Instead of being ashamed of herself, she undertook to fix it upon me the repetition and said she w[oul]d make me know her displeasure. Which she exhibited by a most lofty manner every time we met, which was not often. However when her friend Miss Platt died she sent me a card to inform me, being somewhat touched perhaps that I had daily gone to Miss Platt's to enquire. I laid aside vexation & wrote her a kind note offering to come to see her. She asked me to come next ev[enin]g, which I did. She received me stretched out on a chaise longue, I said I was sorry to see you are ill, no she said I am not ill, but without offering to rise she pointed to a seat at her feet. . . . Then came Harnisch who in a frightened way shook hands, and taking up the only chair which was beside me, he carried it quite round the circle & sat down there! When I spoke Anne answered studiously looking away. In a few minutes I had had enough so I got up to come away. Then according to her custom she began, ["]oh don't go you have just come in. I have so much to talk with you about &c." & I said I came to condole with you on Miss Platt's death and having done that I will go. And I went. Harnisch ventured to the door with me. I said I have just painted an old woman, come up & see it. He did, looked a minute said it is very fine, I must go since those young ladies are there, and he ran like a terrapin with a fire on its back.

Albert E. Harnisch, bust of James L. Petigru. Collection of City Hall, Charleston, South Carolina.

Then there appeared a certain Capt & Mrs Dawson[3] from Charleston. Anne gave them a dinner, charging those asked to the dinner not to let me know—& invited me in the ev[enin]g. I accepted. Did not go of course—and the next morning sent her a note thanking her & Mr Harnisch for paying me the compliment of an invitation, but I did not think it worth while dressing for a small after dinner party, nor did I consider it suitable for a lady of my years and pretentions to be brought in like the children to des[s]ert. This dumbfounded her & she replied not a word. Tho' she complained that I had no cause to object as Mrs Greenough came in the ev[enin]g. Mr Ropes[4] said perhaps Mrs Carson took exception that as these Dawsons were from Charleston she was the proper person to ask to meet them. But Anne caught on her claws, that the Dawsons being secessionists she could not ask us together. She knew I had called on the Dawsons, and she had confederated with me to meet the Montgomerys who were flaming secesh. Now comes the point. He [Harnisch] got my photographs for Mr Petigru's bust. I went of my own accord to see how it was going on, it was awful, and I staid ever so long getting it put in shape. I returned a second time and said it was better, and I took my finished photo saying when he was ready to finish the clay to send for it & I w[oul]d come again. I heard nothing for weeks. Then I wrote to ask for my photographs I had left with him & to ask how he got on. He replied by note that the bust was done, cast in plaister and was going on in the marble, & he w[oul]d bring my photographs in the evening. I was so shocked that he sh[oul]d presume to go on to the marble without asking me to see if I was satisfied with the model, (which every sculptor does) that I wrote him a letter to be handed when he came in the ev[enin]g. He did not even give me that satisfaction for he sent up the photographs by the maid. My letter was to tell him he was not complying with the terms of the contract which were that I sh[oul]d be satisfied entirely with the likeness & the artistic execution. For which I said I could not answer. I got a most insolent note dictated by Miss Brewster, that he was surprised at my harsh letter, that I had expressed myself quite satisfied with the bust, and I did not consider that Mr Petigru's bust was not the only work he had to execute. That he had other & more important works besides the Calhoun monument. He was sorry that I felt myself aggrieved but did not see in what he was to blame. I was hot and furious. I sent down a note that if he could not see that it was his duty to submit the bust to me before proceeding to put it in marble neither could he see in what he had offended me.

And I wrote a letter to Judge Magrath enclosing one to Mr Courtenay which would blow-up the whole matter. I said I was disappointed in the artist I had selected, who having gone on too hastily without submitting the bust to my criticism, I could not be responsible for it, and I felt I ought to tell Mr Courtenay so, that he might by telegraph stop it—or do what he sh[oul]d think fit. I went to bed with my feet like ice & my head aflame. Next morning there was my letter with the stamps upon it, but when I came to say my prayers I could not for the first time in my life with a clear conscience ask to be forgiven as I forgive. I am not sure the bust is quite what it sh[oul]d be, but I feel to send the letter w[oul]d be a terrible retaliation, and perhaps ruin this poor creature in the Calhoun Monument too. So I held back the hand that was burning to revenge myself. I went to the artists meeting that AM, of which I send you the resolutions in a roll of photographs today. Harnisch ranged up & insisted to walk home with me, protesting he meant nothing. I came down upon him without stint. I said he & his prompter having got out of me all they could hope for now tried to discharge themselves from all obligation by a system of disrespect seeking to quarrel with me. That I would not allow Miss Brewster nor any one else to put their feet upon me. He counted on my good nature & he was repaid of Miss Brewster, if he pleased to be the laughing stock of Rome that did not matter to me, but personally I found I must exact the deference due to me &c & he said Miss Brewster had invited him to come up in answer to my letter but he was so tired after working all day. I said however Miss Brewster dictated that note of yours. He could not deny it. But he is so stupid and so dazed he don't seem to understand the rudeness of his conduct. I told him to say to Miss Brewster that whatever she had against me to come and say it, and I would give her the plain truth. That she had exploited people's patience with her bad tongue long enough. That the things she says are infamous and I sh[oul]d tell her so to her face whenever she chose. He was very humble, and I let him go, and I was glad I had escaped the great temptation to avenge myself. I don't know how it will end, after all. Whether or not I should go to see the bust at once. Of one thing, I am resolved, to write to Mr Courtenay if he wishes other busts done to have another artist. It is all a plot of Anne's to get rid of Harnisch's making any return for all the trouble I have had. I don't care about the Calhoun Monument. But it is a cruel pain to me to have the likeness of Mr Petigru mixed up with such mean contention. It is unworthy of him and of me—and I will try to possess my soul in patience and act as my father would have done in the case. He would have scorned to avenge himself. But I am too sorry I did not give it to Simmons.[5] If Simmons had been nice about it! but he was so disagreeable when I proposed it to him, and Harnisch asked so properly to be allowed to do it. And the disagreement about the monument was so likely to be strengthened by giving the bust to another that I gave it to him, of which I heartily repent.

1. Mary Lowndes March.
2. Anne Brewster lived on the floor below CPC's 107B Via delle Quattro Fontane apartment.
3. Francis Warrington Dawson (1840–89), publisher-editor of the *Charleston News and Courier,* and his wife, the Civil War diarist Sarah Morgan Dawson.
4. A young Boston tourist whom CPC had taken up.
5. Franklin Simmons (1839–1913), another American sculptor resident in Rome, whose work CPC greatly admired.

May 27, 1883, 107B Via delle Quattro Fontane.

In my last I told you my vexations with Anne & the wretched victim Harnisch. I am very glad I did not wreak my vengeance on him. It would have been very unworthy me, and especially unlike what Papa would have done. But I had up H and drove into his thick skull that he had been guilty of great disrespect to me. He was quite horrified, and all he could say in excuse is that he had not seen it—and that he is stupid. Yes he said I am stupid, but I do not mean to act badly. So I have condoned the offence. Tho' when the marble is advanced enough to pronounce, if I find it wrong I shall say so to the person who ordered it. But [I] beg you will not mention it in any letter or to any Charlestonian, for it seems Courtenay is a most tenacious man, and he wants the bust kept a perfect secret, till he himself unveils it to astonish and delight Charleston by his munificence. . . . And he refuses to take the bust if any wind of it gets abroad. And this idiot Harnisch keeps this particular back from me, so I might have blown it in any letter, by a mere mention. And then making me angry it was the nearest thing that I did not send off my letter which w[oul]d have made a complete explosion.

Miss Brewster has so subdued the poor creature he can't say his soul is his own—and I believe he will be swamped in every way. I hope he may not make a failure of the Calhoun. I shall keep out of the way of that, as the best I can do for one I have befriended, which gives him a claim on my forbearance. But as for Anne, I am done with her. Our relations are limited now to the Galignani[1] which I daily send her as of old, & she reciprocates with the Revue Des deux Mondes.[2] But I shall not put my foot in her house unless she comes to call as every body else does. She grins upon me in the most mincing way when we meet on the staircase &c. But I will not be drawn in.

1. *Galignani's Messenger or the Spirit of the English Journals*, a newspaper published in Paris, 1814–95.
2. French literary, political, and scientific journal founded in 1829.

June 22, 1883, 107B Via delle Quattro Fontane.

I hope I may be able to do good to May [March] and that the summer will turn out well. As I go as a guest it is convenient at the low ebb of my purse, but at the same time it takes from me the joy of being able to make a sacrifice to friendship and gratitude to Mrs Lowndes[1] & Major. I do sacrifice my Summer—and my independence, but it will not be so handsome as if I c[oul]d go on my own charges. However, I am in for it. I had a telegram from Alex Hamilton, answer prepaid, to be assured I w[oul]d meet May in Paris. Lorenzo had to rout out of bed in the dead of the night to despatch the answer that it might reach on 19th, May being to sail 20th. I leave on 28th and will be in Paris 30th D[eo] V[olente]. . . . You know I hate Paris, and it is a pest to me to go there.

1. Sally Buck Preston Lowndes, May March's mother and Carolina friend of CPC, who had left the South with her husband, Major Rawlins Lowndes, in 1861 and who had frequently provided a New York haven for CPC when she was ill.

July 8, 1883, Langen Schwalbach, Hotel Alle-Sale [*sic*].

I left Rome June 28th Thursday 2,40 PM and reached Paris Sat[urday] at 5,30 AM. I went to hotel Castiglione according to letter from Clem March—it is just across from the Liverpool so I felt quite at home. I bathed and rested, and Miss Goodridge & Mrs Randolph came in the afternoon, and I went out with them to see a beautiful gallery of pictures and dined with them. Sunday morning Charles March came up from Venice. I went out with him to Notre Dame, & the Luxembourg. 4 PM the passengers of the Amérique arrived, and after that I had to give myself up to them and a little shopping. Mrs March bore the journey better than had been expected. G[eorge] L S[chuyler] was quite exhausted, by the poor food of the Amérique & hot state rooms next to the boiler tubes. But he soon began to pick up. We were only three days in Paris, leaving Wednesday ev[enin]g by 8 PM train. we did not reach Schwalbach till the next afternoon near six. It was a long hot journey, and it is very encouraging that May bore it so well. The family politics induced Charles to return to USA leaving Clem with his mother. He is devoted to her, tho' he hopes when she gets regularly occupied with her baths he may run off on excursions. It is going to be awful dull of course.

This is a very nice place & we have the first cut,[1] but there is not a creature we know but deLancy Kane & his wife (Miss [Edith] Isselin),[2] and all the people look ugly & unattractive. There is a fine band of music playing all the time. I went to the English church this morning, which was much more hearty than Mr Nevins,'[3] rendering of the service. We shall have to stay here six weeks! Heighho! So you can write one letter after you get this to the hotel Alle-Sale, Langen Schwalbach, Germania. When I get my drawing box & begin to paint the flowers I shall do well enough. But unluckily I was too conscientious to drag that box all the way round by Paris, & I gave it to Stein to send direct to Schwalbach. I have just had notice that it is at Wiesbaden & the charge is more than my three other trunks from Rome to Paris. . . .

The Schuylers want me to move to Washington and open my studio there, before the ground is occupied, and while they are alive and can help me. But it is a serious thing to begin over again in a new place, and if I fail I could'nt come back to my Roman snuggery. It requires much

Caroline Carson, "Self Portrait in Blue." Courtesy of Ashton and LaVonne Phillips.

Caroline Carson, Self Portrait in Pink. *Courtesy of Ashton and LaVonne Phillips.*

thought & fine action. They w[oul]d have me come this winter. But I am sure I ought to spend this winter in making oil studies of hands, so as to go there as a competent painter of portraits. It scares me to think of making the move. Tho' now Mrs Tilton has gone I believe I shall feel very solitary in Rome.

I mean to let the Harnisch affair alone. I will say nothing of the bust, and let them judge themselves if they like it. Honestly I do not. And I fear the Calhoun is going to be a prodigious horror. The merit that was in H. seems to have been crushed out of him by his old woman of the sea, and he will never have the spirit of Sinbad the sailor to break her skull & get himself free.[4]

1. Presumably the first choice of food, specifically the choice cuts of meat.
2. New York socialites.
3. Robert Jenkins Nevin (1839–1906), the high churchman who was the rector of St. Paul's Episcopal Church in Rome.
4. In one of *The Thousand and One Nights* stories, Sinbad the Sailor was enslaved by the Old Man of the Sea but ultimately escaped by making him drunk and then dashing his brains out with a rock.

July 23, 1883, Langen Schwalbach, Hotel Allée Saal.

We have been here so long I forget when we came but I think it was the 6th July. It seems an age. It has rained incessantly, and is so cold I wish I had my winter clothes and furs. The people who know about German Baths one can easily recognize for they come to the Spring wrapped in furs and good cloaks. There never was anything so dull. Not a creature we know, or are likely to scrape acquaintance with. Everyone seems especially dull and preoccupied. There is a band of music playing at all hours. Nothing can be more dismal than hearing them at 7 AM playing waltzes under the dripping trees. There are nice long shady alleys to walk in if the rain would stop and anything like summer set in. There is a fine Kursaal[1] with restaurant on one side [and on the other] reading room where are all the papers, and a lofty elegant ball room between. There are concerts nightly, & twice a week a ball. The ladies go in walking dress and hats, and all who sit on the two first rows indicate thereby that they will dance with any man who comes up and makes a bow. When Clem dances, May and I watch him from the window, and that is our wildest entertainment—all shut up at 11 PM. May drinks & bathes punctually, and Clem sees improvement in her, and he tells me that every hour of the day he blesses the inspiration of my coming with them, that he never could have got on without, and he thinks my influence with her most salutary. That consoles me for the dreary waste of time, for I can paint very little even if there were much to paint, which there is not. I supposed when we got to Spa among people she knows, May would be tired of me, & very glad to have me take my departure for Italy in Sep[tember] and so be relieved from the expense of me & Esterina. But now Clem & she anxiously inquire if I can stay till they sail, which will not be till end of October. I suppose that I must see her through to make the sacrifice complete. But I do long to get back to my own life. If I can however see her quite restored I shall be glad to have given up the autumn as well as the summer to the daughter of my kind friends.

1. Treatment center.

August 5, 1883, Hotel Allee Saal, Langen Schwalbach.

I am having the dullest time of my life. It has rained every day & nearly all day the whole of July and it is cold & miserable. If the thermometer gets up to 64 Fahrenheit we <u>rejoice</u>. As for summer heat it is hopeless. The sun has come out today but large watery clouds threaten to swallow up his rays. May is as gentle and amiable as possible, but her good & bad days alternate just the same showing no improvement so far. It is very discouraging. Clem keeps up his spirits wonderfully, and his patience and cheerful devotion to his mother are admirable. He never leaves us for half an hour. She cannot bear to be alone. You may imagine how heavy is the task. I find I can do nothing neither paint nor write. Partly from the charge to keep I have, and partly that the atmosphere is so depressing I feel fit for nothing and am sleepy all the time.

We shall have to stop here 20 days longer, and then go to Baden. I hope the [Robert] Cushings will not have left Baden before we can get there. Baron Osten Sacken came 7 hours journey from Heidelberg to see me, he stopped two days & went on to visit at Ems another friend, so as not to make it too particular coming to see me! Nillson[1] is here escorted by old Lydig Suydam[2] who trots after her like a poodle. He can talk of nothing but the honour he enjoys in her friendship, and assures us over & over (of what we do not question) namely that there is no "sentiment in his connection with Nillson." She has still a handsome face but she has grown so heavy and big behind, and she stalks about like a grenadier.

1. Probably Christine Nilsson (1843–1921), Swedish operatic soprano. In 1883 she sang at the opening of the Metropolitan Opera House.
2. David Lydig Suydam, a socially prominent New Yorker.

September 6, 1883, Baden-Baden, Hotel de l'Europe.

We came on 22nd Aug[ust] to this place, coming into the midst of the Races, which made a great turmoil in contrast to Schwalbach where quietude reigned. I can't say the bustle of the Races is very amusing [?]. I went one day (the first) with the Cushings. It was a hot drive of an hour at 1 PM. The course is an oval [of] more than a mile, so the races for the most part were a single round which is not half so exciting. And under the broiling August sun the horses ran with distress. Moreover it was [an] awfully long five hours. I was bored to death and declined all invitations to go again. The only thing that pleased me was the hurdle race, where one of the horses tumbled his rider off (unhurt) at the first hurdle, and then ran the race out by himself coming a length ahead of the other horses. But for all his good will the poor fellow could not take the prize. Imagine the rage of his owner at the stupid rider. The great attraction was the Prince of Wales,[1] who took himself about very freely, and went to a fancy ball as a cook—and looked it very completely. The Grand Duke of Baden came also, and there were grand illuminations for him, and he drove around all night with the Prince of Wales in an illuminated carriage preceded by another with red lanterns and tinkling bells. . . .

I have found in the gravel a splendid diamond ring. I waited three days for advertisement of reward, then I cautiously advertised, but no one claiming it, I shall consider it a grain of good luck, and when I get to Paris I will see about selling it.

1. From 1901 to 1910, King Edward VII.

September 26, 1883, Baden-Baden.

We leave today for Paris, and will be at the Metopolitan Hotel 8 Rue Cambon till Oct[ober] 27th when Mrs March sails in the Normandie, & I will make a bee line to Rome. We wanted to go to the Liverpool, but could not get rooms to suit us.

October 7, 1883, Hotel Metropolitan, 8 Rue Cambon.

I am quite knocked about the ring. Clem has taken it to several jewellers who say it is worth $700, but when asked to buy it they either decline altogether or offer less than the third! I supposed diamonds bought their value sure, but it seems the selling & the buying value is quite different. This accounts for my getting so little for the diamonds the Gov[1] gave me when I came to sell them. Consequently I will not give away the ring at this rate, but keep it & try some day to sell it to someone for the price they w[oul]d have to give if they were buying in a shop. Meantime I have not in hand the 5 or 600 I had expected to have.

1. CPC had used her wedding gift from her husband, William Augustus Carson, to pay for James's education at Columbia College in New York.

October 30, 1883, 107B Via delle Quattro Fontane.

With what joy do I write the above address! How glad I am to get back to my own place, and to the blue sky of Italy, after the rains of Germany and the smoky lead of Paris! After all I did not see Mrs March off. She expected to leave from Havre on the 26th & I the same ev[enin]g to take my flight straight to Rome. But some hindrance in the Normandie made them substitute the Labrador in which she did not wish to go—so she waits for her favorite Amérique of the following Saturday. They wanted me very much to hold on, but I felt as if I must get home by first of Nov[ember], and as May is much better and has her two sons with her, and plenty of friends at hand, I could not consider it desertion to come away. So I went off with

Esterina Friday ev[enin]g 26th at 7 O'clock, & arrived at 7 AM Sunday 28th. . . .

So far from being well off for having lived at free quarters for 4 months, I find I was never so hard up. There were many incidental expenses I sh[oul]d not have made at Corpo di Cava, and . . . [they leave me] short $200. I really have but $100 for Nov[ember] & Dec[ember], & how I shall make out I do not know. I must pinch very hard. . . .

I long to get to my brushes. Tho[ugh] art has not been remunerative this year. . . . W[oul]d you believe the pig Harnisch has not come up to enquire after me?

December 2, 1883, 107B Via delle Quattro Fontane.

I have finished Arnoldus,[1] & got him a superb frame, for which Adele will have to pay $40. Costa the great[2] came yesterday, and professed himself entirely satisfied with the workmanship. He fell to & touched the background in one place, but he w[oul]d not hear of doing anything to the face, wh[ich] he compared with the photograph. Haseltine[3] came t'other day to see it, & praised it, and he always goes to the root of the matter. "Says he, you will have $200 for that? No I said nothing. He said if your cousin has means you ought to give her a very broad hint to pay for it![")] That I can't do, but I shall ask her to put it on exhibition for a while as I wish it to procure me orders for other portraits. Herr Ross[4] also came to see it, & commended, & offered more suggestions than Costa, and I shall profit by one of his remarks to put in a little touch. . . .

I have taken Esterina's sister Marietta [Servadei] home to paint from. I will keep her all winter looking out for a good place for her later. It does not cost me more than having the models who are a troublesome crew.

I dined at the Astor's[5] Thanksgiving Day. Mrs Astor is very well now, and I hope they will get their sails all properly trimmed this year and make a complete success. They came to call on me two Saturdays ago. But by mistake got into Anne's apartment, where they were kept waiting & Mr Astor left the cards and came away. They might justly have been displeased at not finding me prepared on my day. But for all that Mr Astor told Mr Hooker that they had gone with the intention of getting a piece of mine, and that Mr H sh[oul]d ask me to send him one for the value of Lire 500. Of course I wrote to explain that it was not in my apartment that they had been kept waiting, & sent things for them to choose among. Mr Astor chose the Etruscan vase with the Wild Poppies, which I was glad of, as I like it, and he said very complimentary things of it. Meanwhile I wrote a note to Anne asking for the cards that had been left thinking to be in my apartment, & wondering at my remissness in not being ready. And I added if <u>she</u> had been making her visit to me, I sh[oul]d have had the pleasure of seeing her, & sh[oul]d not have lost Mrs Astor. (I might have lost the 500 lire wh[ich] of course I did not say to Anne) But I said if she w[oul]d instruct her maid to make sure on <u>Saturdays</u> who people were enquiring for we sh[oul]d avoid these imbroglios, also that I had been considering about changing my day to Monday so as to make it easier for the many persons who complained of coming twice when they could make both visits the same day. She wrote a note that I w[oul]d send you, but that I have to keep the document as proof in the war that has ensued. Therein she said that the Astors had asked for Miss Brewster, that the door was opened by her sewing woman the Countess Marconi (!) That when they found she could not receive them they had left their cards and gone away. Those cards she could not send, as she always tore up cards, or her house w[oul]d be filled with such rubbish &c &c.

When I went to dine with the Astors, Mrs Astor at once began that she was sorry having got into the wrong apartment—up spoke Mrs Greenough, Oh Miss Brewster! poor woman. She is so distressed!—But someone took Mrs G off & I said to Mrs A. It is all a fetch of Miss B. She lies in wait to catch my visits, and she wrote me you had asked for her. Said Mrs Astor we came with the servant he asked in Italian is this the apartment of Mrs Carson and the woman said si si, entrate piace[6]—and that they waited 20 minutes at least. (Miss Brewster's maid Emma had told Lorenzo how that her signora had been caught, by keeping some persons waiting as she always did to show her consequence, & it was the American ambassador who put down the cards & went off.[)] Well to go back Anne half an hour after sending me the above quoted note, stopped up with the greatest confidence & was announced by Esterina. I found her in my salon without her bonnet in the fashion of an intimate friend. She was as pleasant as possible, tho' she did refrain from offering to kiss me.

We talked of everything except Astors & days—Harnisch or art. Two days after I got a note wh[ich] I must really copy for you.

Harnisch's impertinences have been pushed so far that I have written to Charleston, if more orders are proposed not to send him them through me, as I am no longer his friend, and that the Bust of Mr Petigru was not sculptured by him at all, but turned off in a marble yard on the Tiber, and he only signed his name to it. Keeping me in ignorance till the last day I was in Rome in June—so that I had no time to warn Mr Courtenay of how he was executing the commission. As the piece of marble was fine & the general effect tolerably like it was better not to interrupt Mr Courtenay's plan of presenting it at the Centennial. But the work was not his, nor the likeness the perfect one I had been asked to guarantee and I had been cheated about the execution of it. Also I have written to Henry Young to tell him the Calhoun looks pretty bad, & he had better order it inspected before the casting. I have hesitated before doing this, but the Calhoun is really too big a thing to let go in this way, and I am really frightened to see how much is wanting, and how incompetent & conceited Harnisch has become.[7] The truth is this last year Anne seems to have crushed out of poor Harnisch the little manhood he had, and an artist cannot put into his work that which he does not himself possess.

1. Arnoldus Vanderhorst (1835–81), whose portrait she had painted for his widow and her cousin, Adele Allston Vanderhorst (1840–1915).
2. Giovanni (Nino) Costa (1826–1903), a prominent naturalist painter who had studied landscape painting with Jean Baptiste Corot and John Millais and who influenced CPC's renditions of landscape.
3. William Stanley Haseltine (1835–1900), an American landscape and marine painter living in Rome and part of the Storys' and Terrys' circle.
4. Denman Waldo Ross (1853–1935) had just finished his Harvard dissertation "The Early History of Land Holding among the Germans," which is probably why CPC constantly refers to him as Herr Ross. Only after his father's death in 1884 did his career as an impressionist artist, critic and teacher of design and painting technique, and collector of oriental art begin.
5. American minister to Italy William Waldorf Astor and May Dahlgren Paul Astor lived in the Palazzo Resfigliosi.
6. Come in, please.
7. Harnisch's Calhoun, which was dedicated 26 April 1887, was, except for part of the base, replaced in 1896 by J. Massey Rhind's Calhoun monument.

December 16, 1883, 107B Via delle Quattro Fontane.

I had written to M[ary] E W S[herwood] that she had better come to Rome for change and keep house with me this winter. She is quite disposed to come after New Year. It is my duty & my pleasure to return to her some of the kindness she showed me so largely. Would I could invite her to free quarters & the best of everything. But this I have not the means to do. But what I have I will freely give her. I should give her my bed wh[ich] is large & comfortable, & turn myself into the corner you occupied and I will try to comfort her all I can.[1] Though my spirits are low enough. First the heavy draft on me all summer to keep up May had broken me down [a] bit. I felt as nervous as she. And then the persecution from Anne & Harnisch. . . . However I am finding relief in work, and in praying to God for patience and cheerful submission to what it pleases Him to lay upon me.

1. About this time financial reverses forced John Sherwood to sell their New York home with all its furnishings. Mary Elizabeth Wilson Sherwood (1826–1903), lecturer and writer of novels, ettiquette books, and memoirs had been a prominent New York socialite until her lawyer husband declined financially and mentally.

December 30, 1883, 107B Via delle Quattro Fontane.

Mrs Lee & Miss Tracey[1] have elected Rome for their home. I am going to the Pal[azzo] Bonaparte to a grand eggnog reception they give on New Year's afternoon. Mrs Haseltine[2] had a superb Xmas tree for all the noble children of Rome, & their noble parents as well. I did not have the heart to put on my new French bonnet while you lay ill in the hospital.[3] But I will make a resolute effort & put it on for N[ew] Year. . . .

I have Marietta, Esterina's other sister in the house for a model and dear old Miss Shirreff is sitting to me for her portrait at Mrs Grey's request.[4] If I succeed in it I shall be set up as a portrait painter. Arnoldus has been packed and sent two weeks ago.

1. Katherine Parker Tracy and her sister, Mrs. William P. Lee, were both New York socialites.
2. Helen Marshall Haseltine, wealthy wife of the artist William Stanley Haseltine.
3. CPC believed that James Carson's sciatica and rheumatism came from his failure to pursue homeopathic preventative medical self-treatment.
4. Grey and Shirreff were English ladies passing the winter in Rome.

1884

January 15, 1884, 107B Quattro Fontane.

Oh! I must tell you about Anne. I was determined to give her a back stroke, and I lay in wait for her. New Year's day I was infuriated by getting the letters about Dean Hall. I had to go to a grand reception at Mrs Lee's. Who should I see but Anne going up with Mrs Story with whom she has a great recrudescence of intimacy just now. They stopped to puff on the first landing, I drew up & we passed blandly the compliments of the season. Then I turned to Anne and with the sweetest smile I said "I am sorry Miss Brewster that we cannot make the combination to receive the same day, as I hear you no longer receive on Mondays." ["]Yes[,"] says Anne, ["]I have given up general receptions and I receive only my particular friends when I am able to do so." "That is very well," says I ["]but at all events we have derived a great deal of amusement from the correspondence." "Indeed" sniffed she, "Did you find it amusing?" "Oh very amusing I assure you, and not only I, but all our common friends, for I show your notes to every one, and they are highly diverted." Anne turned blue with rage, and she hissed out, "You take a great deal of pains for what is not worth the trouble." "By no means["] replied I most graciously, "the notes are well worth it, every body thinks you never wrote anything so entertaining"—and I sailed on feeling a great deal better in my mind and quite restored to good humour. Of course Anne is perfectly ferocious. But as she can't be more abusive and malignant than she was before, it is better to have her for an open enemy. I wish I had a good way to retaliate upon her and Harnisch. I dare say I sh[oul]d not use it if I had.

January 20, 1884, 107B Quattro Fontane.

I have painted Marietta three times, and I am now painting a portrait of Miss Shirreff which Mrs Grey ordered. I am to get $100 for it. Costa came to see it & pronounced it very fine—but just now I feel rather discouraged it does not look to me as like as it did. But the few judges to whom I have shown it, think it a capital likeness. I hope when quite finished it will be all right.

February 3, 1884, 107B Quattro Fontane.

Mrs Stokes has beaten the Vatican! Miss Stokes has been distracted to marry Soderini,[1] and he demanded of the old woman a living otherwise no marrying. The old woman w[oul]d have him put up more than the vague promises of advancement that his mother always announced he was to have from the Pope. Mrs Stokes held out and for six months it has been pull Pope pull Stokes—and the engagement remained imposto (not proclaimed). At last the Pope has given way, and promoted Edouardo to some post in the Dateria[2] which gives him something more than his pay as Guardia Nobile.[3] Immediately Miss Stokes has run round to declare her happy prospects & ask for congratulations, and is to be married at Easter. The Duke & Duchess de La Roche are sulking in Paris. It is very funny! Soderini has not made a great catch—for it is said Mrs Stokes really has'nt much money. It is all in her hands during her life, and sh[oul]d the daughters die without children old Stokes disposed of the propertually [perpetuity?] eventually. The Duchess has no child & this one may not either, in that case "my dear Plume a jump for nothing."[4]

1. Count Edouardo Soderini either as scholar or Vatican insider later collaborated with Francis Marion Crawford on a biography of Pope Leo XIII.
2. Dataria, the Office of the Curia Romana that distributed papal charity, conferred marriage dispensations, and served as the bursary for the Vatican.
3. Papal guard that recruited its men only from the nobility.
4. The duchess was Mrs. Stokes's other daughter. Plume was a character in George Farquhar's play *The Recruiting Officer,* written in 1706.

March 30, 1884, 107B Quattro Fontane.

I was at the Storys Friday ev[enin]g, impromptu charades and interludes. Nina Moulton was charming acting with Waldo Story.[1] The great amusement was Herr Ross dancing on an imaginary tight rope. It was indescribably funny. Then he made a speech going through the whole gamut of passionate utterance, and all merely reciting the alphabet! It was overpoweringly comic. Annie Von Rabe has come all alone. The children left in the custody of their Prussian Grandmother, and Annie free as air and slim as wire running about to amuse herself. . . .

Countess Gianotti is going to join the Catholic church this week—& the Reverendo Nevin will send many more into the catholic church while he is crowing over Campello & Savarese.[2] Instead of sticking to the simplicity of service we were brought up in, he lays on ornaments terces & tunes, till the half of his congregation think it better to go to the real thing instead of lodging at a half way house where the sign is changing every few days. The Rev himself trooped off to America this winter to give lectures at Andover in abuse of the Pope—and got the Rev Payne already a sick man to take his place. Payne surrendered to the fever, and the Rev is on his way back. I for one will be sorry to see him. . . .

I have made a success in the likeness of Miss Shirreff. I am painting Mme Cortazzo & making her a beauty.

1. Like his father, William Wetmore Story, Thomas Waldo Story was a sculptor.
2. Enrico Campello (1831–1903), a Catholic priest who attempted to reform Catholic church practice and had just established the Chiesa Cattolica Italiana to do so. G. B. Savarese was his colleague.

April 13, 1884, Easter Day, 107B Quattro Fontane.

[For the past week] I have been shut in the house with an outrageous cough. I got out only this morning to church. Glad to be there. . . . The Reverendo did not get back to Easter as he said he would tho' he is on this side. He has most likely stopped to pay his court to Lady Windsor (Gay Paget).[1] I wish he w[oul]d stop away altogether, and let us get Gouv

Wilkins to come. Dr Huntington[2] the new Rector of Grace church N Y preached an admirable earnest cheerful sermon. His topic was that in Religion only can we have Hope, freedom and gladness.

I am always dwelling in my own mind on the gladness of Religion, and with the hope of the immortal life in the company of the righteous all the troubles of this life may be borne with cheerful patience. I have never been willing to look on Religion as a thing of gloom[y] restraint, or ceremonial etiquette, but of cheerful active well doing and well bearing. All these things are more prominent from [for?] the christians around us. C[ounte]ss Gianotti has quit the sawdust with which the Reverendo Nevin has been choking us, and has gone to the Catholic church so as to be in unison with her husband & children—finding no longer the home in the church of her life time. Mrs [Mary Crawford] Fraser has followed Daisy [Margaret Terry] into the Catholic church and using [Hugh] Frazer's consent to her abjuring for her children also—and C[ounte]ss Gianotti tells me of several ladies of the Reverendo's congregation who are on the verge of defection. While the Reverendo goes off to abuse the Pope at Andover, his own flock is skidaddling! It is really comic, tho[ugh] so serious.

1. Recently married daughter of the British minister to Italy.
2. William Reed Huntington (1838–1909).

May 11, 1884, 107B Quattro Fontane.

Arnoldus [Vanderhorst] must have got to Charleston & I want to hear from you of it. There is in "the Queen"[1] at London a flattering notice of my portrait of Miss Shirreff, written I believe by Mrs Taylor. Mrs Grey has written me to get the portrait photographed, that she may give copies to her friends in England.

Annie Von Rabe . . . is wound up in "her brother-in-law" Fraser. Mrs Mimolee's deserting to the Catholic church & taking the children without asking him & getting them rebaptized Annie looks upon as lesé majesté to her duty as a wife—and so it is. Frazer is a sour, saturnine, shy man no doubt. But Mimolee captured & married him much against his will, & she ought to have stuck by him. As it is she has gone with the eldest child to the Tyrol wh[ich] is ordered for his health there to remain from 1 to 3 years! The younger boy of 8 is with Mrs Terry bring[ing] a French governess & servant man affected to his use—Fraser paying board for all. Then he has to break up his house wh[ich] of course he can't keep, & go to England & apply for some foreign post—he has a sister dependent on him & he thinks he will get her to go out with him probably to one of the South American stations. So the poor man is quite broken up & of course very much hampered for money, and all this because Mme Mimolee must have a priest to tell her woes to. Annie takes Fraser's part, & spends all her time condoling with him in his misery, for he is nearly crazed by the break up. As soon as he goes she will take up other friends. What most disgusts her is to see Mimolee and Daisy burning little greasy tapers before tuppenny (two penny) little pictures of the bambino and the Virgin in strong blue & red with 7 lath daggers in her heart. Annie says when their artistic sense is not revolted by such coarse images it is a sign their minds are utterly vitiated. All the world commends the Countess Gianotti joining the faith of her husband & children, and the same would from the Queen down, say "Mrs Fraser cannot love her husband" to do such a thing. The Countess has no little coloured prints about. All the change I see in her is that she sends me more things & seems anxious to prove that change of form does not change her heart.

1. *The Queen*, an illustrated journal and review, was published in London 1847–99.

June 1, 1884, 107B Quattro Fontane.

By the way Adèle [Vanderhorst] had the portrait three weeks before putting pen to paper to acknowledge it—and then she is tolerably cool about it tho' she thanks me for my "kindness" She does not mention the beauty of the frame, the skilful choice of colour of the coat—and tho' "she thinks it wonderful I could do it from photos—& the features are very like" she is not enthusiastic at all. It may be her dull way, but it disappoints me. Especially as I asked her to put it on exhibition before shutting it up in her house where I suppose few persons go! But that she does not touch on at all, but says it is hung in the Dining room! I wanted H E Young, Crafts and all Arnoldus's friends to see it—and I am vexed & disappointed at its falling so flat—as it seems to have done on Adèle. . . .

In my art I find my only consolation. I paint every day better, and I shall soon not be afraid to face any public with my portraits. I am painting Phyllis Shakspeare Wood,[1] and it is coming wonderfully well. Mrs Wood said this winter "Oh! that you had painted Kitty for me." And then she asked me to paint Phyllis who is the beauty of the family. You know every family has a beauty. . . .

Annie Von R[abé] . . . is sitting for Jack Elliott[2] (you remember that slim dark young man at Mrs Terry's) for her portrait full length and it takes all her time, now Fraser has gone. Herr Ross seems to have seen nothing of her this year. Sam Ward's death was very opportune just as the old fellow was reduced to indigence again by the failure of Mr Keene[3] who made him an allowance of $4500—a year! I wonder somebody does not make me such an allowance. I w[oul]d be gay & lively too like Sam.

1. Daughter of Shakspeare Wood (1827–86), the British sculptor and vice-consul in Rome.
2. American portrait painter resident in Rome who later married Annie's cousin, Maud Howe.
3. James Robert Keene (1838–1913), American businessman and speculator, who had just failed in a disastrous attempt to corner the wheat market.

June 22, 1884, 107B Quattro Fontane.

Annie has as usual gone off at full speed on another hobby. I told you how that she gave herself up to propping up & comforting Fraser on his wife's desertion (for her manner of going into the Catholic church is nothing less) As soon as poor Fraser went on his doleful way to England to seek some other post, Annie was pounced on by Elliott that slim young man with the black eyes you used to see handing the cake bucket at Mrs Terry's, & who looked made by nature to pose with a mandolin & a velvet cap and feather for genre pictures. Well he is himself a painter, in love with Maude Howe,[1] and on the strength of that sentiment he appealed to Annie to pose for him to paint. And she gave in and he is doing her full length, and she passes the whole day at the studio & is entirely absorbed in the work, & in spurring up Elliott to paint better than he knows. She drinks tea sometimes in Ross's studio, but she sees little of him or any one.

She dines every ev[enin]g at her mothers, being in a high state of disgust at Daisy, and it must make a pleasant dinner party.

I am painting Phyllis Wood, and it is coming extremely well. The Trollopes[2] were here yesterday to see it, and said many commendatory things, and sent love to you. Mrs Grey wrote from England after that notice (you may have seen quoted in the Charleston papers) in the Queen, to have the portrait of Miss Shirreff photographed, and I enclose you a copy. I am also copying in the Gal[leria] Borghese Mr Morgan[3] gave me an order & paid in advance £20 to copy something whatever I pleased. . . . I have done Mr Morgan's a head of a woman by Gian Bellini. . . .[4]

It is so cool that I do not mean to budge till middle of July. I can't get the rooms I engaged at Corpo di Cava. Scappolatiello found 8 persons ready to stuff into my three rooms & he threw me over. Mrs Newbery has written to ask me to stay with her a month, but I do not think I can do that. She is very delicate, and ordered by the Doctor to have nothing to do with housekeeping; so to have a guest in the house cannot be convenient. I may go to Sorrento for August. . . .

Mrs Taylor has published in the Phil Evening Bulletin of 7th June a most flattering notice of my work. Much good may it do me.

1. Maud Howe (1854–1942), the daughter of Julia Ward Howe and Samuel Gridley Howe, was a prolific writer of travel description and fiction.
2. Thomas Adolphus Trollope, the brother of the novelist and correspondent for the English *Standard*, and his wife.
3. Junius Spenser Morgan (1813–90), American banker based in London since 1854 and the father of John Pierpont Morgan. He became a dedicated art collector in the 1870s and financed major purchases for New York's new Metropolitan Museum from 1872 onward. His commissioning CPC for an unspecified copy may, therefore, have been motivated by a suggestion from his mistress and CPC's close friend, Alice Mason.
4. Giovanni Bellini (1426–1516), Venetian Renaissance painter.

July 13, 1884, 107B Quattro Fontane.

It was so delightfully cool till a week ago that there was no call to leave Rome, and indeed the wise in affairs of the Cholera say that Rome will be the safest place if the Cholera forces the blockade they have made against it. I had two pictures to finish indeed three that I want to have quite done before leaving Mr Morgan & Chs H Marshall[1] each gave me an order to copy whatever I please for £20 sterling, & paid in advance. I did not like to trust to the chances of life to depart in debt to them. So I have been to the Borghese Gal[lery] & copied a proud head of a woman by Gian Bellini for Mr Morgan—and for Marshall I am doing a lovely piece of the Carracci[2] ceiling in the Farnese Pal[ace]—(which you did not see, it being in the private apartment of the French Ambassador) But when Mme de Noailles[3] was here I took a note book one night to a reception, & set down the list of the colouring—and now I am working it out by photograph. It is coming very well. I shall finish it this week as well as a small portrait of Mr Petigru I am painting to the order of a Mr Gaston of Wash[ington][4] wh[ich] Jas Lowndes procured me. When they are done I propose to push to Sorrento, & thence to Corpo di Cava. It is so hot now I will be glad to get away. Grace [Bristed] goes Wed[nesday]. . . . She like many others is hesitating whether to leave Italy—for sh[oul]d the Cholera not penetrate to Italy, when the time comes to return in Oct. they will be submitted to such severe fumigations, it is a serious thing especially to such as have weak bronchi. As it is most letters undergo such a fumigation & stabbing that it takes me by the throat to read one & I keep sneezing all the time I have it out to answer.

I went last Monday to the marriage of Miss Stokes & Sodderini, as you take a lively interest in the couple I enclose you the pious part. They were married in the extremest heart of catholicity yclept the private chapel of Card[inal] Jacolini in the Propaganda Fide. The chapel being very small the company had to be very select—so I was surprised by getting a very nice little note from Miss Stokes herself asking me to be present. Of course I went & sent an elegant bouquet. There were but 14 ladies asked—and a few more men. The bride looked refined & went through the immensely big service with the heroism that only delicate females are capable of. Sodderini acted like a man who had made up his mind to do his part. Old Madam Stokes having beaten him as well as the Vatican—for after withholding her consent to the engagement until the Pope sh[oul]d have done something for Sodderini, as I wrote you—the old woman then fenced so well that she brought him up to the marriage without binding herself to make them any given allowance to live on! Nevertheless the affair was very elegant, and after the ceremony there was a handsome collation in one of the halls of the Propaganda Museum and a china box of confetti was given to each lady, and a satin bag of the same to each gentleman. I was amazed not to see Anne among the select few—so when I made the visit to Mrs Stokes I asked her how that was. She promptly said "I don't see why I sh[oul]d spare Miss Brewster"—and proceeded to say that the invitations being so few she intended them as a great compliment, and they had given them verbally to those they had seen, in preference, as being less formal. She met Miss B in the Babuino,[5] and she asked her & she accepted—her daughter had written a note, but she having given the invitation viva voce, they did not send the note. They did not mean to ask Harnisch, he having failed to show them any civility all winter. But the morning after meeting Anne she called at 11 bringing Harnisch with her evidently to force an invitation for him. But Madam Stokes who can withstand the Vatican was not going to give in to Anne—who persisted in asking all the details of the wedding, and finding Harnisch was not to be asked she rose up to go—saying 9 Oclock was early for her to come out so if she did not appear Mrs Stokes must understand she wished the young people well! Mrs Stokes is furious. Harnisch however sent a superb bouquet (he had made 2 years ago the bust of Mr Stokes) and now Anne gives out that she was not invited! I hope the old cat will show her claws to so many that she will come to be treated as she deserves. The Duke de La Roche came to the wedding but the Duchesse[6] remained in Paris. It is said the poor woman has an internal cancer.

1. Charles H. Marshall, son of a Philadelphia shipping magnate.
2. Bolognese artist Annabile Carracci (1560–1609) painted his frescoes in the Farnese between 1597 and 1603.
3. Wife of the French minister to Italy.
4. Perhaps William Hawks Gaston, a merchant and farmer in Oregon and Washington.
5. Via del Babuino runs into the Piazza del Popolo at the foot of the fashionable Pincio.
6. The bride's sister.

August 3, 1884, Hotel della Sirena, Sorrento.

I have invitations to the wedding & breakfast of Miss Tracy & Hurlbert,[1] to take place at Kirkstall Grange Leeds, the residence of (Louey) Mrs Beckett Denison on 9th Aug[ust]. It never entered into my head to egg Hurlbert on to propose for Kitty. It seemed preposterous when first I heard the report. He came to lunch with me, & I told him as an "on dit" of the day. He protested he would leave Rome for its gossip, that he never heard of such a notion. Thus enjoying a last fling of dust in my eyes. I had a very gushing letter from Kitty, and the Invitations were directed in his hand, but he has not written to me about it. They are to spend the honeymoon at Lord Lymington's county seat, put at Hurlbert's disposal—and in November come to Pal[azzo] Bonaparte.

The quarters there are so small that Hurlbert must perforce live like Achilles among the nymphs. For fear you are not up in your classics I must tell you that Thetys [*sic*] the mother of Achilles knowing through the oracle that glory & death w[oul]d come to her son in the Trojan war, dressed him as a woman & shut him up in the custody of the nymphs. But Minerva who knew the triumph of the Greeks depended on Achilles sent Mercury disguised as a bagman to sell finery to the nymphs and ladies. He exhibited [a] store of veils & ornaments that the ladies rushed upon, but Achilles stood uninterested by till a sword was produced by Mercury, that he seized, and as he drew it, Mercury recognized him, & easily persuaded him to throw off his disguise & hurry to the war. How

Twentieth-century hotel letterhead reproducing an 1890 print of the Hotel della Sirena. Courtesy of Carmine Berton.

long think you will Hurlbert dwell quietly in the lap of Kitty with [her sister] Mrs Lee to tie his night cap?

Marion Crawford[2] has made a great coup in getting Miss [Elizabeth] Bardan [Berdan] daughter of the Albany General who sells rifles to the sultan. They are to be married at Constantinople, & pass the winter in stuffy pal[azzo] Altemps with Mrs Terry who is delighted. The girl is very pretty, very rich & they say, very nice.

Annie [von Rabé] has only now left Rome for Lesnian.[3] I told you she was posing for Elliott, & for a bust of Aspasia for Simmons. . . .

I went to the Cocumella on the 20th It is an old Gesuit [*sic*] convent turned into a hotel, wonderful old ins and outs, in the midst of an orange grove overhanging the sea, which at least 80 feet below you get down to through a series of grottoes. It is a mile distant from Sorrento. But I was driven away by a dog that howled all night right under my window. I came over here where Col & Mrs Montgomery were staying, and found I could be lodged in this elegant hotel for 12 fr[anc]s a day & I was paying 11 at the Commella—that is for self & Esterina. I have two beautiful rooms & everything in first class style. There are innumerable corridors at my disposal for which I pay nothing, & I have the little contadini pose for me at a lira a morning. So I am living cheap and extremely well. Would I had you here!

1. William Henry Hurlbert (1827–95), a childhood friend of CPC, had recently retired as editor of the *New York World*.
2. Francis Marion Crawford (1854–1909), novelist and son of Louisa Ward Crawford Terry.
3. The Prussian estate of the von Rabé family.

August 10, 1884, Hotel della Sirena.

How I wish you were here! The air so soft & delicious. The waveless sea so warm that I go down the hundred feet to the bath every morning at 6,30, and am back at 7 to make my usual toilet. I have a room about 16 feet square with excellent spring bed and all the furniture as nice as possible—the floor in blue tiles opening on a stone balcony overhanging the sea. Esterina has a nice little room along side. The table is abundant &

good—and I have all this for 12 fr[anc]s a day! with no extra but my wine 2 fr[anc]s a bottle of which I drink 2 a week—and a franc for the bath. But that we manage famously, the whole family bathing for the one franc. Lorenzo to whom I allow a subvention of a lira the day in my absence from Rome, & who says he always spends two more at the Osteria of his own, has been persuaded by his loving spouse to come here. She has made an arrangement with the padrone to take Lorenzo for 3 lire a day, for this he has an excellent room at the top of the house & all his food. So he has no more expense than the journey from Rome wh[ich] cost him 15 lire 3d class. So the santa famiglia[1] being reunited go all down to the bath together. There are little houses, I pay my lira for the use. Esterina comes with me & we put on our bathing costumes & plunge in, then Lorenzo has the box for himself to undress—and presently he plunges in head foremost, for he swims like a duck. I am satisfied with a short bath, & come out & dress & come away. Esterina follows, & lastly Lorenzo, and we have had the bath all three for one lira. Lorenzo goes again in the afternoon & disports himself for an hour or so, while Esterina goes out on the balcony and admires his evolutions in the water down below. He has brought a sheet from Rome to dry himself withall, so I believe his afternoon bath costs him only one or two sous to the old man who keeps the bathing houses. You see it is very economical. . . .

I am going to spend Sep[tember] with the Newberys at Corpo di Cava. Oct[ober] will I hope find me in Rome. If I decide to return to America I sh[oul]d sail in Dec[ember] or Jan[uary]. I might let my house for the winter months wh[ich] w[oul]d lift some expense & give me the chance to spy the land in U S. But I don't know if I can compass it. I paint every day from 9 to 1 from the models I get here at a lira. They are not pictures I can sell—but it is practice for the portraits I want to do—and each one I gain ease of execution.

1. Holy family.

August 24, 1884, Hotel della Sirena, Sorrento.

I am studying the ways & means and probabilities of going in Dec[ember] to N. York for the winter & summer—leaving my apartment to be let for the winter. Esterina & Lorenzo w[oul]d have to be paid off & left to shift for themselves; which w[oul]d be a good discipline for them, but I sh[oul]d never get them again on my return, and I don't know what revolution it w[oul]d make in my housekeeping. I sh[oul]d have to give a hundred dollars to them on quitting after 12 years of service to me. How I sh[oul]d make out in U.S. I cant anticipate. I w[oul]d go to a hotel in Wash[ington], and set up my shingle to paint portraits, & perhaps get two sitters! Then the summer at Lenox & try there how it w[oul]d go. But I don't see the way clear. And it looks to me as if I sh[oul]d never get a settled home again, but have to board all the time in one place or another. That is misery to me. . . . I am awfully afraid to give up my pleasant apartment in Rome to risk myself in the vortex of American life, without money. . . .

I ponder the ins and outs, and can arrive at no conclusion definitely. I have done what I laid out to do last year, namely given the summer to studying painting heads in oils. In four weeks here I have made 8 studies, none of them highly finished of course, but yet each a good likeness and on each I gain facility of handling. I wish I had had the means long since to have learned oils, & to insist on portraits. But I went on from hand to mouth painting flowers, because I could do them well & sell. But now nobody wants to buy flowers any more. They buy embroideries & stuffs for ornamentation, and I find I must do some thing else, or accumulate unsaleable inventories.

On the 28th I go to Corpo di Cava, to stay a month with my dear Newberys who have invited me to their house, the hotel (tavern) being quite full. . . .

There is some cholera in Italy—but it does not seem to spread violently, and I never think of it. They say there is some in Naples. I believe it is a case we sent from here. A horrid, affected little English old maid undertook to eat oysters they passed round the table one day last week Almost every one had the wisdom to decline, so she took the portion of several and swallowed them down with lemon—and soon she had diarrhoea, and as soon as she was better, she ate everything, & it came on again, so as she was alone, and nobody was disposed to give themselves up to nursing her, she was fain depart to a very good English hospital in Naples. And we are well rid of her, for she was an awful bore.

September 11, 1884, Corpo di Cava.

In these cholera times I suppose you and Willie are rather uneasy about me. I staid at Sorrento till 28th Aug[ust] & then took a carriage which brought me & my luggage & Esterina to Corpo di Cava where I am hospitably entertained by my dear Newberys. Up to my leaving Sorrento tho' there was a flurry of suspected cholera at Naples it was not declared. But two days later it broke out with fury in the low quarters of the city. You will see by the papers the consternation, the riots & the devoted King's visit to Naples & the Hospitals. Had I foreseen the trouble I sh[oul]d have gone direct to Rome; for though up the mountain the danger of infection is less than in most places—I w[oul]d rather be in my own place, and not add to the anxieties of my friends here.

As many as could rushed from Naples to Cava—and the Cavese are in such terror they mobbed their syndic[1] & made him (nothing loath) put such restriction on intercourse, that we are really shut up—from the outer world—and begin to think of how the provisions will hold out. They fumigate every body who even takes a long drive in the neighbourhood—and all who come by R[ail]R[oad] are put in a close room for 7 min[utes] with such powerful fumigations that some have died on being taken out and many remain very sick. The smoking is not the least use—but they persist in it. One man got here last night from Naples rather sick—they were afraid it was cholera & they took him to the cemetery & locked him all night in the dead house! This morning they took him out, the populace wanted to burn him up alive as he is, but the Syndic rescued him & packed him back to Naples. These things are liable to happen at each little commune one has to pass through. I don't feel the least fear of cholera, but I have great fear of the fumigations. The letters & papers make me sick when they arrive. When I go to Rome I shall have to undergo the fumigation there if I escape it on the road. But they do not make the stuff so strong there, so one may survive. There is no cholera in Rome so far. I wish I were safe there with the fumigation passed through instead of hanging over me.

The steamers are all taken off the lines—and nobody knows when they may run again. My notion of going to N[ew] York this winter grows more vague with all this.

1. In Italian, *sindaco,* the administrative head of a commune, who is elected by the communal council.

September 30, 1884, Rome.

I arrived last night safe from Cholera, but not sound as I took one of my worst colds some days before leaving Corpo di Cava. I came armed with a certificate from the Syndic of Cava that Mme Carson & maid had passed the previous month under his eye, guiltless of epidemic, and, we passed Naples barely in time to take the first train for Rome, so that I had to pay my fare on the Roman R[ail]R[oad] in the carriage. The trunks c[oul]d be expressed direct from Cava to Rome, but passengers must pay on going into the carriages of the other company. I was in great dread of the fumigation at Rome—so I made my way with my certificate in hand to the Doctor, and coughed before him so awfully, that he excused me & my hand bag from smoking—but Esterina & the little impedimenta all were made to pass through fumigation of phenic acid & sulphur. The trunks they w[oul]d by no means give up. So Esterina & Lorenzo returned this morning at 8 with the keys. They have opened everything, hung up all the dresses in Sulphur smoke, & shut the whole into a room for two hours. Esterina has to go back at 11 to get them. I hope they will not have picked out a few articles of wear suitable for wives & daughters of impiegati.[1] Esterina is very much aroused by what she saw. Some of the trunks opened were filled with clothes so dirty they deserved to be burnt, & she enjoyed seeing them thrust into an oven & the fire set to them. My things may have caught infection by being opened in such company!

I am glad to get home. There is no Cholera in Rome, and any way I am not afraid of taking it. But I w[oul]d not like to see & hear the dreadful things that take place. The cholera interferes with my projected trip by the Florio. The steamers are all taken off the line—& no doubt all vessels from Italy will long be subjected to quarantine, which I should never think of running. Moreover I have the most discouraging letters about going for artistic purposes—and unless I were sure of getting many portraits to paint I sh[oul]d be swamped at once. Unless something more favourable than I have heard yet, turn up, I cannot try it.

1. Clerks.

October 26, 1884, 107 B Quattro Fontane.

Of cholera I have no fear. The epidemic is dying out at Naples, and it has never been to Rome at all. But it will make an empty house of all Italy this winter. . . . The picture I painted of Phyllis Wood is hung up in their salon with applause. If people would only sit to me in numbers! . . . The first chance I get I'll send that miniature to Jane Postell I painted so long ago.

December 7, 1884, 107B Quattro Fontane.

I have cut down my own expenses in every way I can—but the prospect of selling pictures is very poor. The box of pictures I have sent to N[ew] York, & written about to Willie contains one picture No 3 which is to be paid only. It is of Mr Petigru ordered by Mr Horace Grey of Boston to add to a gal[lery] he has of the eminent lawyers. Of course he will not wish to pay for it at the rate of a portrait of one of his family. I shall charge only $30 with the frame for he will have so much to pay on the transportation & taxes that it will mount up to about $50 before he gets it.

December 28, 1884, 107B Via delle Quattro Fontane.

I have such a lot to tell you I am like a bottle too full. Last Sunday as I got to the street I met Harnisch coming in gaily with Miss Brewster's maid Emma the little serpentine, as Esterina calls her. Harnisch bowed I returned it. The little girl flew at me & kissed my hand, as she always persists in doing. Harnisch raised his hand & said "Mrs Carson I wish to present her to you as my future wife!" "I congratulate you" said I without a moment's hesitation; said he "I intended to write you a note to inform you of it" I congratulate you said I again & shook hands with him & with Emma—and said "You will have a nice little wife—you could'nt have made a better choice!" He thanked me, and the interview ended! If he had set himself to revenge me on Anne he could not have done better. I forgive him all his behaviour to me, for this. I feel like a righteous little jew with my foot dipped in the blood of my enemy. The thing has been going on a long time, & I have been wishing the little minx sh[oul]d capture Anne's slave—but I never gave it utterance for fear of premature disclosure. Anne it seems dismissed the girl about ten days ago, but condescendingly told her she would inquire of Mrs Story & other friends of hers to get her a place. To which Emma replied, non s'incommodi signora. Il padrone l'ho io.[1] Thereupon she went at Harnisch, and declared he must marry her at once. The great passion of love conquering fear, he actually mastered courage to declare his intention so doggedly to Anne, that she is forced to see her game is played out. However with the power she really has of suppressing her rage when she chooses, and covering her defeat—she sends for Wood the vice consul, and tells him that of course she would have wished Mr Harnisch to make a more suitable match in his own sphere, but since he is determined, she wishes to have every thing done in order, & that the due legal arrangements sh[oul]d be made. Harnisch likewise becomes a catholic, which Anne had never obtained of him to do. He has gone into retreat. Is to be received in a few days & the marriage will take place as early in June as possible.

He has furnished his rooms out at the studio & will take his bride to live there. Meantime they are still in Miss Brewster's apartment & as he paid half the expenses of course she can't turn him out till he chooses to go. But it must be a funny party. This Emma is the daughter of old Anacleto Anne's cook & drudge, the most shabby miserable old man you ever saw. The girl can read & write having been brought up in the charity school where one of Esterina's sisters got her education on the Duke of Sermoneta's foundation. The girl is not even pretty, but a trig little piece as full of tricks as Anne herself—so H has fallen from the frying pan into the fire. I did not desire to do any harm to Anne & Harnisch, but I am enchanted with this blow he has dealt her & himself at the same time. . . .

Mrs Sherwood has come, and I devote myself to her all I can. Yesterday she was here at my reception and I lighted up the chandelier as I did for you. It was all I c[oul]d do to make a show for her. She is very pleased with my apartment. She is stopping at the Londia in Piazza di Spagna travelling in company with Mrs Bob LeRoy & Miss Hunt[2] of Brooklyn they divide expenses. I am very glad to see her, and I wish I could do something for her, but I am too poor this winter. I can't ask her to dinner even in a small way. I embraced "my sweet girl for you" and she returns the embrace with interest to you. She was here yesterday when M E W S & her two ladies, & Mme de Hegermann[3] & Nina Moulten came in. I confess I had not the courage to introduce her to them. I am afraid she was mortified, but it will not do to introduce people who are of a different set to each other. Simmons now says he w[oul]d like to marry Miss Dexter[4] and wants me to give him a shove. So I had him here yesterday & introduced him to her, and I must sound his praises & take her to see his statues. He has done a Penelope wh[ich] is the finest modern statue I know: and as Marshall does not come forward who knows but the fair Maria may incline to the one who does come forward.

1. Don't inconvenience yourself, madame. I have a patron.
2. New York socialites.
3. Anna Lillie Greenough Hegermann-Lindercrone, wife of Johan Henrik Hegermann-Lindercrone (1838–1918), Danish minister to Italy 1880–90.
4. Maria Dexter was a friend of James Carson.

1885

January 11, 1885, 107B Quattro Fontane.

M E W S[herwood] is enjoying Rome very much the bad weather notwithstanding. I had her to breakfast one day—and I wish I c[oul]d do more for her but I am too miserably poor. I dare not spend a penny extra. I am really frightened. I hope by this [time] that business will be rising & you & Willie get employed, for I can do no more. . . .

I have just rec[eive]d a letter from Mrs Grey in London. Miss Shirreff's portrait arrived, & she likes it better than ever, & it is approved as a painting as well. Mme Carra has brought her little girl[1] to sit for me, only as a decoy duck, however—and I am going to begin on the Sig[no]ra Capecelatro on the same empty terms. One must do so much unpaid work to get a name.

Harnisch was married Thursday & took his bride to Naples. Anne was determined not to own up to defeat, so she assumed the whole thing & had them married under her auspices, when she found she could'nt stop it. She catches every one to tell them that she did not wish the marriage, she wished Mr Harnisch to marry in his own sphere—but that the girl is a sweet creature, well educated, utterly incapable of learning any thing. That Harnisch has very German notions of a wife, does not propose to make a lady of her. . . .

I met Harnisch once again in the staircase and he told me he had become a Catholic, & the first thing they demanded of him was to be at peace with every body—wherefore he had spoken to me! I told him I tho't it was I who had much to forgive, but we w[oul]d let the matter rest, and

I w[oul]d send him as a wedding present the candle sticks he had sent me, and he must take it in good part. And I did send them—because Anne had said Mr Harnisch had made lady Carson a present of beautiful candlesticks that cost 250 fr[anc]s. They cost I sh[oul]d think about 30. I am so glad to wash my hands of the pack—and truly I forgive Harnisch all he has done me, for this marriage which is such an affront to Anne. By the way Mr Court[e]nay has sent me a photograph of the bust. It is awful—much worse than it looked in the marble. It sets me on edge to see it. I have poked it away. . . .

I am going to dine with the Harrimans this ev[enin]g. I wonder if they will bring out the Chateau Ykem.[2]

1. Elesina Carra, daughter of Clara Field Carra.
2. Chateau Yquem, generally esteemed the best Sauterne wine. William H. Harriman was a vestryman and benefactor of St Paul's Episcopal Church in Rome.

March 3, 1885, 107B Quattro Fontane.

Mr Thenay Consular clerk is just returning to America, & has kindly taken a small parcel for me. It is a small portrait I send to Aunt Adèle [Allston] of Papa, she to leave it to Ben & Louise in token of my gratitude to them for their kindness to you. . . . There is also the miniature of Jane Postell,[1] I wish you to keep till a convenient moment to send to her. If you know her address you c[oul]d send it express at once. Also that of Mary Louisa Ravenel which I want sent . . . to Henry Young who will give it to any Ravenel survivor. . . .

M E W S[herwood] boomed off at last in a hurry. She had a great success, and is much wondered at into the bargain, which she is happily unaware of—she thinks she has the pearl of French dressmakers, and instead it is the most astounding flyaway, hanging garden sort of costume ever seen.

1. CPC's cousin Benjamin Allston (1833–1900) had married her cousin Louise Gibert North (1836–96) in 1882. Jane Postell was a cousin on CPC's mother's side.

Il Duca d'Andria Ferdinando Carafa e la Duchessa d'Andria Maria Serra Cassano hanno l'onore di partecipare il seguito matrimonio del loro figlio Riccardo Conte di Ruvo con Donna Enrichetta Capecelatro.

Napoli Aprile 1885.

Antonio Capecelatro dei Duchi di Castelpagano e Calliope Ferrigni de Pisone hanno l'onore di partecipare il seguito matrimonio della loro figlia Enrichetta col Conte di Ruvo Don Riccardo Carafa d'Andria.

Roma 19 Aprile 1885.

Invitation to the wedding of Ricardo Conte di Ruvo with Donna Enrichetta Capecelatro, 19 April 1885

[April 19, 1885]

I send you these as a specimen of how they do things and to amuse you. You remember the Capecelatros. They lived in the same Palazzo della Congregazum [sic], V[ia] Nazionale where do the Greenoughs and the Trollopes.

Don Camillo Massimo claims lineal descent from Fabius Maximus,[1] and much he has come down, having wasted his money on a photographer[']s wife & the like, reducing his family to comparative poverty tho' they still inhabit the old Pal[azzo] Massimo. But he has been interdicted by a conseil de famille[2] & the remnant of the property taken out of his hands and put out to nurse. Nonetheless he drives about with his wife & daughters & is always on hand like the most exemplary Paterfamilias. The Princess is a Lucchesi Pali daughter of the Duchess of Berry by her 2nd marriage with the Count Lucchesi Pali, & consequently half sister of the Comte de Chambord.[3] The Princess looks a true Bourbon, and is a saint of good will and sweet manners.

Mme Bonnier is an American married to a rich Frenchman—& I met her at Vevey. Her mother was a Mrs Hepburn of Georgia who had had a stormy career shooting one husband to marry his cousin, or something of the sort. I had been shy of mother & daughters at NY hotel when they were going abroad in the time of the Empire to seek fortune in France, and they found it it seems in old Bonnier—& she looks like a French woman with white hair & was most gushing & affectionate to me!

1. Roman consul and general, 322–296 B.C.E.
2. A judicially sanctioned family agreement instituted to preserve the assets of a minor or incompetent relative.
3. Henri Charles Ferdinand Marie Dieudonné, comte de Chambord (1820–83), was the Bourbon pretender to the French throne in the early years of the Third Republic.

May 24, 1885, Florence.

By the way old Mrs Stokes has played Soderini again. She brought him to the pass of marrying her daughter without any settlement, and he had a small capital which he spent in furnishing the apartment, old madam—not even doing that but promising an indefinate income in money. Now the old woman leaves Soderini in the lurch, pays for none of the furniture & even claims things that he had from his father. His mother then stepped in to the rescue. But after all poor Edouardo finds himself to have gone to the shearing & come home shorn.

June 21, 1885, 107B Via delle Quattro Fontane.

I am trying to get ready this week to make my journey. Clem March writes me from Venice such appeals to come there first for a fortnight, that I have yielded—tho' I w[oul]d rather go to Venice in Sep[tember]. . . . It will break the long journey to go to Venice, and perhaps so also it will be better for me, as I do not feel strong. . . .

I enquired in Florence about Mr Elizabeth Murray and heard he returned with the new wife & daughters, and has made no attempt to introduce them to the people he knew in Mrs Elizabeth's time. It looks very queer, for although everyone w[oul]d have perceived he had married very soon, no one w[oul]d have questioned it; but not trying to present the new wife looks as if he were conscience stricken about something. . . .

Mrs Hurlbert [is] awfully cut up about Hurlbert's getting no appointment, tho' she bears herself bravely. They were so sure of it that she had gone to negotiate for the Astor apartment in Pal[azzo] Rospigliosi,[1] & it is said they had cards ready struck off as minister and ministress.

Mrs Heywood was ill all winter while Heywood[2] stalked around in his majestic fashion & dazzled M E W S[herwood] by his splendour. It comes out, that he has exploited her so unconscionably, spending all the income on his books, carriages, & things that she has at last turned upon him. Has taken back her money into her own hands, & will perhaps end by making him an allowance! You were right in saying he watched her like a cat, it was part of his system of subjection. With that large income she never had any money she could call her own, and he had run in debt for the household expenses & equipages, half of which she never used. Last year she was ill, & the Dr ordered her away in May, it was not till late in July Heywood w[oul]d take her, because he was correcting the proofs for one of those dull old poems of his he was reissuing & reprinting in England at great expense—& he w[oul]d not budge for fear he sh[oul]d not conveniently do his proof reading. He w[oul]d'nt let her go to Mme Folchi who was at a cool place on the Adriatic. This winter it was the same, she was ill, with a sister of charity nursing her, and all he w[oul]d do for her was to read to her another revision of his poem of Kuliphilas,[3] the Wandering Jew! wh[ich] she had been suffocated with again & again. He has got to the point when they travelled to take a valet to attend on him, and make her leave her maid at home on account of expense! At last she c[oul]d stand it no longer when she found that debts were making—& she has rebelled—but he sticks to her like a leech & is out at Albano[4] where she is waiting Mme Folchi's confinement with a 3d baby. Poor Mrs Heywood is so worn by it all, her face is no bigger than a cup. It must be an awful life she leads with such a cold blooded selfish tyrant. Really I fear sometimes he may strangle her when he has her alone in that great Palace. But she has taken back the control of the money and he may return to the modesty from which she raised him. All the same it must have come to be a dreary existence since she has found out how utterly selfish and ungrateful he is.

Don't tell this if any one happens to know her, for it has not yet become publicly known. But nothing can be kept secret in Rome of all places.

1. Palace facing the Quirinal where United States minister William W. Astor had lived.
2. Probably Joseph Converse Heywood (d. 1900), author, inter alia, of *Lady Merton. A Tale of the Eternal City.*
3. Cartaphilus, porter for Pontius Pilate, who had mistreated Jesus after his trial and was condemned to live and wander forever.
4. Albano Laziale is about fourteen miles southeast of Rome on the Appian Way.

[July 1885,] Pension Kaiser, Innsbruck, Austria.

I rec[eive]d No 78 & 79 two days before I left Rome and having written No 90 & sent you the June parts the day before, I waited to tell you how I had made out the long hot journey across Italy and over the Brenner. It was hot & heavy. I did it however without stopping on the way in 26½ hours. Arrived at the Golden Sonne, washed ate a little and went to bed and slept 15 hours.

I already feel better for the Alpine air. Innsbruck is in a high valley with mountains all around, and the Inn [river] runs thro' it to join the Danube very far away. The Hydes arrived next day after me, and we came & got our rooms in this Pension, which is very plain living but much sought after. A set of old frumps in it now.

August 12, 1885, Pension Kayser.

I feel my poverty in all this.[1] . . . Alas! I can barely scrape along. The occasional presents from friends (especially the Delanos) are what keep me afloat now—for my returns from Appleton w[oul]d not do it now that the sale of pictures has so fallen off. I might live on by giving up my apartment, and going to board in a pension & keep no servant—but that will come hard to me and as long as I can manage to get on, I will not reduce myself to that—for it w[oul]d involve giving up my painting wh[ich] is my greatest pleasure. . . .

There has been the grandest Schuzenfest[2] going on in Innsbruck for a fortnight. The decorations are extremely gay & pretty. The Kaiser[3] came, and they gave him a serenade of 500 Tyrolean Singers, Illuminated the Mountains, had fireworks, and a procession wh[ich] was the prettiest thing I ever saw. All the cantons of the Tirol & Austria sent companies of sharp shooters in national costumes, each company had a full band and every man was decorated with a bouquet, many had wreaths thrown to them wh[ich] they put round their necks, hung on their guns and piled on the drums. Many banners were torn to shreds in the wars some as far back & [as?] the great Frederick's[4] wars, and were carried all the more proudly. The streets they paraded are very wide & they passed before us down to a large cross place where they turned round a monument, & took down another street and round back again so we saw three movements going on in perfect order at the same time. It was very pretty. They have an enclosure for the shooting wh[ich] is incessant all day long. Almost all the shooters wear medals gained in other smaller trials and each man has a tall white cocks feather stuck at the back of his hat, sometimes two feathers and bunches of flowers. It is funny to see grown stout old fellows so decorated & evidently enjoying it. On the fair grounds there are of course menageries, giants, dwarfs, go-rounds and the like. There is a great rustic booth where the tables are crowded all day & till midnight with men & women drinking beer & eating bread & sausage, and bands overhead playing the gayest music. In the centre is a kiosk where secure under glass are displayed all the prizes wh[ich] will be distributed when all the shooting is over. Cups & watches, & gold pieces, & all sorts of handsome things, so that I came to Innsbruck as a quiet place and I have chanced on the greatest festival ever held here.

I shall go Sep[tember] to Venice, & Rome Oct[ober].

1. CPC's own reduced income and the tenuousness of her sons' employment.
2. Schüzenfest is a rifleman's festival or sport.
3. Wilhelm I, Emperor of Germany from 1871 to 1888.
4. Frederick II (the Great), Prussian king from 1740 to 1786.

September 6, 1885, Venice, Hotel de Rome.

I painted but two things the time I was at Innsbruck—for I had no convenient place for painting. One was a likeness of Clem March—& the other of Henry Young. They were not finished while Clem was with me, & were sent after him to Paris. He however decided suddenly to go home, and I do not think they were in time to reach him in Paris. If it turns out so, I will get the excellent Goodridges[1] to send them across by some one or other. If they arrive safe in N[ew] York, I shall have Clem hand over Young to you. You are to judge if it be a good likeness—for the photo he sent me did not at all recall him as I remember, and this is more like my recollection—only I am not sure of the colour of hair & complexion. If you think it good then I w[oul]d ask you to have it properly framed, putting a strip of wood top & bottom to make it a little more in proportion, as you will see I had the canvas widened. I will pay for the frame & the sending it to Young. But I don't want it sent to him unless you consider it a good likeness I want you to endorse this letter "directions for portrait of H Young" so as to lay y[ou]r hands on it whenever the picture turns up.

I painted last winter a head of you that is superb—& it is handsomely framed. It is a great consolation to me, and some day it will be pleasant to you to own y[ou]r likeness painted by y[ou]r Mamma. I have begun one of Willie this summer, & it promises well. . . .

Sep[tember] 9th

I was interrupted here by a visit from Paul Tilton, who has been hanging on by the eyelids here in Venice for 18 months. Literally by the eyelids, for he is so lazy and hazy that he will never come to any good. I am more sorry for Mrs Tilton[2] than ever, when I see Paul such an unsatisfactory being. . . .

Damaresq is the brother in law of Haseltine.[3] Posi ran his bank as he now does Handley's—but he had an awful time, in respect that Damaresq & his wife were a miserable crew. She was swelled up to a blubber, but dressed nevertheless like a cocette, and acted like one, & ran up debts and as Damaresq was not much better & drank awfully they got wound up—ran away, & left Posi to sit in the empty bank for six months enduring the abuse of the tradesmen they had defrauded. It was Damaresq (who was vice consul) who under Schuyler Crosby's inspiration showed up poor McMillan, & got him turned out for drinking. Crosby himself wanted to be Consul General—but he did'nt get it, tho' they ruined McMillan who was an excellent consul, tho' he did get merry sometimes of an afternoon after hours. People can't be destroyed by their enemies if they keep themselves straight. . . .

I am so troubled by your state of mind, that I had to fly to my art for relief. I was enjoying the leisure of Venice, to sail around & visit all the lovely things. But it was no use with your fate[4] like the sword of Damocles over my head. So I went to the Academy, procured a permit to copy, stretched my paper, made my squares & drew in Santa Barbara—and today at 1 PM I shall go to the Sta Maria Formosa[5] and begin copying it. It is very fatiguing work, but it is better than fretting and when it is done I shall send it to our dear Mrs Daly, who especially admired the picture.

1. Probably New York socialites Frederick Goodridge and his wife, a member of the Grosvenor family.
2. Mrs. Tilton had left Rome and her husband to live with her sister in New York state.
3. Presumably the artist, William Stanley Haseltine.
4. At this point, as so often in the past, James Carson was on the verge of losing his job.
5. St. Barbara was the central figure in an altarpiece by Jacopo Palma (ca. 1480–1528) in the Church of Saint Maria.

September 27, [1885,] Venice.

I have not found Venice very pleasant this time, and I am eager to get away. Though it is still hot, I shall depart on Wed[nesday] to arrive in Rome Oct[ober] 1st. It cannot be hotter in my large rooms than it is here. Having finished my picture I have nothing special to do. Paul Tilton is a perfect thorn to me here. He is really a hopeless case of idleness, discontent, conceit and envy. No good can possibly come of him, and I think of his poor mother and shudder. I shall not write her again till I get back to Rome, & then I shall skip all mention of Venice so as not to say I have seen Paul. He is so destitute I can scarcely refrain from giving him fr[anc]s 100 but I know he w[oul]d just stalk into the Club & spend the money as if he had a fortune behind, and in a few days be as near starvation as he is now. It is no use for me to strip myself of what I need, to supply the wants of so incorrigible a sluggard. So I shall be glad to be some where else before a catastrophe arises.

I hav'nt heard from Mrs Heywood for some time. Heywood keeps her so under surveillance that she can seldom write, and often he suppresses letters written to her. He keeps her like a ticket of leave[1] woman, only watched still more closely. He is afraid she will get off somehow to the American Consul, and revoke the power of Attorney she gave him by which he draws all the money. She has'nt the firmness to withstand him. My belief is he is deliberately trying to break her down to insanity, so as to have the entire control. The wonder is he does not fear to kill his golden goose. But he has got her will made & everything she has, and this is the way he rewards her. I never imagined such cold blooded, selfish cruelty. It is incomprehensible, but as she will not take her own part resolutely, I shall try to keep out of it when she throws herself upon me.

These things wear me out. It was the contention with Nevin last winter in behalf of poor little Proctor that made me so ill at last. I hope I shall never back down when my help is invoked, but I shall not put myself forward when it can be avoided hereafter.[2]

1. A colloquial name for an "order of license" giving a convict restricted liberty before the expiration of her or his sentence. It could be revoked if the person acted badly or was insufficiently industrious.
2. See explanation after 8 November 1885.

October 17, 1885, 107B Quattro Fontane.

I am really tired of Rome, and I wish I had the resolution to go to Florence. Rome has become too populous. It makes food dear, the streets so thronged one can't walk without jostling wh[ich] is a great fatigue. The roads out the gates are cut up into holes & bogs by the carting of material for the enormous number of houses building, and they are so badly built some tumble down.[1] Almost all my friends are gone away. Even the Terrys will go next year to Florence, or this winter if they can let the gloomy apartment in Pal[azzo] Altemps. Arthur[2] is to be taken into Maquay's bank at Florence, and the rest will follow. Annie Von Rabe has had much sickness in her family but all are doing well now, Mrs Terry says. The widow Van Rensselaer is still in US. I hear. Mrs Tilton's son you saw in Paris is Paul the eldest, now in Venice expected to make fame & fortune as a painter, but neither will he by reason of his extreme laziness and conceit. Poor Mrs Tilton. . . .

I have seen no Charleston papers so the particulars of that horrid eyesore are veiled from me, but when I returned from Venice Mrs Posi told me St Michael's steeple is overthrown![3] I shed tears. I have no letters from Henry Young since. Also Mrs Posi has heard of the tragedy in which her brother Dr Bellinger is involved.[4] It is most horrible. I have seen Mrs Dawson's letter to her, saying how difficult it is now to live peaceably with the negroes. It is a dreadful question that is sure to give great trouble before long. . . .

All these things seem to cut the ground from under my feet. I do not see my way to attempting such a difficult problem, for I have no longer the strength or spirits for new enterprises. When General Sherman[5] is retired at 62 how can I with more years on my shoulders undertake fresh departures. If you were permanently set up, and I could come and sit down near you in a snug little way, that is what I w[oul]d do. But otherwise I don't think I can make any change of base. I w[oul]d like to move to Florence for there I have Mrs Hyde & Mrs Huntington whom I love, and other friends who are companions. Here I have only Countess Giannotti, most kind & affectionate, but she lives more and more in a circle quite apart from me. When I go to an ev[enin]g party I find scarcely any one to speak to, & when the Terry's go I should find myself quite neglected in general society. . . .

Esterina & Lorenzo are acting specially well. Lorenzo gained a thousand lire last winter in the Lottery (you know Italians are always risking a few sous in the lottery) and on the strength of it he came while we were in Venice and spent a fortnight. What he saw and heard in the hotel seems to have opened his eyes to the comforts he enjoys in my service, and both of them appear to have taken out a new lease of good behavior. Sh[oul]d I go to Florence they doubtless w[oul]d come along. But I don't know what will give me the wrench to go. If Maldura sh[oul]d raise my rent I w[oul]d depart at once. Otherwise scarcely—for the expense of moving w[oul]d be at least $500—and tho' living is cheaper in Florence, it w[oul]d be two or three years to make up the saving of the outlay—in five years I shall have accomplished my due term of existence, and it seems scarcely worthwhile making a fuss. . . .

Harnisch's Calhoun is cast & was on exhibition at the public foundry. I went to see it. Since statues were made never has there been one as bad as this. Every one is agreed that it is the worst they ever saw. It is quite deplorable. He seems to have lost the wits he possessed, for whereas he made busts & figures in anatomical correctness, this is utterly out of all relation to nature or to art. I wrote to Henry Young they ought to pay some one, Old Crafts for instance, a thousand dollars to come out and inspect it, but by no means to allow it to be shipped before they knew what it is like. That it is only fit to be sold for the weight of the bronze wh[ich] is enormous, & will cost a great deal to transport. They have so much more money, they could do this let Harnisch make the Allegorical figures for the base, wh[ich] perhaps he may do better, and they could have another statue made before it is too late. I now wash my hands of the concern. I heard last year Miss Brewster said it was <u>she</u> not Mrs Carson who had got the order for H—and I am glad to hear it so. It is true they made inquiries concerning his competence of others than me & took the model he offered them on their own choice. So there is no need for me to assume the shame of this thing. It <u>is</u> shameful.

1. To accommodate the government of Italy after it became its capital and to house a population that doubled from 1870 to 1890, Rome experienced a massive building boom that significantly altered its geography as well as its architecture.
2. Youngest child of Luther and Louisa Ward Crawford Terry.
3. A major hurricane struck Charleston on 25 August 1885, damaging or destroying an estimated 90 percent of all residences but not toppling the steeple of eighteenth-century St. Michael's Church that stood at the city's center.
4. Killing a black man.
5. William Tecumseh Sherman resigned his command of the United States Army in 1883. He had been a friend of the Petigru family since the 1840s when he was stationed at Fort Moultrie, South Carolina.

November 8, 1885, 107B Quattro Fontane.

I gave a party yesterday. Not on the pattern of that "barty" of Hans Breitman[1] that our dear [Charles Astor] Bristed was so fond of quoting. At my party they drank only half a decanter of Marsala, and gallons of tea. I was moved to this enterprise by the inauguration of the new regime. I tho't I would ask them before the season opened with finer display than I can make. It turned out extremely well. Every body seemed pleased to meet after the summer to compare notes, as well as to make acquaintance with the new Consul Gen. Alden. The Stallers did'nt come, they said they were engaged. I lighted the chandelier as I did for you. Your loving friends the Trollopes were delighted with your portrait—which hangs in the dining room quite low, so when I am at dinner you are just in your place. Alas! it gives me almost more pain than pleasure, for it makes the want of you the more sensible.

The Heywoods have just come back from Paris. He watches her more like a jailer than ever—she seemed lively however and begged me to come to dinner today. I shall try my hand to keep from being thrust between the bark & the tree. If she had the courage to assist herself she has the power in her hands; but if she submits to his tyranny nobody can help her. Her sons are no account. Neddy was her stand by, and in his death she lost her only prop, poor soul!

I did not tell you the Nevin[2] imbroglio last winter because it was so long & so bad. Gouv Wilkins came in at the end, and he knew a little of it. Nevin was monstrous sweet to Gouv this time. I remain on terms of "observation" with him. I invited him to my Tea and I have this moment received a note from him that he was out of town & got back too late to come. If you care to hear all the ins and outs I will make up a package of the correspondence & send it to you. It was about a poor little clergyman he brought out last winter as assistant; and whom he turned upon & treated most shamefully—and every one passed by on the other side, except Mrs Field Princess Brancaccio & I. It was an awful fight, but we sustained the poor little man, & dragged him out of the arena, & bound up his wounds, pouring in oil & wine. . . .

The Signorina Capecelatro has passed at once to the title of Duchess.[3] The father of her husband Count Ruvo died a month ago still a hale man he was—so Ruvo becomes duke d'Andria. Wurts is on a visit to his house for a few weeks He is delighted with his present chief at St Petersburg Mr Lothrop.[4] Mr [Junius] Morgan will come in Jan[uary] to Wurts' apartment, again—but he is not married to Mrs [Alice] Mason, and nobody can tell how it will turn out. She seemed to rule everything in his house last winter, but the marriage does not take place.

1. Pseudonym for Charles Godfrey Leland (1824–1903), American author, editor, and student of the Roman past.

2. See following entry for the Nevin affair.
3. See wedding invitation enclosed in CPC to JPC, April 1885.
4. George Van Ness Lothrop (1817–97), lawyer and at this time United States minister to Russia.

[The Reverend Robert Jenkins Nevin, to whom the following letter was addressed, was pastor of St Paul's Episcopal Church in Rome. Carson had long objected to his introducing high church practices into the Episcopal services. A long letter from Nevin to Carson, dated 22 June 1884, contains his response to her complaints about his chanting or "monotoning" parts of the service. His response, rather abrupt although long winded, was that as priest he knew best and conducted services just as he always had and just as he had learned to do in seminary. Clearly CPC had referred to church members, namely Countess Giannotti, who had converted to the Roman Catholic church—a phenomenon Nevin brushed aside as irrelevant to his ways, which were, as he defined them, to read the lessons and to address the congregation in a normal speaking voice but to chant or "monotone" the prayers and other parts directed to God. This practice was necessary to satisfy young church members who expected such practices. Older and stronger members like CPC who were accustomed to different ways should be willing to tolerate change for the sake of others.

With those tensions as background, the issue of C. H. Proctor boiled over in February 1885. Nevin had hired Proctor, a young American priest, to be his assistant and do all the parish work while Nevin worked at the literary and theological writing his bishop had urged him to pursue. Proctor, apparently sickly to begin with, had contracted a bad cold, taken leave, and then collapsed in the middle of the service after his superior's return. Moreover, he had preached a sermon on St. Peter so heretical in Nevin's eyes that the rector had rebuked him in front of others. As a result Nevin decided to fire Proctor without giving him any previous notice.

Carson came to Proctor's defense at once, backed, she wrote, by many if not most of her fellow parishioners. Nevin first held his ground, then wavered in the face of her suggestion that a middle ground be found in which Proctor would be given a financial settlement compensating him for the months he had served. Nevin, however, insisted that Proctor leave Rome at once, a condition that both Proctor and Carson believed would be seen as a disgrace that would follow him home and damage his relations with his American parishioners. Nevin contended that it would make no difference since Proctor was in trouble with them already. And so, rejecting Carson's compromise proposal, Nevin turned the matter over to the vestry, which backed their rector.

Whether or not the vestry sanctioned the private collection of funds for Proctor that Carson then proposed is unclear. In any case, vestryman Hickson Field refused to head the subscription list because he believed the matter should never have gone to the vestry. Nobody else came forward to organize the collection. And shortly thereafter, Nevin returned Carson's twenty-lire contribution. A note from Louisa Ward Crawford Terry suggested that Carson had done all she could do and that the matter should now be left to Nevin.

The following is a draft of Carson's final letter to Nevin explaining her role in the controversy as she saw it.]

Friday, [February] 13, [1885,] 107B Quattro Fontane.

Dear Mr Nevin,

I am not by any means the chief adviser of Mr Proctor, he did not come to me the first person, nor have I seen him since last Friday wh[ich] is a week. I have been trying, as you know, if by good will some way out of this difficulty, so deplorable, might be found. The proposition of your letter today seems to open that way. Since you authorize me to do so, I will send for Mr Proctor, and try to get it settled so.

You doubtless think me one sided in my view. But you must remember that the greater part of my life I have been a slave holder, accustomed to have my fellow creatures absolutely in my hands; and that I was taught by my father's word and example to be extremely careful of the failings and happiness of those dependent on us; and that when their interests & passions clash with ours, we must as the strongest put up with a great deal, and look at things from their side, before our own. It has I suppose, given me the habit of mind of taking part with the weak. I am sure you are yourself too strong not to have the generosity that belongs to strength. But in dealing with Mr Proctor you have not considered it a matter between you and him only, but that you were responsible for having the service of the church discharged with decency and order. Recrimination can only wound the Church our mother. It is useless to speculate on what might have been had Mr Proctor been encouraged to go on, if he could have done so, or if he would have manifestly broken down & justified unmistakeably your apprehensions. The thing is now done. If Mr Proctor will listen, it seems the best solution of the difficulty. As the order of the services are no longer at stake you may give free scope to your benevolence, & treat him with the great tenderness due to a man as sick as you hold him to be.[1]

1. This final sentence, although it is written at the end of this draft copy, seems intended to replace two others that CPC had crossed out.

November 27, 1885, 107B Quattro Fontane.

By the way poor Mme [Clara Field] Carra who is a cousin of the Haseltines is at the point of death. She has been ailing since summer and it has run into so bad a fever there is little hope of her coming round. Hendricks death must have been very sudden. How many pres[idents] & vice pres[idents]—die![1] It is curious of two men picked out of the nation, the lot of death falls so often. This poor young Alfonso's death is sad—and the more so for the Regent & her baby daughter. We shall see some more Spanish troubles. Don Carlos was sailing around in a Gondola at Venice, and he will be very likely to begin another fight for the crown against the baby Queen.[2]

1. Vice president Thomas A. Hendricks (1819–85) died November 25.
2. Alfonso XII ruled Spain from 1875 until his death in 1885. Because his grandfather, Ferdinand VII, had set aside Salic law to make his daughter sovereign instead of his brother Don Carlos, she ruled Spain as Isabella II until her death in 1868. From 1868 until Alfonso's accession to the throne in 1875, Spain was torn by Carlist uprisings. Under a constitution adopted in 1869, a son of Victor Emmanuel II of Piedmont (Victor Emmanuel I of Italy after 1870) was made king and ruled as Amadeo I from 1871 until 1873 when a republic was proclaimed. It was put aside in 1875 when Isabella's son, Alfonso XII, came of age and was placed on the throne by a group of generals. In February 1876 the Carlist War ended in defeat, and Don Carlos went into exile. After Alfonso's death, his young queen, Maria Cristina, reigned as regent for their son, Alfonso XIII, who was born in 1886.

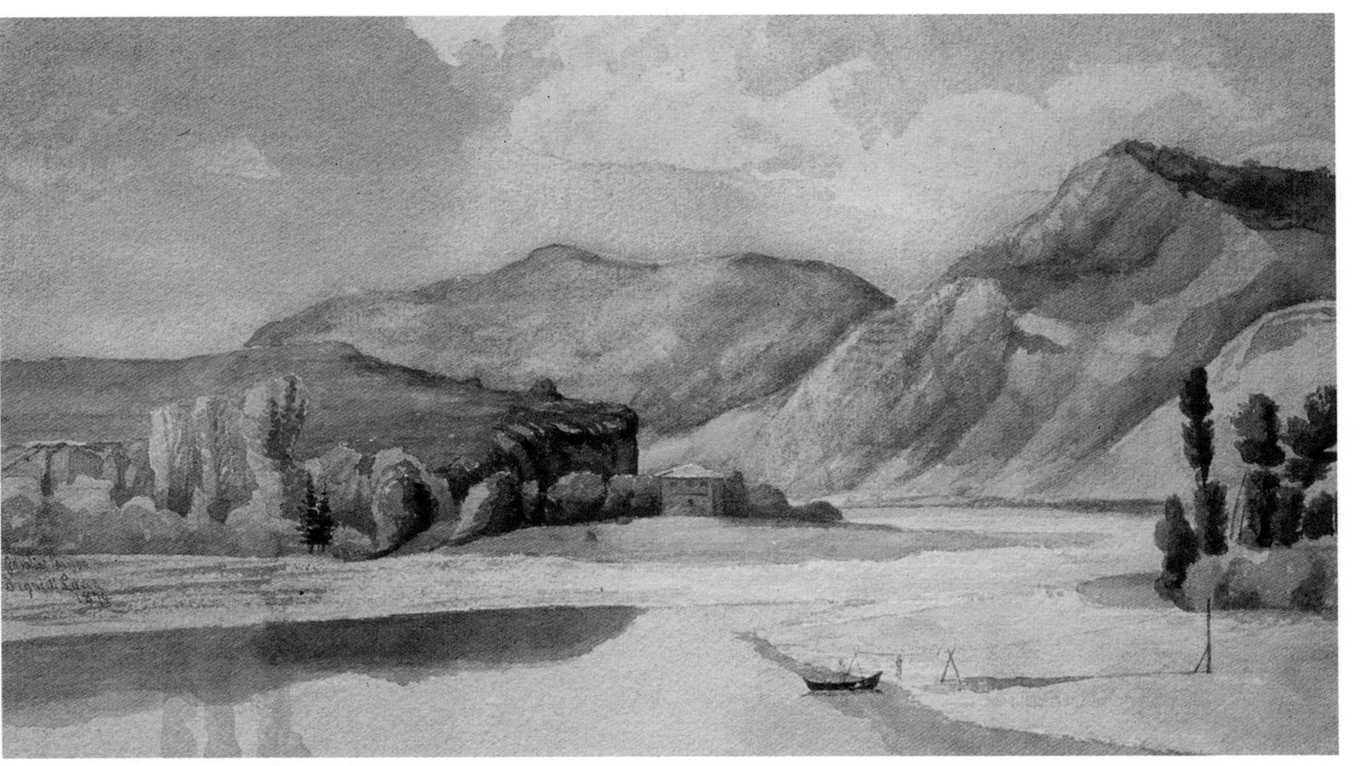

Caroline Carson, Bagni di Lucca, 1874. *Courtesy of Ashton and LaVonne Phillips.*

Caroline Carson, Piazza del Campo and Palazzo Pubblico, Siena, 1874. *Courtesy of Ashton and LaVonne Phillips.*

Caroline Carson, Villa d'Esté, 14 May 1875. *Courtesy of Ashton and LaVonne Phillips.*

Caroline Carson, Bridge over the Moselle at Coblentz, July 27, 1875. *Courtesy of Ashton and LaVonne Phillips.*

Caroline Carson, "Pomegranate Branch." Courtesy of Ashton and LaVonne Phillips.

Caroline Carson, "Pomegranate Branch" (detail). *Courtesy of Ashton and LaVonne Phillips.*

Caroline Carson, "Flowers of an Unidentified Leguminous Plant." Courtesy of Ashton and LaVonne Phillips.

Caroline Carson, Ehrenbreitstein, July 1875. *Courtesy of Ashton and LaVonne Phillips.*

Caroline Carson, Perugia, 14 July, 1876. *Courtesy of Ashton and LaVonne Phillips.*

Caroline Carson, Corpo di Cava looking to Mt Postiglione from Villa Guariglia 6 AM, Sep 8th/78. *In the authors' possession.*

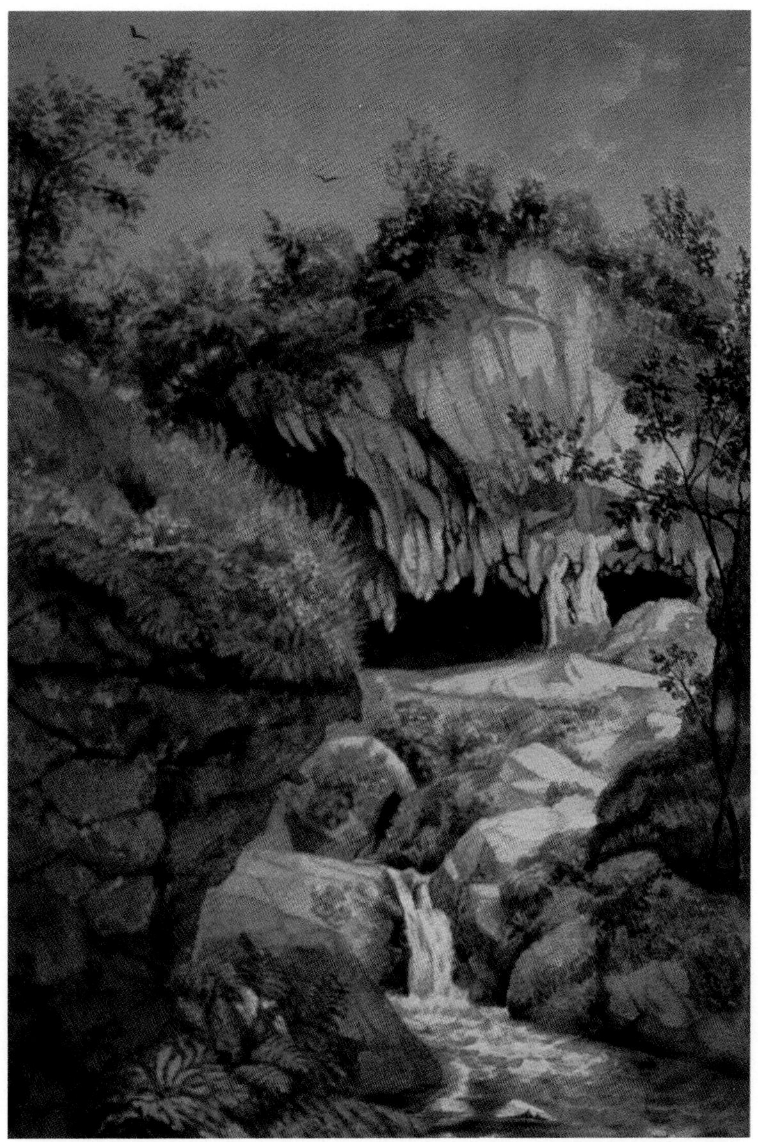

Caroline Carson, Grotto of Bonea Cava, May 3, 1876. *Courtesy of Ashton and LaVonne Phillips.*

Caroline Carson, "Still Life, Decorated Vase against Yellow Damask." Courtesy of Ashton and LaVonne Phillips.

Caroline Carson, Andermatt 1874. *Courtesy of Ashton and LaVonne Phillips.*

Caroline Carson, Colle Savelli, 2 Maggio 1880. *Courtesy of Ashton and LaVonne Phillips.*

Caroline Carson, Saarnen. July 21, 1882. *Courtesy of Ashton and LaVonne Phillips.*

Caroline Carson, "Self Portrait in Blue." Courtesy of Ashton and LaVonne Phillips.

Caroline Carson, Self Portrait in Pink. *Courtesy of Ashton and LaVonne Phillips.*

Caroline Carson, Sorrento-Amalfi Peninsula, Sep 14 1886. *Courtesy of Ashton and LaVonne Phillips.*

Caroline Carson, Christian Edward Detmold, 1878[?]. *Courtesy of Ashton and LaVonne Phillips.*

Caroline Carson, copy of Andrea del Sarto, The Holy Family. *Courtesy of Ashton and LaVonne Phillips.*

1886

February 5, 1886, 107B Quattro Fontane.

Mr Wood went out like a candle in a puff of wind. The girls & Tom were here Sat. and I asked after their mother whom they said did not come because Papa had a little cold, & she stopped to give his medicine. He had had one or two colds already this winter (just like me). Monday the fever went down—they were so little alarmed that the girls kept an engagement to lunch. Tom was with him all night, and at 2 AM his mother & he saw a sort of change on the face of Shakspeare and by 7 AM Tuesday he passed away without agony without any sense of leave taking. It is a dreadful thing to lose not only a kind father of the family, but the breadwinner. How they will get along I can't imagine. What little means Mrs Wood has are in Ireland. . . .

They are all very good & patient. I have been with them all these two days, and I shall go presently, for they like to have me sit down beside the poor woman. The funeral is this afternoon, but I shall not go tho' the weather is fair at last. But I have neuralgia in my face so badly—& I take fresh cold every time the wind blows on me.

To turn to the other side of life here is Nina Moulton's[1] engagement. Last year she was with her mother in Denmark—where by the way M de Hegermann suffered so painful an operation for stone, that his life was in peril, tho' now happily he seems well again. It was reported that Nina had captivated the best match in Denmark. But as it all went off & nothing more came of it last winter, it was supposed a thing desirable, but not to be. Now however the young man has come to Rome after her, and all is settled to the great satisfaction of all well wishers. . . .

The Trollopes are going to remove to England in June. Mrs Taylor remains in charge of the Standard correspondence. We are all dreadfully sorry to lose the Trollopes, & Mrs Taylor will find it hard work all the year round & living alone. It is true she is to get all the pay, but the Standard had cut down the pay, whence old Trollope threw it up altogether. How the Shakspeare Woods will manage to live I know not—it is dreadfully sad.

1. Mme Hegermann's daughter by a previous marriage. Lillie Suzane Moulton, known as Nina, married Count Frederick Christopher Otto Raben-Levetzau (1850–1933), a Danish diplomat, in April 1886.

February 28, 1886, 107B Quattro Fontane.

I have not been out to a single evening party this winter, and to dinner only with C[ounte]ss Gianotti sometimes, and once with Miss Goldsmid, and Friday last with Mrs David Sears of N[ew] York and Boston, a cousin of Mrs Daly whom I knew as the lovely Emily Hoyt—and lovely she is still in mind and manners. She bought, by the way, the dark Medici Bambino I painted in 77—and I immediately set to work to make a replica of him, for I thought you would miss him. He hung in the Salon between the Copy of Claude by Paul Tilton, and the Roses on the yellow back ground, right over the tea table. A week ago the Princess Brancaccio sent me two superb pheasants wh[ich] the King had sent to her. I had Mme Cortazzo and Mrs Strong (!) to eat them, and Lorenzo plucked the feathers carefully laying them in bunches, wh[ich] I mounted by pushing the quills through coarse bobbinet and gumming them down. I remember Mamma having Early to make her yards of trimming of guinea fowl feathers in this way. I shall have trimming for several bonnets, and I wrote the Princess I sh[oul]d write to you of her kind attention in sending me the birds, and I knew you would be pleased at her kindness to your mamma, and so the pheasants w[oul]d be enjoyed on both sides of the Atlantic. She is really very sweet, sometimes she sends me great baskets of flowers. People who have great plenty of those nice things, seldom think of sharing them with those who have not.

Last Thursday Mrs Field asked me to a ball she was giving to the children to open her apartment, which is only completely finished now. When you saw it, half the rooms were still incomplete. I think you only saw the dining room and the little morning room. The ball was in a great room in the centre of the apartment, hexagon shaped. The walls of grey satin great mirrors in the panels and all the cornice painted with cupids & flowers,—this was filled with the children—and from the arches around the grown people (a select party) looked at them. The children were beautiful. They showed blood, breeding and good nurture. They all danced with the utmost propriety without ceasing, and the extreme little ones jumped up and down to the music like little fantoccini,[1] but all in good humour & perfect gravity. Mrs Field the Prince & Princess assisted by Haseltine & other gentlemen were busy distributing beautiful presents to every child. There must have been 20 large French dolls superbly dressed, helmets & breast plates for the boys, fine toys, little clocks, fans, &c. One boy got a pair of shoes in papier mâché two feet long full of nine pins. There were cabbages of papier mâché bigger than the biggest, full of balls & toys. I saw one little mite at the last—very tired sit down on her cabbage, and she looked for all the world like a bit of a fairy story. I wandered round with Mrs Terry into the empty grand salon that looks out in the garden over the Coliseum in the fading twilight it was a scene of enchantment. The globe lamps in the chandeliers of the salon reflected through the plate glass of the great window fell upon the thin foliage of the trees making them look as if hung with garlands of light. Mr Field himself looked on in pleasant contentment and everybody seemed perfectly delighted. There was of course a fine collation, but I did not even go into the tea room, as I was going straight from there to Mrs Sears to dinner at Hotel Bristol. But I got my share of the feast for all that, for the next day Mrs Field sent me a delicious mountain of cake, wh[ich] had not been touched. She had brought me from Paris at Xmas a dozen p[ai]r gloves and a jersey embroidered in jet. They are really very kind to me—and so is C[ounte]ss Gianotti as constant as her name.

1. Little puppets.

March 24, 1886, 107B Quattro Fontane.

What a strange thing it is that people go to hear M E W S[herwood] talk of places they all know much better than she does. I wonder how she has brought it about. Three thousand dollars however is substantial proof of the charm of her talk whether inspired by an "original mind" or not. Only I wonder. The more that I heard so much of her talk last winter, and between you and me I thought her sadly gone off in conversation. Everything was said in such a loose-haphazard style, and she said so many things . . . like one who had forgotten what was fit to speak of, and what was not. I am glad she has made the money, for she works hard for it. The Storys have quite turned round upon her, for her talking double about the Hurlberts and chiefly that she has praised [Franklin] Simmons's statues. That is the sting. She has sent Mr Story a copy of Verses dedicated to the Greatest Sculptor of the Age—from a neophyte. The Storys pretend that the verses can't be meant for him but for Simmons! She says the Angels inspire the master's work. Story says no angels but himself inspire his work—and as Simmons has made a statue of Abdiel[1] "the faithful from among the faithless" it must be he whom Mrs Sherwood means to vaunt. So they reject M E W S well meant effusion. What she means by inscribing herself as a neophyte, I can't imagine. She has not gone in for sculpture that I have heard so she can't call herself a beginner in that act. All this I hear second hand from Alice Mason—for Mrs Sherwood being in disgrace with Mrs Story and I being a friend of Mrs Sherwood Mrs Story, very comprehensively invokes me in her displeasure, and she has left me out of all her parties this winter! It don't much signify however as my cough has been so bad I have not been able to go out a single evening all winter. I went this PM to a small tea at the de La Roche's, the first they have had since the death of the Sister, and I was seized all of a sudden with such a convulsion of coughing I had to come away at 5 O'clock. . . .

I went to a grand Ladies' Lunch at Mme de Hegermann's a fortnight ago. In drinking Nina's health—Mme de H turned to me and drank yours. Nina is to be married next month. I gave her your congratulations and she bade me cordially thank you. I am busy painting for her a group of the Farnesina, the same I did for M E W S—but this I am doing on parchment, so it is like miniature on ivory. It is coming very handsome.

1. A Gadite. 1 Chron. 5:15.

April 18, 1886, 107B Quattro Fontane.

I have been very poorly all winter, as I have told you, with a cough, and colds in the head that come on with pink sneezings even without leaving the house. So I have seldom been abroad, and never once in the evening. I am awfully dull & desolate. . . .

I have only ventured out once or twice in the day. Of course I must go to Nina Moulton's wedding with Count Raben wh[ich] took place on 8th at the church, and I went for a few moments to the reception. She was lovely of course. She had a necklace of three strings of pearl[s] the gift of Mr Morgan & Count Raben gave her sapphires set in diamonds. She is as happy & contented as possible, and is gone on to Denmark stopping now at Florence where they are being fêted. I painted for my present The Mercury & Psyche of the Farnesina. The same that you saw at M E W S[herwood]'s but handsomer for I did it on parchment which is like miniature on ivory. . . .

Thursday afternoon I went to a garden party of Lady Louisa Legge at the Villa Chigi out of Porta Salar[i]a.[1] The campagna was most exquisite in colour, and all the élite of Rome was there, but in ten minutes the sky was overcast and a few drops of rain fell, and I hastened away, leaving all the party walking in the alleys of Ilex, for the drops of rain were few & far between. As I came away I met carriage after carriage of people going, but I was too afraid of this horrid cough to turn back.

1. Villa Chigi lay in the outer northwestern reaches of Rome.

Easter Day, April 25, 1886.

I had run down so low when I last wrote that I really did not know how to get on. So I asked Mrs Field the next time she went down to Porto d'Anzio to let me tag on, for I c[oul]d'nt screw my courage to go alone as the Dr recommended the change. Thursday 22nd she sent for me all in a hurry that she had decided to go—by the 10,30 AM train. I c[oul]d'nt get ready, but I followed by the 4 PM, and found the whole family at the station for me—Mr & Mrs Field Prince & Princess & the two children. The Princess is building a villa half way between Anzio (Anticum) & Nettuno[1] and they were all camping in the hay loft that is to be when the horses shall be inducted into the stables. The villa has only the stone walls built as yet. The P[rince]ss had nailed Turkey red[2] on the walls, and made a really pretty room in which we gathered. The french cook was on the train with me & was immediately turned into a cellar below where a stove was flaming & he was put to preparing the dinner. He had brought pâté becasse[3] & all sorts of good things, & he had fish right out of the water, and by 8 O'clock we had a most luxurious dinner, some sitting on camp stools for chairs were scarce, but fine china & linen and every body gay. After dinner Mr Field & the Prince walked back about ¾ of a mile to Anzio to sleep at the hotel, a boy lighting them with a candle inclosed in a loose roll of paper from the wind. Mrs Field & the Princess slept in two little beds in one little room. Bebella, and the maid in another, and Marc Antonio and I in the third. Marc Antonio is as pretty as ever and he behaved like an angel; I don't know a child of 7 told a strange lady was to sleep with him, that would not have cried and resisted. But he looked a little perplexed only & did not object. I said I would tell you & I knew you w[oul]d enjoy it so much. The little fellow slept on a little chaise longue, & I in the bed, and the maid came early and carried him off in a blanket, and we made the most harmonious couple.

On Good Friday we walked to Nettuno, a delightful quaint old village on the sea—and we went in the woods & gathered cyclamen—and after midday breakfast the Princess read the Litany and the Gospel for the day and we felt more edified than by the Reverendo's rendering of the service Then we sat on the Terrace of the new Villa to see the sunset. Saturday morning I went on to Anzio to see Mrs Heywood who is down there for a change, but they had gone to Rome for Easter. At 12 we took the train back to Rome, that is Mrs Field Princess & I. The Gentlemen & the two children came back in the ev[enin]g. It was a real gypsy life of three days and it did me great good and has carried of[f] the cough almost entirely. I feel like my old self again which I have not done all winter. . . .

The Trollopes have pulled up stakes, sold every thing & return to England in June. Mrs Taylor remains as correspondent of the Standard. They cut the salary down so T Adolphus refused the reduction & Mrs Taylor took it. She will be the richer—but the Trollopes the poorer and after 45[4] years in Italy every one believes the first winter in England will carry off T Adolphus. We are all very sorry to lose them.

1. A coastal town about thirty-seven miles south of Rome.
2. Bright red cotton cloth.
3. A pie baked in an oval mold lined with forcemeat made of woodcock livers and leg meat, filled with woodcock breasts covered with sliced truffles, and topped with a pastry crust.
4. Thomas Adolphus Trollope had come to Florence in 1843, but had moved to Rome only in 1873 when he became Roman correspondent for the London *Standard*.

June 8, 1886, 107B Quattro Fontane.

I have a faint hope Willie may come out by the Florio & spend the summer with me at Sorrento. I shall go 1st July. Cholera never has gone to Sorrento, and what is flying on the eastern coasts of Italy is a very attenuated character. I live better for less money at the Sirena than any place I ever have been. . . .

Miss Goldsmid is in despair for her apartment in the Cortanzi. The hotel has been sold to the German Jesuits those fellows with the red cloaks—they offered such a large sum the proprietors could not resist the temptation. They are buying up all the best places in Rome as usual. They are dispossessed by the Gov[ernmen]t—and make an outcry—& say the church is in such poverty & affliction, and behold they buy whatever they want,—the expropriated Capuchins have built, in Via Meralana beyond the Fields's towards St John's Lateran, an enormous monastery as big nearly if not quite as the huge Ministero delle Finanze in the Via 20 Settembre you remember on the way to the Pagets & Porta Pia. The new apside[1] and the restorations of St John's were open on Ascension day. It is most splendid work—all done since Leo XIIIsth accession. The old mosaics are transferred to the new vault perfectly—and the frescos and painting and gilding are gorgeous.

Simmons invites me to go Friday to see a new statue of his. He has made a monument for the Hospital the Delanos have built in N York—and he has a mon[ument] to Longfellow[2] for Portland—and the Storys hate him like poison. By the way the Storys, Lees & Hurlberts are furious at M E W S[herwood]—and breathe fire and brimstone at her. If she should make some great coup however they w[oul]d all be her very humble servants. She is sailing around in England, & gives out she has come into an inheritance! Poor Mary Elizabeth, I fear she must collapse. It is impossible people will go on flocking to her talks like a band of ducks to a pond of water where every thing is thrown in. She really frightens me, one can't trust to what she may say. She is not like Anne [Brewster] treacherous from malice, but she talks "copy" and to make an effect she sticks at nothing. It is deplorable, and I feel guilty to feel about her so—for she was very good to me, and thinks me her friend, and so I am, but I shrink from intercourse with her. This is confidential strictly, don't let this opinion escape you. She was good to us all three, but she is awfully changed in running to seed. . . .

Poor Mme Carra was buried 5th Dec[ember] & Carra is going to be married in July, & takes the little girl away from Miss Field though he promised on her deathbed to his wife never to separate Elesina from her Aunt. He is to marry a catholic who requires him to hand over the child to her to bring her up a catholic.

I have an awful threat hanging over me. Esterina is suspected of being enceinte,[3] and if it prove true I don't know what sort of a revolution it will bring about. I am in an awful fidget—but she seems to take it very coolly. Lorenzo summoned a jury of matrons yesterday, and they strongly lean to the opinion. Time will show. I shall suggest nothing, and wait further developments.

1. Misspelling of *absides,* Italian for apse.
2. Henry Wadsworth Longfellow (1807–82), poet, professor, and a native Mainer.
3. Pregnant.

July 16, 1886, Sorrento, Hotel della Sirena.

Here am I established for the summer in the same rooms I occupied two years ago. The sea and the land are as lovely as ever & I and Esterina live first class hotel for 12 fr[anc]s a day all included, cheaper & better than anything I have found yet. But Vesuvius disappoints me! The eruptions last winter, and the great one of Ætna have drawn off the fire, so there is but a faint smoke from the cone instead of the beautiful light I used never to weary watching as it went & came like a great light house. The flurry of cholera has frightened every one away so there are but three persons in the hotel besides myself. I have not a creature to speak with. Last ev[enin]g I dined with Marion Crawford[1] & his wife who occupy a charming villa, two miles off. It is a perfectly ideal spot, and they are there like people in a romance—wh[ich] he might have written. . . .

By the way a moving circumstance is impending. It looks as if Esterina is enceinte. This will be a bomb exploded in my quiet household! She insists it is not so, she has consulted two doctors and a levatrice[2] and none of them can pronounce. Meanwhile she grows rounder regularly, and I think it can't be long before she has some notice wh[ich] she cannot mistake. By the way she says you told Lorenzo you w[oul]d be Godfather to his child if he c[oul]d get one. So you had better prepare to make a gift!

1. Francis Marion Crawford (1854–1909) had, in 1883, written two novels set in Italy: *A Roman Singer*, a story about artist life; and *To Leeward*, the tale of an English girl unhappily married to an Italian marchese.
2. Midwife.

August 1, 1886, Sorrento, Hotel della Sirena.

Wed[nesday] 4th Monday ev[enin]g the Hotel gave a children's ball. It was one of the prettiest things I ever saw, and nobody asked to contribute a cent. The Terrace which is 80 ft long & very wide was the ball room. It is covered with sail cloth with curtains of the same all around, and it is there we take all our meals, looking to Vesuvius over the sea that lies 108 feet or more below the terrace wh[ich] is built into the perpendicular rock. All this was decorated with Ivy & oleander blossoms, & innumerable lights, and beyond two open terraces & the garden all filled with flowers coloured lights & flags—big & little A buffet set out with cakes & wine & ices—a band of music and about a hundred of children some mere little mites, but all dressed up like dolls, & all dancing with the utmost gravity & decorum under the impulse of several of the gentlemen. They even had the cotillion for them, some so little they c[oul]d just scramble up into their chairs, but each had a ribbon given or a card case of Sorrento wood with the date of 2 Agosto on it. At 11½ the children went home, & then the grown persons kept it up till 3½ AM! I retired when the babies did. . . .

Caroline Carson, Sorrento-Amalfi Peninsula, **Sep 14 1886.** *Courtesy of Ashton and LaVonne Phillips.*

Esterina still hangs like Mohamet's coffin[1] uncertain. I know the comfort of my household will go with her baby's coming.

1. Legend has it that Mohammed's iron coffin hung in midair above Mecca, held by the magnetism of lodestones.

August 22, 1886, Sorrento, Hotel della Sirena.

I have just witnessed a sad spectacle a man found drowned in the shallow water on the rocks below. They dive to bring up the sea moss for the apothecaries, and this old fellow was reaching down for it, and never lifted his head again. There he lay for hours watched by the coast guard until the coroner came, when he was drawn ashore and after verifying his death he was put in a boat & carried off to his village near. Nobody had come to claim him, poor old man. It made me think of the dirge in Cymbeline

Fear no more the heat o' the sun,
Nor the winter's stormy rages.
Thou thy worldly task hast done,
Home art gone, and ta'en thy wages
Golden lads and girls all must
Like chimney sweepers come to dust.[1]

The other two verses are beautiful, and you had better read them in y[ou]r Shak[e]speare. Pity he should have marred so exquisite a song with the conceit of the chimney sweepers.

Some very pleasant people have turned up. Barone & Baronessa Colletti, with four of the nicest sweet graceful children. The young Duke & Duchessa d'Isola. She is the niece of Bentivoglio Middleton's wife,[2] and she delights in talking of them; I do not let on my appreciation of Benty's merits. The little duchessa is very pretty, nice & well educated, speaks English & German as well as French which all Italians speak with a bad accent. The duke is a regular gamin but amiable and no fool. One day a band of mandolinists came while we were at dinner on the terrace. After playing their repertoire the Duke called for the tarantella, jumped up from the table, and taking out little Titine Colletti they danced with the utmost spirit to our great enjoyment. He said he w[oul]d bring his Tarantella costume the next time he went to Naples. But the Duchessa has forbidden it. She don't think it dignified that he sh[oul]d <u>often</u> skip about in a mixed assembly in the dance of the contadini.[3] They all learn it in Naples of their dancing masters, and have the costume in velvet & silk wh[ich] they wear at fancy balls. There was a beautiful children's ball given by the hotel two weeks ago, and there has been a subscription ball at the Vittoria and there is to be one at the Tramontano. But I take no part in these.

I enjoy Sorrento immensely. I dine with the Crawfords often at 8 Oclock and sometimes I feel a little scary coming home at 11 in a little carrozzella[4] driven by a sleepy boy. They say the roads are quite safe, but as this part of the world has turned out such crops of brigands one does'nt

[k]no[w] when another may sprout up. It is the only drawback to going to the Crawfords who are extremely agreeable and hospitable, and seem never to have enough of my company. Our talk turns all on art and literature so that our meetings are really symposia, & it has grown up quite unaffectedly. We get accustomed to talking with some people in a strain we c[oul]d never think of touching with others. . . .

I am not at all pleased at the prospect of Esterina's progeny. I do believe you are at the bottom of it. You condoled so much with Lorenzo, and stimulated him so much to assert himself that this is the consequence. Esterina says she sh[oul]d send the baby off to Lorenzo's paese[5] to be suckled, but it cant remain in that state forever, and I know it will end by breaking up all the comfort of my house. I can't think of harbouring creature,[6] but I am sure Esterina will be spoiled for my service. It will be another link broken to my residence in Rome. If I c[oul]d see the way to any possible place for me in America I w[oul]d pull up my tent and go. But I can't go and live in one room in a boarding house, and that is all I could get for my money anywhere there. I am weary thinking it over, and now I will do nothing till I find myself driven by unforeseen circumstances as I have been in all my moves hitherto.

1. William Shakespeare, *Cymbeline*, act 4, scene 2, speech of Guiderius on the burial of Cloten.
2. After the Civil War, South Carolinian Henry Bentivolgio Van Ness Middleton had returned to Italy, the country of his birth, and in 1869 had married Countess Beatrice Cini, the grandniece of Pope Leo XIII.
3. Peasantry.
4. Cab.
5. Village.
6. In Italian, *creature* are babies for whom one harbors special affection.

September 26, 1886, Hotel della Sirena.

Could my hundred dollars prop up St Michael's I w[oul]d pinch very hard to give them, but it w[oul]d be a mere drop in the bucket, and I lose my nearly $3000 City Stock[1] by the Earthquake, and I sh[oul]d be a recipient of help rather than a benefactress.[2] The lawsuit has taken a new twist that will call for longer litigation, & whereas the interest on my City Stock has hitherto sufficed for the expenses I shall now have to provide for them out of the money turned over by the receiver. Sh[oul]d I be dragged before a SC jury they w[oul]d have no scruple in despoiling me whether I gave thousands or nothing to the victims of the Earthquakes. . . . I have asked Henry Young to give for me $20 for St Michael's—and $10 to Amelia Parker.[3] The general mass who profit by the mayor's fund will do well enough without my obolus.[4] . . . I will not have to get a pistol (tho' it is a suggestion to consider) to visit the Crawfords, for I shall return to Rome in a few days, and the skies are so full of rain & wind that I shall not venture so far of an evening. Esterina grows apace, but your Godson has made no movement tho' it is high time unless he be a mere sham of wind.

Two weeks ago I went as the guest of Mme Reggio on a cruize to Capri. She took a six oared boat & we set out in gallant style escorted by her courier & maid. Fortunately I declined taking Esterina along. We were kept in the broiling sun two hours at the débarcadère[5] for wharf it can't be called when wharf is none. The Douane[6] allowed none to land without a clear ticket of health from the continent. We had to telegraph back to Sorrento. At last we were permitted to step on shore, and whereas the women had been threatening with doubled fists lest we bring cholera to Capri, now they pressed around us to buy coral and with difficulty we got in the carriage that had been waiting all that time. It was too late to visit the Blue grotto that day. So we went up to the hotel, refreshed, and in the afternoon we had a lovely drive round the Island to Anacapri as far as a road can be made up the steep rocks. Next morning we set out in great glee in our boat to make the voyage round the Island and visit all the grottos some of which are thought nearly as beautiful as the Blue. But round the first point we fell into a chopping sea from the gulf of Salerno, and still as we went it got worse, so that to turn back was worse than to go forward. First Mme Reggio turned faint and really frightened me for the discomfort went entirely to her head. After a while I succumbed to sea sickness worse than I have suffered on the Atlantic. None of the grottos c[oul]d we see, till we got round to the Blue where the water being comparatively tranquil we landed and sat awhile to recover. Then each got into a little boat to enter the blue grotto which is only 4 feet open at the mouth. But inside it was as hot as a steam bath, and I was too sick almost to open my eyes on the wonderful blue that seemed thick as if you could spoon up liquid turquoises. we came out in three minutes. Mme Reggio in transferring to the big boat was lifted by the waves made a false step and twisted her ankle. I remained so sick we had to give up returning by boat & stopped a night more to take the steamboat back next afternoon. We arrived in sorry plight. It was a week and many podophyllins[7] before I came right—and Mme Reggio is laid up with her foot & cannot yet put it to the ground. The surgeon says it will be a year that it will continue to pain her. I also got my fingers full of prickly pear through my gloves, and with tweezers and mutton suet laboured three days before my hands were out of the stinging.

1. Municipal bonds.
2. On 31 August 1886 a major earthquake, followed by a series of aftershocks, inflicted great damage on Charleston's St Michael's Episcopal Church, on whose vestry Carson's father, James L. Petigru, had served for over forty years and in whose churchyard he, his wife, and their three other children were buried.
3. An old Charleston friend.
4. A small Greek coin.
5. Landing.
6. Customs house.
7. The resin from podophyllum, the dried rhizome of the May apple, used as a cathartic.

December 4, 1886, 107B Quattro Fontane.

Winthrop Chanler came last week, and he and Daisy [Terry] are to be married on the 15th & 16th for it takes two days now to get married with the necessity of going to the Town Hall for the civil marriage. A most disgusting thing to have to do! I don't know if we shall be invited, but I was at the Capitol to see Edith Story married, and though she & Peruzzi were treated with special honour & taken into the best rooms, & the Syndic himself with his scarf girt round his loins administered the oaths, I thought it an odious proceeding, to be dragged into a common hall with clerks sitting around with pens stuck in their ears and cracking jokes in whispers, while we and the Bride stood around forlornly, and the Bridegroom & the witnesses fumbled with papers before the Syndic—& then he had the Bride up to sign papers also, & finally to receive an exhortation from him on the duties of matrimony. . . .

Your Godson will be putting in an appearance about Xmas, and you had better pluck up. I don't know how I shall manage. As it is Esterina is quite unfit to appear on the Saturdays. So she is shut up in the kitchen to watch the soup, & Lorenzo has to figure at the tea table and I put off my dinner till 7½ when Lorenzo can return to his gridiron and broil me a steak as he has done today. It reminds me of when July meddled with Sarai Cook—and Blanche wanted me to make a great row, which I did not see my way to do. But I waited, and the thing happening to fall out in April, July accompanied me to Dean Hall expecting to have a gay time with a gun on his shoulder to take his pleasure for the month. Great was his dismay when I called him up, and said very coolly, "July you have seen fit to disable my cook, you will now go into the kitchen and take her place." He was dumbfounded and without a word he slunk down the kitchen stairs, and took to the pot. He fathered no more children for Sarai.

December 27, 1886, 107B Quattro Fontane.

Xmas has gone by without my writing you . . . Because I was too ill for the purpose—I shall have to go back to Daisy's wedding which took two days to tie all the knots. 15 at the Capitol the Civil marriage & 16 at S Luigi dei Francesi the religious service, & then a Protestant benediction in Pal[azzo] Altemps.[1] Fortunately I had been summoned the Monday before to see the trousseau which was very elegant. Mrs Delano[2] having early sent Daisy $2500—so that she was not limited in her taste. The presents were very pretty—all of them—and some handsome. . . . Winthrop says he means to choose her jewels in Paris. He will have the satisfaction of paying double price than in Rome. Daisy's dress for the Capitol was myrtle green satin with cream satin bonnet trimmed with myrtle satin ribbon & feathers. She is the happiest creature in the world, except Winty who is just as pleased as she.

1. The Terrys now lived in the Palazzo Altemps. Daisy herself had become a Roman Catholic, but her parents and Winthrop Chandler remained Protestants.
2. Mrs. Franklin H. Delano, the daughter of John B. Astor, was Winthrop Chanler's great aunt.

1887

January 3, 1887, 107B Quattro Fontane.

Your Godson was born this morning at 8,15. We had an awful 24 hours. Narrowly escaped having to call in the Ostetrico[1] with his instruments. But she had the first midwife of Rome and with two attendant wise women they encouraged poor Esterina and finally drew to light the creatura. They brought him to me to see all done up in his swaddling clothes and crying like a good fellow. He looks as big as Willie did at his age. Lorenzo has just informed me that if he had known what it was he would never have married, "per fare cosi tribulare una donna."[2] When they brought to me Giacomino Carlo, Angelo, I put into his little fist a gold piece of ten francs and he gripped it well, and carried safely to his mother, showing an excellent natural[e][3] for holding on, which may prove very advantageous to him in life. He will be packed off to Lorenzo's paese in a few days as soon as he shall have been baptized, and I hope the house may return for a while to its accustomed tranquillity.

1. Obstetrician.
2. To make a woman suffer so.
3. Aptitude.

February 8, 1887, 107B Quattro Fontane.

Esterina has resumed her ministrations about me wh[ich] is a great comfort, but Lorenzo has been laid up for a month with a slow ulcer on his leg, it has been laid open, but it is likely to take a long time yet to heal. We got in a brother of Esterina a shoe maker to draw water make the fires &c & I got my dinner from the trattoria. They gave me a great deal for my money, and it was very fine, only after two days I c[oul]d'nt eat it. Then Gigi under Lorenzo's directions has made my soup & broiled a bit of meat—but Gigi got a w[h]itlow[1] on his finger and so I have but one hand & one foot at my command. However Gigi can go with me & fetch me back when I am invited to dinner wh[ich] my kind friends make very often. Giacomino reigns in Ceccano[2] (Checcano pronounced) He is reported to be as fat and round as a plum.

Mme de Hegermann went off to Denmark to see the countess Raben through. There was a little arm of the sea to cross to get to Copenhagen. A perfect tempest arose and the steamboat was nearly lost. She was lashed to the mast. Her son-in-law from the shore stretching his arms to her nearly in despair. But by the mercy of God they reached the wharf and she has escaped even an illness. At Mr Story's they said there is an American slang about the Chesnut bell,[3] and we want to know how it is used, what it means. Maud Howe is married to Jack Elliott. Annie says he is a dear nice fellow, but she w[oul]d'nt like a man she w[oul]d need have to wake up in the morning. It seems Jack rivals the sluggard of Watts[4] in his reluctance to get up for the day's work.

1. Inflammation of the deeper tissues.
2. The Pizzuti family came from Ceccano, a village fifty-two miles southeast of Rome.
3. An old or stale joke.
4. Isaac Watts (1674–1748), Nonconformist minister who wrote hymns and *Divine and Moral Songs for Children.*

March 6, [1887,] 107B Quattro Fontane.

I had got through the winter so much better that in fine weather I c[oul]d sometimes venture out in the ev[enin]g—so ten days ago I went to the

Valle to see Coquelin in Tartuffe.[1] I took Milly Wood with me, and it was the most enjoyable ev[enin]g I have had since the one you and I went to see Rignold in King Henry V. Coquelin however is an artist far out of reach of Rignold, but the balance of Milly Wood instead of you leaves the other performance the best. . . .

This letter is meant to set you more at ease about Giacomino. Had you $50 convenient to send it w[oul]d have been seen as 500!—but as it is $25 will fill his cup. His name is Giacomo Carlo Angelo Pizzuti. But I think you had better have the check made out to me & I will hand it over—or to Giacomo Carlo Angelo Pizzuti on order of Lorenzo Pizzuti. They are so funny here they might insist of having Giocomino[2] come in person to sign the draft.

1. Constant Coquelin (1841–1909), French actor known as Coquelin ainé, played in Molière's comedy *Tartuffe*.
2. Giocomino, which the child was always called, is the diminutive form of Giocomo.

March 27, 1887, 107B Quattro Fontane.

After dinner came Simmons. He has sold his Penelope to Mrs Gerry[1] through my launching C[ounte]ss Gianotti at her old friend Mrs Gerry—of NY. And Simmons has come up to scratch and under the disguise of buying some water colours, he pays up. . . . Of course you are too discrete to let on about Penelope You will hear of her for Mrs Gerry is the daughter of Robt L. Livingston. Of course you w[oul]d say you knew Simmons, and how much you and your Mother admired his works—which truly are far beyond the others. He is finishing his Longfellow wh[ich] is very fine. Ernest Longfellow[2] happens to turn up at the moment, and it is the greatest benefit to Simmons to have his criticism at this point of his work. Ernest L is quite enthusiastic about it. I shall have no more occasion to push the sale of Simmon's statues for these will spread his reputation so that he will need no more trumpeting.

1. Mrs Elbridge T. Gerry, a New York socialite.
2. Ernest Wadsworth Longfellow (1845–1921), painter and son of Henry Wadsworth Longfellow.

May 18, 1887, 107B Quattro Fontane.

Mr & Mrs Heywood were received into the Holy Roman church at Easter by Card[ina]l Gibbons.[1] Heywood says "in high places they desire that Nevin be not removed from St Paul's Via Nazionale, as he is considered to have a great gift for sending people to the true church." As Miss Wolf did not execute her will in his favour, I fear the Vatican will have its wish of retaining Nevin.[2] In some places there are fierce fishes trained to go out in the harbour and drive the finny tribe into the nets set near shore. Such an one is Nevin unconsciously.

1. James Gibbons (1834–1931), American Roman Catholic prelate, was named a cardinal in 1886.
2. Rumor had it that Wolf's will had bequeathed $50,000 to the Reverend Nevin.

June 5, 1887, 107B Quattro Fontane.

By the way it was Château Yquem we enjoyed at Mrs Harriman's. She sent me the opera box at the Costanzi last week, but no Chateâu [*sic*] Yquem. I took Mrs Posi along, & Costa & his wife, and to my great joy escaped an increase of catarrh. . . .

Princess Brancaccio has invited me down to her Villa at Nettuno this week. We shall sleep in the house this time, not the stable, and I will have a room to myself—but it will not be the fun of the gipseying last year with Marc Antonio as a room mate. . . . I am going this ev[enin]g to Miss Stearn's at the Trinitá dei Monti to see the fireworks on the Pincio.[1] They have built up a complete enormous structure of scaffolding representing a palace wh[ich] is to be illuminated with 4,000 jets of light—and all sorts of coruscations. They will do great damage to the trees & grounds of the Pincio—and though this is said in every Newspaper they persist in doing it. Every 5th June they celebrate the Statuto (constitution) which is their declaration of Independence; by illuminating the Castle of St Angelo, and all the fireworks on the banks of the Tiber fell without damage into the water. But this year the guardians of the Castel said the fireworks scaffoldings injured the masonry & so they cast about for another spot for the display, and pitched upon the poor little Pincio, the only garden the Roman public has to walk in. They have gone to enormous expense & set up tribunes[2] in the Piazza del Populo[3] for dignitaries, and those who pay for a seat. It will be very fine I dare say; but the damage to the Pincio disproportionately great. They had to cut down ever so many trees—& the showers of sparks will injure so many more. It is too stupid.

The last news of Giacomino is not favourable, the poor little creature vomits a great deal—it may be the beginning of teething. I w[oul]d really be sorry now if he sh[oul]d die. Esterina is going to Ceccano to see him the day I go to Nettuno. I have made a very fine copy of the Madonna del Sacco of Andrea del Sarto.[4] Do you remember the fresco on the door in the cloister of the Annunziata at Florence? Mine is done from a picture in oils by the Master, wh[ich] Mr Greenough had the great luck to find & buy from a tumble down old palace in Orvieto.

1. Viale Trinitá dei Monti is a street leading to the Spanish Steps and is at the heart of the tourist district of Rome. It borders the nearby Pincio, a park atop the Pincian hill, which is still the largest public garden in Rome.
2. Platforms.
3. This square at the northern entrance to ancient Rome lies directly below the Pincio's western edge.
4. The Italian artist Andrea del Sarto (1486–1531) is buried in the cloister of the Church of the Santissima Annunziata.

June 26, 1887, 107B Quattro Fontane.

I went down a fortnight ago to visit Princess Brancaccio at her Villa on the sea at Nettuno near ancient Actium. I stopped five days and enjoyed it very much. In the bosquet[1] where we took tea I read to the family circle a poem I composed on the way down by rail, & scribbled on my orario (timetable) If I can find it I will transcribe it for you. They were all delighted & the Princess said she w[oul]d have it set to music & printed. But they have all swooped off to Paris now—& the poem never will be thought of more I suppose. . . .

C[ounte]ss Gianotti went yesterday to Chambéry[2] where she has rented a villa for the summer & invited me to stop on my way to Zurich.

But I go by St Gothard as more direct. Grace [Bristed] went a month ago to put her villa at Innsbrück in order to receive [her son] Charley & a college friend. Her servants, three of them have trooped back swearing vengeance on her. That they were starved & could'nt stop, & now they claim wages for the whole summer, which is preposterous—& of course they will not get it. Meanwhile they pester Posi, but the excitement rather does him good. Of course Grace must be in a mess of troubles, and it will be but the beginning; for she is sure to find the whole Innsbrück venture a failure. The idea of her buying a house, having only seen it twice in one afternoon's drive. Away from the town, in the broiling sun all the afternoon, & she will have to drive ever so far before she can reach shade. I, who am not a coward, would not like to go and put myself in such a lonely spot—especially with the reputation Grace is fond of giving herself of being very rich. She will be put upon by all the traders, besides being perhaps robbed by burglars, if nothing worse. . . .

Giacomino pulls along at Ceccano, but he is not as fat and flourishing as when he was sent there. I hope he will pull through however, and that Esterina will not be tempted to try it again.

1. Grove.

2. On Lac du Bourgen in southeastern France.

July 13, 1887, Pension Itten, Thun.

I crossed the Alps 29th June in company of the Hydes & Mrs Robt Gracie. we are an antiquated company—and we are to have added to us today two more old ladies, Mrs Grey & Miss Shirreff, who come purposely to spend a week with me before their final journey to England. The dear souls especially Miss Shirreff, are so worn out & infirm they have taken leave of Italy forever more—and when they reach England Miss Shirreff expects never again to leave it. But my being in Switzerland they w[oul]d not say adieu in Rome but come to pass a week with me here. This is a very pretty place, very comfortable and very cheap. I pay fr[anc]s 10 a day for self & Esterina—which I have done before in Switz[erland]—but never had so much for the money. Thun is a pretty little town on the Aarve[1] where it runs out of the Lake of Interlaken. We do not see the lake from this house. But before us is a very green meadow fringed with trees above which we see the range of the Jungfrau 20 miles off. The walks on the banks of the river are lovely. Curling by beautiful tall trees, and furnished with seats at comfortable distances—and above all smooth & level, which is a great relief to the feet aching from the toil & stones of the seven hilled city. I would willingly pass the whole summer here, but that I want to try if the air of Uetilberg will cure this persistent catarrh, and that my dear Goodridges have settled to come there to meet me. Although I no longer sneeze and blow my nose incessantly, the obstruction in the breathing apparatus is not removed. I will try Uetilberg, and if that fails I will make up my mind to bear it as well as I can.

1. Aare or Aar.

Caroline Carson, Christian Edward Detmold, 1878[?]. *Courtesy of Ashton and LaVonne Phillips.*

August 11, 1887, Uetliberg prés Zurich.

The funeral services for our dear Detmold stood clearly before me in your account. It is painful to think we have parted with such a true friend. Every day I feel more solitary on the down hill of life, as one by one drop off of those who have borne me company so long. . . .

I really am not strong enough to encounter much change and worry. I have not found the elixir I expected in the air of Uetilberg. It is very good air but the catarrh hangs on—and my heart beats so at the little ups & downs of the one walk that I don't know what to make of it. The hills of Rome have not caused me so much difficulty, perhaps it may be the beginning of a permanent trouble. . . .

My dear Goodridges have been with me nearly three weeks and the Baron [Osten Sacken] also. He is as full of good talk as ever, and faithfully escorts me around and even plays piquet with me in the evening. When they go away I dont know what I shall do with the rest of the time. It is an awfully dull & uninteresting spot. The Landscape a mere panorama too distant to sketch, & no flowers to be had, still less any living models to paint. The first day of Sep[tember] I shall put for Italy, & stop at Milan & then at Florence so as to reach Rome after an autumnal rain shall have made it safe to return.

September 28, 1887, Florence.

I am very unhappy. I got Mr Sewards very kind & explicit letter yesterday and at once wrote to Posi to prepare the necessary steps for me to make this renunciation.[1] It is a cruel pass I am put to, nobody conceives what pain it is to me to renounce my country and ask to be received into another. It is only a little less horrible to me than to have seen the Flag of Fort Sumter fired upon. The strongest feeling in my nature is the love of my own country the Union. It seems too hard that having been driven out of my native state by secession, I should now be expelled from my country by the persecution of an old secessionist. Were I a man I would never do it. I sh[oul]d return to USA though I was chased through every state in the Union. I know it is all a sentiment, but it is the strongest feeling in my nature. I make the sacrifice because Mr Seward thinks it the proper thing for me to do, and because I hope some good may come to Willie and you from it. But the mortification to me and the desolation are unspeakable. I hope Mr Seward will make a strong point of my being driven out of my country by the malice of my enemy. I have written to Posi & to Mr Hooker not to mention the subject in speaking or writing to any one. It is odious to me to hear of it. . . . I feel as if the old Jewish imprecation were upon me "That soul shall be cut off from his people"

I don't know how much it will cost me in fees—but I am sure it will make me liable to taxes which as a foreigner I was not called on to pay. Moreover when I sell a picture I can't send it home free of duty—and when I come to die how will you get all my pictures and things home? —And what effect will it have on my will which is in Appleton Blatchford's[2] hands. You had better show this letter to Mr Seward that these things may be considered. I am ashamed to trouble him so much. I am on my way to Rome. If any thing turns up wh[ich] w[oul]d arrest my action, pray telegraph me. . . .

29th

On the whole I don't think you need show this letter to Mr Seward. I will write to him myself, as soon as I can ascertain what effect the Italian law would take upon my status as citizen, and on the sucession to my goods & chattels. Sending them home as the paintings & the furniture of an American used abroad, they w[oul]d go in free of duty. But to pay duty on all my things as an Italian would ruin you & Willie—and yet it is the greatest interest to me that you should have & keep my remnants after me. In Italy a heavy tax is laid on sucession to pictures as well as real estate. They might not set a high value upon them, but there w[oul]d be something to pay diminishing the little I have to leave.

I have slept on this letter and woke up at 5 and thought it all over and I am very near resolving rather to make the voyage and go to New Jersey, if that will do. While my pen was on this sentence, I got from Mr Hooker the copy of his letter to Mr Seward, showing what a lot of documents w[oul]d be required from Charleston itself as my birthplace before doing anything to be received as an Italian. This w[oul]d show our hand at once to the ordinary long before the protection c[oul]d be obtained. I am afraid New Jersey is my fate. I dare say it will kill me, but that is not what

I dread, but passing the rest of my existence in a boarding house. Still there is no remedy I can see, unless it be to wait the appeal from the S C court which Judge Waite indicates.

I must study it out & do nothing rashly. What time w[oul]d it be necessary for me to put in my appearance in Jersey? I sh[oul]d have so much to do before leaving Rome.

1. Clarence Seward had advised CPC to change her legal residence as a way to escape the jurisdiction of both the South Carolina and the New York courts in her battle to regain Dean Hall. The choice he proposed was either establishing that residence in New Jersey or claiming legal residence in Italy and renouncing her American citizenship.
2. Samuel Appleton Blatchford was a partner in the New York law firm of Blatchford, Seward & Co., which his father, Supreme Court Justice Samuel Blatchford, and Clarence Seward had founded.

November 17, 1887, 107B Quattro Fontane.

Giacomino is said to flourish, and reigns the prince of Cecanno (pronounced Checkcano). He will come back in April after he is weaned, and what he will do in this apartment I am sure I don't know. Perhaps it will not be so bad, and he may prove an amusement to me. The weather is so bad I seldom get out, so I have taken to playing ball, for exercise. You w[oul]d laugh to see me skipping about to catch my ball. The only vacant spot on my walls, is over the chimney in my bedroom. Anne [Brewster] must think I am dancing about to spite her.

December 7, 1887, 107B Quattro Fontane.

Grace [Bristed] is very fine. I was at an elegant lunch given by her two days ago, to Mr Wurts who is here from his Legation at St Petersburgh. He brought me a lovely piece of tapestry from Bokkara Central Asia.

1888

January 1, 1888, 107B Quattro Fontane.

I got a funny note just now from Miss Beresford whom I ha[ve]n't seen for 18 months she was in America. She writes "Dear Mrs Carson. Is there any place here where one can buy white silk for painting fans? I generally got mine in Paris. Does the silk require any special preparation? Excuse me for troubling you, & believe me to remain Very truly yours C M Beresford." Cool don't you think? I have answered "Dear Miss Beresford, I often buy silks at Bianchi's. You can sponge the silk with Isinglas. Truly yours Caroline Carson" Of course she will be in a stew to know how much Isinglas & how to apply—and all the rest. It is a complicated troublesome job—and I don't mean to enlighten her any further. As the Italians say she may go and fry herself. . . .[1]

By the way I have to leave off wine altogether. Not even one wine glass. It throws me into a heat, & next day I have one or two red spots on my face. So that shows it is bad for me, and I resolutely give up the wine I like, and moderately drank—and now I confine myself to cold water. It is a daily act of self denial. But I will never be got the better of by my palate.

1. The Italian idiom is *mandare qualcuno a farsi friggere*—literally, "to send someone to fry him or her self."

February 5, 1888, 107B Quattro Fontane.

Posi we miss;[1] Grace [Bristed] already has had occasion to do so. The other day she was out with the manservant and her French maid let the cook & scullion go out for a walk, remaining alone in the house. The door bell rang & she admitted a man—whom Grace had had for a waiter but had dismissed—as soon as he found by the woman's unguarded words that she was alone in the house, he accused her of being the cause of Mrs Bristed stopping his pension! fell on her with a stick and beat her about the head & breast—she got the door open screaming murder, he pushed past ran down stairs got into a cab and made off. When Grace returned she found the woman bloody and desperate. She went at once to Mr Handley who was very sorry, but did not offer to leave the bank—as Posi w[oul]d have done instantly. She went herself to the questura[2] & reported her case. The man had decamped with his wife, and is at large still, for all I know.

1. Giulio Posi had died in December 1887.
2. Police headquarters.

March 10, 1888, 107B Quattro Fontane.

Nothing but dreadful news has filled this long, cold, horrid winter. The death of so many friends, the general malaise of society, the bad appearance of political affairs at least on this side of the Atlantic. The awful situation of the Kronprinz[1]—and now his coming to the empire at such a moment. He sets off today for Berlin, & the cold journey most likely will precipitate his end. At least however he will die Emperor and the sad princess Empress—which will secure her at least a better position in Germany where she is hated most unjustly.

The tragedy of Crown Prince is accentuated to us in Rome by the condition our dear Fields are thrown into by the disease of Mr Field. He was operated for cancer in the jaw last spring, thought to be cured—came back this autumn in high spirits. The sore broke out, Mrs F & the Princess hurried back to Paris with him. There they called in Desclat who has made such wonderful cures. He refused at first—for he said after an operation he had little hope of doing good. But they insisted, & he is trying to arrest the disease. He has come down with them at enormous expense of course. But Mrs Field & the Princess count not money nor fatigue. They do not leave him for a minute. No one is received in the house, their whole time is given to the sufferer. I only have been let in. They asked me to breakfast and kept me all day, & Mr Field sent for me to his rooms. . . .

I tho[ugh]t to be sure to find among [old books that William Carson had recently sent her] Papa's letters & Tom Appleton's—and being disappointed, in an evil moment I decided to reach into the package of letters inscribed to be burned at my death. They were however only my correspondence with Mr Everett from 58 to 64.[2] They revived so many buried regrets that I had put behind me. Every thing came back with the joy & the intense sorrow as poignant as 27 years ago—without the courage that carried me through the acting those scenes. The pain is intolerable, & there is no remedy for the past which was so pleasant once and bright. But I must go on my journey to the end and try not to look back & dissolve into a river of salt tears.

1. The crown prince of Germany reigned as Frederick III, emperor of Germany from 9 March until 15 June 1888, when he died. His wife, whose period as empress was equally brief, was Victoria, the eldest daughter of Queen Victoria and Prince Albert of Great Britain.
2. Edward Everett (1794–1865), onetime Massachusetts governor and United States senator, minister to England, and secretary of state. He and CPC formed an intense personal relationship in 1858 that lasted until December 1860 when Everett withdrew his offer of marriage. Their correspondence, however, continued until shortly before Everett's death in January 1865.

March 31, 1888, 107B Quattro Fontane.

[John Rollin] Tilton was found dead in his bed last Thursday 22nd. Mr Hooker & Nevin hurried him into his grave Saturday without so much as putting the notice in the Italie. There were only 10 persons at the Cemetery counting Nevin & Paul [Tilton] who arrived by the train from Venice.

All Rome cries out shame upon it. Why it was done nobody can say. Nevin buried him out of the way of Sunday when he is very busy, & Hooker lost his head. As the body was taken out to the deadhouse Friday night, there is no reason why they c[oul]d not have waited till Monday, and given decent notice. Most persons did not hear of his death till after the burial. I did not go. The ground is very wet from the incessant rain, & it was raining hard at the hour, and C[ounte]ss Gianotti a year ago exacted a formal promise of me never to go to that Cemetery in bad weather. . . .

Paul Tilton I have on my hands pretty much now, and a heavy burthen it is. I have been every day to the studio with him sorting the mass of bills, receipts & letters, the accumulation of years—most of which was to be burned. It was dismal work: but it is done. Now Paul will try to make a sale to cover the final expenses. But I fear the purchasers will be in no proportion to the debts. It is all most depressing. Besides I have just learned the death of Lizzie Boott,[1] Mrs Duverneck whom I had a great regard for.

1. Elizabeth Boott (1848–88), who married the American painter Frank Duveneck in 1886, had lived in Rome when Carson first arrived. She is reputed to have been the model for Pansy in Henry James's *Portrait of a Lady.*

April 12, 1888, 107B Quattro Fontane.

It has rained in Rome since the 15th Sep[tember] steadily, they say 15th April it will stop, and there seems some sort of preparation going on in the skies for the desired change. Yesterday AM it hailed—at 3 the sky was without a cloud & a cold wind blowing on which I relied to sall[y] forth with only a sun umbrella. Before I reached Mrs Terry's, (now at Pal[azzo] Odescalchi in the P[iazza]. S S Apostoli hard by Font di Trevi[1]) it poured down on my new mantle: the umbrella only protecting my bonnet.

1. Trevi Fountain.

August 23, 1888, Bagni di Lucca, Hotel du Pavilon.

I got . . . a letter from Harriette Lesesne Smith,[1] telling me her husband Robert died last winter, that his parents as well as Aunt Adele[2] have offered her a home, but she longs desperately for a change after all she has gone through, and she wants to come & spend the winter with me at Rome, and to be of no expense to me, as she has between $500 & 600 a year! I really did not know what to do. I w[oul]d like to be kind, but I could not encourage her to risk such an adventure. It is all I can do to make my ends meet, and the least added to my expenses w[oul]d break me down. If Leila sh[oul]d fall sick it w[oul]d be ruin. Her money w[oul]d not at all suffice for her maintenance. Nor did I feel like having a lady who is virtually a stranger to me pass through my room night & day for six months. . . . So I told her I c[oul]d'nt encourage her to try it. Don't tell any body, for she asked me to keep it secret, until she c[oul]d know if it was practicable. I am very sorry to refuse, but I really do not think it reasonable for me to assume such a responsibility.

1. Harriette Leila Lesesne Smith (1855–99?), CPC's cousin.
2. Adèle Theresa Petigru Allston (1811–96), CPC's aunt.

September 13, 1888, Venice.

I left the Bagni 6th and I am expecting Miss [Annie] Porter[1] to join me here 15th. We are having an awful visitation of sirocco, and the smell from the small canals is very bad, and even here on the Grand Canal at low tide it is awful. I hope it won't give Miss Porter an attack of malaria. There are to be great festivals at Rome on 10th Oct[ober] for the visit of the new German Emperor,[2] who is going round making calls on all the sovereigns since his accession except his Grand Mamma of England.[3] Mrs Hyde has asked me to make out the visit to her that fell through last year on account of the flurry of Italian citizenship. I think I'd rather see Mrs Hyde than Kaiser William and so I'll stop in Florence. . . .

I never told you about Giacomino, when he came from Ceccano last April. He turns out a fat, handsome little fellow, never cries and amuses himself and everybody else. He is a universal favourite and many are the presents he has received. Esterina fetched him out on a Saturday & he was always very much admired. He was taken back to the village for the summer, but now he will come as a permanency! He is'nt so far as troublesome as a dog and much more amusing. Bearing your name gives him an interest for me that surprises me. I must in justice to Lorenzo & Esterina say they impose him upon me as little as possible, and they are so happy with their baby it is a pleasure to see them.

I must leave off now, for Clem [March] ordered a little picture of Venice which I must go and work on now that the light serves.

1. A woman CPC had met recently in Rome.
2. William II succeeded his father Frederick III in 1888 and reigned until 1918.
3. Queen Victoria.

October 7, 1888, Florence.

I sh[oul]d have enjoyed Venice with Annie Porter much more if I had not had a violent attack of arrest of circulation, which laid me up for a week; and I hav'nt felt strong since. We stopped the 4th Oct[ober] in Padua wh[ich] is a beautiful town with some of the finest churches I have ever seen. Baron Osten Sacken left us there. Miss Porter went on direct to Rome, and I have stopped for a fortnight with Mrs Hyde whom I prefer to see rather than Kaiser Wilhelm for whom they are turning Rome upside down.

November 1, 1888, 107B Quattro Fontane.

I returned to Rome 22nd Oct[ober], having spent a pleasant fortnight with Mrs Hyde, and having improved the time to make a small copy of the Madonna del Sacco from the original fresco in the cloister of the SS Annunziata. My big copy made from Mr Greenough's[1] old oil painting done no doubt as a study in Andrea del Sarto's studio, I have sent as an offering to Clarence Seward, being as important a work of art as my famous P[rince]ss Eleanora Gonzaga which is your inheritence. I c[oul]d have stayed longer in Florence with pleasure Mrs Hyde's hospitality shining only brighter the longer she c[oul]d keep me—and Mrs Huntington returned, and wanted me to remove to her house the very next day. But the wind was so cold I could not stand it especially in my summer clothes. So I came home and have found most delicious weather.

I am very much in confusion in my salon. The chimney never has drawn properly, and yearly I grow colder & need more fire. Last winter I was often obliged to take refuge in my bed room where a good fire warms up easily. So I have resolved to put in a grate that will burn coke but I am still unsettled about it; meanwhile the room is dismantled no carpet nor curtains. 1st Nov[ember]. however warns me to move on, and tomorrow I will resolutely have the thing done.

I did'nt care to see the Emperor, but I accepted the C[ounte]ss Giantotti's invitation to visit the apartments prepared for him at the Quirinal.[2] No wonder he was delighted! He never certainly had anything so fine before. In Berlin the furnishing is very simple. The rooms were all made over new—ceilings gilded and frescoed with gallant designs which were not monastic at all. It is true in the Vatican there are rooms painted for Alexander VI[3] (Borgia) any thing but clerical. Cupids, Graces Apollo and the rest—and Giulia Farnese his favourite mistress in the guise of the Madonna! But the arrangements for William II are sumptuous. Exquisite modern work, and many cabinets and objects of art brought from various royal palaces in Italy to deck the nest of this bird. The very night of our visit about 11 Oclock a fire was discovered by one passing the Quirinal. It was burning immediately under the wing of Emp[eror] William—and it was not got under [control] for 2 hours, so inexpert are the pompiers.[4] It burned up some furniture stored in the room and nearly reached the Plate room. The flames burst through one grated window on V[ia] 20 Settembre, and through the grating on a door where were sculptured the arms of the Pope Paul Farnese—which have half burned & fallen while the mitre & the keys are aloft—but the arch of the door around the grating of stone is burned & scaled. The door itself of metal or heavy wood escaped. Inside the Palace nothing was known, & it was the chance of a passer by alarming the guard that aroused them in time. The Royal family is absent. The burned stone gives me some idea how Rome could twice have been burned in the old time. It is strange for all I see the burned stone. There was never much furniture so to speak in the old Roman houses, nor could there have been much woodwork, I can't divine how they could burn.

1. Henry Greenough (1807–83), American painter and brother of Horatio, the much better known sculptor.
2. Count Cesar Gianotti was prefect of the royal palace, a largely ceremonial position.
3. Pope from 1492 to 1503.
4. Firemen.

December 2, 1888, 107B Quattro Fontane.

I am sorry NYork sh[oul]d be captured again by Tammany.[1] Hewitt[2] is too honest for them—but I think his example will not be lost, and after being plundered again, the people may demand another Hewitt. As for Cleveland[3] he deserved to be turned out for his miserable subservience to the Irish. I am afraid the Rep[ublican]s. have come back into power too soon however, they have not had time to purge their offences. If however Harrison[4] is the man to stand up without Blaine, he may do well for the country. It is <u>our</u> hope that the Rep[ublican] zeal for civil service will not have to take exactly the form of leaving Stulle in office. If there were a real civil service Wurts w[oul]d be advanced to Stulle's place and we in Rome w[oul]d enjoy a jubilee. . . .

The Reverendo has done a queer thing. Bishop Lyman of N C who is Bishop in charge of the Am[erican] Episcopal churches, has come to Rome on his biennial tour, expecting to administer confirmation to the catechumens. Our Reverendo who never came back till three weeks ago, said the time was too short for him to look up any postulants—and he actually has gone off to Sardinia on a hunting expedition with the English military attaché Col Slade—leaving the Bishop amazed and affronted, as he very openly declares—to make it worse Thanksgiving Day fell into last week, and even this National festival Mr Nevin disregarded to go and hunt in Sardinia! The Bishop told me yesterday he sh[oul]d preach today & depart tomorrow—and no doubt Nevin will return laden with spoils of the chace [*sic*] and tell us again of his arduous duties at St Pauls which he says not one clergyman in five could discharge.

Giacomino is very funny he is not more troublesome than a dog in a house—and he amuses me very much. He is a healthy sturdy little fellow and full of sport. I shall not have to play ball this winter, for he thinks me the proper person to romp with him!

1. The Democratic Party organization in New York City.
2. Abram Stevens Hewitt (1822–1903), an iron manufacturer and an active opponent of Boss Tweed and his ring, had won the New York mayoralty in 1886 as a Democrat but lost two years later.
3. Grover Cleveland (1832–1908), Democratic president of the United States, 1885–89 and 1893–97.
4. Benjamin Harrison (1833–1901), Republican president of the United States, 1889–93.

December 14, 1888, 107B Quattro Fontane.

Nothing particular has happened these last days except that I heard of Charles H Dana's[1] being here, and I sent to ask him to call, which he did. Alas! the 30 years that have rolled over his head since I saw it, has blurred the fine outline, and I never sh[oul]d have recognized him again. I fear if he were questioned he would have the same to say of me. However he was very friendly and offered to do anything for me in NYork that sh[oul]d come in his way. We talked of his getting morphine through for poor Mamma[2] in the war. . . .

I have been three times to the opera, Mrs Harriman sending her box to me. I saw Orfeo of Gluck[3]—most beautiful it is, and Miss Heistreller a German American sings most beautifully in the part of Orpheus. 2nd time heard Ambroise Thomas's Amleto[4] very well rendered. 3d Favorita very badly done. Last night I had seats given me for a new opera Medgé by a Greek composer. But I would not risk it, and gave my tickets to the Shakspeare Woods. . . .

Giacomino grows fit and strong is very handsome, and wilful, but we keep him down with a little rod made of corset bone. He is very funny, and he calls me "Toto" which is his version of Signora.

1. Charles Anderson Dana (1819–97) was, after 1868, the owner-editor of the *New York Sun.*
2. Jane Amelia Postell Petigru (1795–1868) had first become addicted to opiates used as analgesics in the 1830s.
3. The German composer Christoph Willibrand Ritter von Gluck (1714–87) wrote *Orfeo ed Euridice* in 1786.
4. Charles Louis Ambroise Thomas (1811–96) was a French composer known best for his comic operas. *Amleto,* however, is the Italian rendering of *Hamlet.*

1889

January 15, 1889, 107B Quattro Fontane.

You w[oul]d be amused if you could see Giacomino toddling about the house. He is very stout, healthy and handsome, very intelligent and considerably wilful. But as neither Esterina, I nor Lorenzo give up to him absolutely I believe he will yield to discipline. He makes a little chirruping sound that pervades the house; as he has nobody to run after him, he hangs onto Esterina's skirts, and he is chiefly troublesome when she is dressing me. He wants to put on my bonnet himself, and he is passionately fond of dress. I had made for him a little red flannel overcoat with some steel buttons off an old dress of mine. He looks like the Queen's footmen in it, and he is as proud as a peacock. He will do everything to get it put on him, and it is always a struggle to get it off. Lorenzo & Esterina redouble their attentions to me for fear it sh[oul]d be said they neglect me for Giacomino.

Mrs Field came back a few days ago but she has not yet sent for me to come and see her—and she has such a shrinking from seeing anyone that I don't mean to go for a while. The Princess [Brancaccio] has just bought another great body of land near Tivoli, on which is a Castle! and that has quite roused up her interest.

February 10, 1889, 107B Quattro Fontane.

I jog along as cheerfully as I can. I do feel the solitude that age must make around one who lives alone. But when I get Charleston letters I see as in a glass how much I have to be thankful for that I am here and not there. I had a letter from my old friend Lynch Hamilton[1] with whom I have had no communication since we parted in 1859 in our glory at the NYork Hotel: when the near disastrous future was unsuspected by us. He was moved to writing by a visit to Mr Miles[2] who lives like a Prince at the Houmas L[ousian]a There he was shown a letter and a little picture I had sent my old friend the Professor by the hands of Bishop Elliott. This roused up all the old memories and Lynch seized the pen. Mr Miles at the head of 11 Sugar plantations left by [his father-in-law] Mr Beirne to his children is bound like a serf to the soil. He can't leave this splendid estate and had not even time he said to write to me just then! So great riches and none at all bring one nearly into the same subjection. Mr Miles wrote me last year the first use he should make of freedom w[oul]d be to come to Europe with his daughters and bring them to Rome to see me. Now he has made a crop of 12,000,000 lbs sugar he can't budge. I wonder what so much sugar is worth!

Friday 9th I sent Lorenzo to get me a cab to go & visit Baroness Schönberg. He came running back to say the town was in an uproar—he had fled before the rioters up the Quattro Fontane, and he hastened to get his bird gun to defend the stair case if we were invaded! Out of the window I looked & saw the rioters with sticks in their hands running along and breaking all the windows as they passed. Nobody tried to stop them. They did not seem more than 30 & they ran loosely scattered, so that if the shop keepers had sallied forth with their yardsticks and shovels they might have had the better of them. One officer Capt Tosi who was just a little above in the street drew his sword and kept them off from shattering the Galleria Margherita you remember a little above us. What we saw was the fag end of the manifestants,[3] they evaporated at Sta Maria Maggiore. But down town it was much worse. They did not try to hurt any body but they broke all the windows making great damage to the shopkeepers, especially the crockery shops, the sound of the breaking china & glass seeming to please them. A few jewellers windows were robbed, but strange to say they did not invade the Bakers, only breaking all their windows. It shows they were led by Anarchists who wanted to provoke a row—they were not a starving multitude. Though there is no doubt there are hundreds starving who have come to Rome expecting work. It comes of the great reaction after the mania for building on speculation which has made Rome a vast quagmire for two years, and now many are ruined and all work suspended. Meanwhile the peasants left off digging and flocked to Rome to carry hods of mortar, and now they starve. The cold summer too made short crops, and the misery is great. Almost all the Roman Princes too were seized with a madness of going into these speculations of which they knew nothing—they have all come to grief—jewels of the ladies sold at a discount—many have moved up stairs trying to rent their fine apartments for which there are no applicants, and many have to quit and go to little country towns where they must vegetate for the rest of their lives on the little they have left. A few little jews have bagged all the money How it will end nobody can tell. We the foreigners might take fright and run away but for the comforting prediction Simmons brought from his astrologer in America—that King Humbert is to be always prosperous and to live to be 70.[4] So while Humbert prospers it is to be supposed we shall be safe.

Giacomino grows so fast that already I can scarcely lift him—not being so attentive to carry him every day as the old woman was with her calf till at last it got to be a cow and she carried it still. But he is very funny—a really pleasant amusing little creature, with the funniest peculiarities. He is as vain as a peacock. He is very much admired in the streets, and you ask him what they say in the street he puts his head on one side, and with all the airs of a coquette he says "bello mimino"[5] I am expected to teach him English, but so far I have only got him to say good morning. It is true he cant say ten words yet. I never saw as much of a child before you and Willie having nurses and a nursery where you mainly staid. But Giacomino follows Esterina step by step—and has to be in the room while she is dressing me, and a fine time he has of it, putting his resolute little paws into everything. Esterina and Lorenzo are so happy with him I cannot grudge the small discomforts that it entails on me.

1. Probably the son of James Hamilton (1786–1857), Nullifier governor of South Carolina 1830–32, later a figure in Texas politics.

2. William Porcher Miles (1822–99), mathematics professor at the College of Charleston, Charleston mayor 1855–57, United and Confederate States senator 1857–65.
3. These public demonstrations were staged largely by construction laborers who had flocked to Rome in the preceding decades and by southern peasants who had flowed into the city as a result of an agricultural crisis brought on by a sharp increase in Italian tariffs in 1887 that, in turn, led to the abrogation of Italy's commercial treaty with France and a consequent steep decline in agricultural exports. In 1889 a financial crisis precipitated by speculative overbuilding in Rome and Florence, a French sell-off of Italian securities, and the massive issue by major banks of illegal banknotes led to bank failures as well as to extensive unemployment.
4. Humbert I, born in 1844, was assassinated in 1900.
5. Handsome little clown.

February 24, 1889, 107B Quattro Fontane.

It is an uncommon dull winter. Every body is poor. The Roman Nobles have gone into the building mania, some are ruined, and all are hard hit. No brilliant forestieri.[1] And the riot though over in an hour, and only a smashing of windows to rouse the Government that the proletaires[2] are exasperated—leaves a painful impression of unrest—and there is great want among the people & socialists stirring them up. . . .

I shall keep Giacomino in his place, never fear—but he is a very engaging little child, and troubles me very little. It is true Esterina can sew very little, but she does all the rest as usual, and Lorenzo is decidedly improved, and he takes great pains that my living sh[oul]d cost not a penny more, but rather less.

1. Foreign visitors.
2. Proletarians.

March 15, 1889, 107B Quattro Fontane.

I feel acutely the pain of your comparison of our lot with that of the prosperous who pass us in the race. But though we know we have not the best place, we must not give way to despair. Many soldiers know they are sent on the forlorn hope—but they do not draw back for that. Would that we keep always in mind our baptismal vows always to be God's faithful soldiers and servants. Then w[oul]d we stand manfully at the post where he has put us, and we fall in our tracks if need be, but never despair, and are never "confounded." Let me never be confounded is the petition which all the years long I have put up—and so far tho' often distressed we never have been confounded. I do not know Foster's writings. I hope they strengthen faith and do not go into the dreary questionings and denials of the day that w[oul]d deprive us of the confidence in God the Father who numbers the very hairs on our heads and will reward his servants who stand and wait his will. There are most of our friends far more prosperous than we, and we rejoice without envy for them. But most of our relations are far worse off than we. There is no doubt all of our time at the South have to bear the burthen of the war, and who can tell what remains behind in the Southern States with that encroaching black population? If I were a man I sh[oul]d think no hardships too much to get a living away from there. Henry Young tells me no body can be happy in Charleston who knew it in the former days. And all I hear from others is in the same strain. . . .

There is a great Dominican friar Agostino preaching the Lenten sermons. Grace [Bristed] with the elect has a seat in a private balcony & goes every day. But I don't even think of going, for people go at 8 AM and wait till 11 in order to get a place. I was invited by the Press Association to a grand reception given last ev[enin]g to Dr Smalley[1] a distinguished writer on political economy & the like. All the big wigs & the diplomats were to go, and I was persuaded to venture. I supposed Borghi the Pres. w[oul]d introduce the Guest & that there w[oul]d be speeches & presentations. Not a bit. The ladies were all seated while the men had to stand on the outskirts—there was a platform, and those who knew Dr Smalley (or Smiles) could see the back of an old gentlemans white head. On the platform was a piano, and one after another performers and singers professional came forward and performed. It was the funniest way to feast a grave professor I ever saw. When it was half over I came away.

1. George Washburn Smalley (1833–1916), American journalist and foreign correspondent for the *New York Tribune* from 1867 until 1895.

April 28, 1889, 107B Quattro Fontane.

Of course I w[oul]d wish Appleton [Blatchford] asked to see Papa's portrait[1] if you show it. I had an awful time getting the back ground dry. I asked Mr Terry what to varnish it with & he said mastic. Accordingly I gave it a coat of mastic, and it w[oul]d not dry for weeks—whence the delay in sending it. At last I sent for my friend Santoro & we scrubbed the background with turpentine to get off some of the varnish, and then I had to paint it all over. I hope it will not stick with the dampness of the voyage. I sold last year the two Medici bambini for $200—& deposited the money with poor Posi—resolved with this to carry out my desire to send the Portrait to Charleston to stand in the place where Mr Petigru spoke for law and justice. I hope no accident will frustrate this act of filial piety.

1. A full-length portrait of James L. Petigru that CPC painted from memory and photographs for the South Carolina Bar. She wished it hung in the courtroom of the old statehouse in Charleston. It now hangs in the portrait gallery of the South Carolina Supreme Court building in Columbia.

June 16, 1889, 107B Quattro Fontane.

By a recent letter from Mrs Daly I see it will be too much bother to exhibit [the portrait of James L. Petigru] in NYork—and you & Willie had better let [the shipping agent, John A.] McSorley send it on direct to Henry E Young Charleston care of Hill, Adger's Wharf. Young will manage the presentation properly & get our dear Ben [Allston] to take a part in it—and Some day you and Willie will go and look at the picture in Charleston, or in Columbia if the Bar carries it there. But I have clearly & persistently expressed my wish it should be hung in Charleston. To me it does not matter what cases they try now in the old Court House. There was the place where Mr Petigru oftenest expounded the law—and that is the spot where in my mind's eye I always see him. There will be a stipulation with the trustees that if the Superior court returns to sit in Charleston it shall be hung in their room. Meanwhile in the City Hall or Court house as most decorous. . . .

Julia McAllister presides over that protestant nunnery at Morristown.[1] I have to answer a kind letter I had from her at Xmas. . . . I have sometimes thought of asking Julia if there would be board and lodging for me at the Nunnery if I sh[oul]d teach flower painting. But I dare say they have teachers in plenty, and room scarce. I have had to renew my lease for 3 years because the Gov[ernmen]t is pulling up all the proprietors who go on renting without taking out new leases—on wh[ich] there is a tax. . . .

The crooked pieces of coral are commonly called la corna contro il mal'occhio or jettatura[2]—because the superstition is that those who cast a spell by having the mal'occhio, are frustrated by pointing at them a horn, or holding up two fingers like horns— and to make sure they wear a little horn as protection from the jettatura. . . .

Indeed all our lives were spoiled by the War—but it's no use grumbling, and it is very undignified. Let us emulate the patient courage & faith of our Cousin Ben.[3]

By the way Miss Brewster is vacating. She pulls up stakes and moves to Siena, where she can live cheaper than in Rome. If she had retired several years ago I sh[oul]d have rejoiced, but now I never think of her & her going or staying does not affect me—only I am really sorry for the old woman that she has to go away from the Rome she thought could not do without her. It is hard in her old age to be so pinched for money. Her brother did not leave her a penny. Perhaps it is a fellow feeling makes me so kind, for I may have to bundle out next, and where sh[oul]d I go?

1. Julia McAllister, to whom CPC had given painting lessons in Rome, had been principal of St. Mary's Hall, an Episcopal school for girls, in Burlington, New Jersey, from 1887 to 1889. She had just become principal of St. Hilda's in Morristown, New Jersey, in the summer of 1889.
2. The horn against the evil eye. Both *malocchio* and *jettatura* mean the evil eye.
3. CPC's cousin, Benjamin Allston (1833–1900), had given up planting to become an Episcopal priest.

July 15, 1889, Hotel della Sirena, Sorrento.

Here I am to my great content. It is hot but such a good air! I enjoy it, and the ample table with plenty of fish to eat. The last week in Rome everything was so hot & nasty—and it cost me for food alone nearly as much as I pay here for board & lodging for self & Esterina namely 12 fr[anc]s a day. We have brought Giacomino along! Esterina has made a bargain with the manager of the Sirena by which she pays fr[anc]s 4 a week for him. When he is sent to Lorenzo's paese Ceccano they have to pay a franc a day. So they save money. . . .

M E W S[herwood] is really constant in writing letters to me notwithstanding all she has on hand. That she sh[oul]d be décorée by the French Academy for her writings is indeed a wonderful piece of luck! It seems impossible those very superficial letters to the N[ew] York newspapers; and a few translations in verse sh[oul]d merit such an honour. She is opportune, and she has great luck, but at the same time she is very laborious. She certainly drives herself hard; and I am very glad indeed of her wonderful success, which she enjoys doubly, because she so admires success.

August 25, 1889, Sorrento, Hotel della Sirena.

It is as much as I can pull through with to have y[ou]r godson in the house trotting about and diving into every thing while I dress. He is the pleasantest little fellow in the world, but it tries my patience to its utmost stretch, and is only possible there being no one else in the house but myself. He will grow however out of the way, and there is an infant school in Via Nazionale where I hope he may go next winter. He is so intelligent he is sure to be cock of the walk.

Annie Porter is here, and as she has a carriage it is very advantageous to me—my feet being quite out of order—whether from vulgar corns only, or gout as the burning & swelling might indicate, I know not—but this is certain I am quite lamed by it & can't put on walking shoes.

There has been a curious incident in the hotel. An old french priest from Brazil arrived accompanied by a plain woman who might be his sister or niece. Padre Curci was here last time with his sister, & no one thought of questioning the propriety—but whether because these were strangers, or what—I know not, but a rumour ran round the house that they occupied the same room; which was simply ridiculous, because they had two rooms, & if they <u>did</u> occupy one only they w[oul]d surely have crumpled up the other sufficiently. However that may be a little old Irish convert ran off in confessional to make accusation of the Abbé. The priest reported to the Archbishop who sent for the Brazilian Abbé, who showed his certificates, proved his relationship to the woman, & was commanded by the A.bishop to make a public refutation of the scandal. He no doubt was very glad to do so, and before dinner one day he stood forth declared the honourability of the lady and him self, and waxing wroth he asserted ["]Il n'y avait que des Anglaises et des protestantes qui auraient pu dire de telles choses."[1] Every one stood aghast—none more than this vile little Miss Evelyn—but Lady Donner [and] myself the only protestants sifted the matter & traced it all to Evelyn. Annie Porter who said she w[oul]d not speak to her nor sit at table with her, we six English speaking being at one table to ourselves on the great loggia where we dine. So the hotel keeper informed Miss Evelyn that she must eat alone until she went away which he requested her to do as soon as possible. She stood it out for two days, and then departed to a second class hotel kept by Germans where she will have less chance to make mischief. The Abbé was so incensed however that he departed likewise. I never before happened to see one calling herself a lady turned out of a hotel. It seems she is a confirmed mischief maker, and nobody likes to have her. We are delighted to be quit of her on any terms. She was a most exasperating, pretentious person, and an intolerable bore. She professed great enjoyment of Sorrento and she had been at the Sirena last summer. I had begun to think I w[oul]d never come back here if she was to be a constant guest.

1. "It was only the English and Protestants who could have said such things."

September 16, 1889, Hotel della Sirena.

I have just rec[eive]d my copy of Mr Benoit's eulogy on our ancestor Gibert. We should strive to be virtuous too—and pray that the sins of our Fathers be not visited upon us to the exclusion of the mercies promised to the generations of those who love God and keep His commandments! Many a time when I have been sore pressed by Satan, have I invoked the memory of my Father's mother and the Pasteur[1] her father, although I knew of them but vaguely.

I have been looking out for the meeting of Mars and Saturn, and I find it will be visible here about 3 AM of the 20th and at that [time] the mountains back of Sorrento will cut off the view of the horizon. So it will be no use turning out of bed. If some horrible convulsion of nature happens as the flood—when they two met about 4000 years ago we shall know it soon enough. The sea is raging now, and the wind makes my door sing like a sounding board. This end of the house is in the eye of the wind E N E—and if it gets worse in the night I shall be cut off by a long corridor with the wind rushing through it. I often think if the end of the world come upon us whether it would be more appalling to meet it in the flesh, or to rise from the grave at the last trump. One way or the other we must face it, now or hereafter. It is amazing that thoughtful persons can class Revelation with the religions that have ruled mankind and passed away. The very sublimity of the words are beyond the reach of human imagination. "And God said let there be light, and there was light.["][2] Just compare it with all the theories of the Creation how poor & mean they are in comparison. "Again at the last day the Angel of God shall stand with one foot on the sea & one on the land, and declare that Time shall be no more.["][3] No human intellect has ever risen to such an awful grandeur. It was not in the heart of man to conceive it.

The summer is over, and I shall soon return to Rome Giacomino has gone already with Lorenzo. Miss Porter left a week ago. The day she went we drove to Pompei spent the day visiting the ruins, and she drove on to Naples, and I returned in her carriage to Sorrento with Mr Halstead Smith a young American, who has now sailed for America.

1. Jean Louis Gibert (1722–73), Carson's great-grandfather and a Huguenot pastor, had led his French parishioners in a migration from France to South Carolina where they settled New Bordeaux, near Abbeville. Her grandmother, Louise Gibert Pettigrew, had died when CPC was only six.
2. This is Gen. 1:3, not Revelation.
3. A rendering from the King James Version of Rev. 10:2, 6 reads, "He set his right foot upon the sea, and his left foot on the earth . . . and sware . . . there should be no more time."

October 4, 1889, 107B Quattro Fontane.

Here I am, back in my old nest, rather rusty it has grown with time and wear, but I am busy furbishing it up, and I am actually buying a carpet for the Salon on the strength of y[ou]r Aunt Maria [Daly]'s paying generously for some fans, & giving me a further order. I wish there were more like her and the Judge! . . .

Henry Young writes me the picture arrived in perfect condition was opened with regard, and gives satisfaction; and he sent me a [Charleston] Courier & a [New York] World with commendatory articles. The World however saw fit to go to the root of the matter and declares my early love of art developed from my birth on 24th May 1819. I wrote Henry Young he might tell the superfluous chronicler that no woman wants her age recorded except on her tombstone, and even on that the date sh[oul]d be correct. That I was not born in May, nor on the 24th of any month, nor yet in the year 1819. The Century had rolled into the twenties when I saw the light,[1] and as I shall not have reached the appointed goal of life when the picture shall be formally presented, I hope the World's writer will observe a discreet silence on the occasion. It is a great relief to me that the picture has reached its destination undamaged. H Young has arranged it shall be committed to the care of trustees for the Charleston Bar, & Ben [Allston], you and Willie are to be on the (nominal) trust.

1. 4 January 1820.

November 30, 1889, 107B Quattro Fontane.

We have heard Carmen with Frandin, a Belgian, singing in it. I never heard it before! I was so delighted with the music, Mrs Harriman's box being sent me, that after I went twice and sat in the pit. Now they are giving Patria[1] but I don't know if I shall hear it. The rain & cold have begun, and I don't like to turn out after dinner. . . .

Miss Porter's portrait has turned out very well—and Berilacqua's a decided success. Unluckily it puts no money in my pocket for he is my homeopathic adviser, and he is devoted to me and charges me nothing.

He has paid for a handsome frame for the picture and it makes a good effect. But to draw other sitters—that is the difficulty. Ross who made the hardest looking portraits has hit upon pastels wh[ich] he uses with skill, and as he draws well the pastel favours his handling and he has a rush of sitters, and has grown fat—jollier he ca'nt be more than of old. But as he has never made me a visit since you were here I am rather stiff with him.

Mrs Crowninshield & her younger son Frank are here for her health. Hers was one of the pleasantest houses when I came to Rome, but they went ten years ago back to America and Fred Crowninshield[2] makes his way as a decorative artist, more saleable than pictures.

1. Probably *Patrie* by the French composer Emile Paladihle (1844–1926), which was first performed in 1886.
2. Frederic Crowninshield had returned from Rome first to Boston and then to New York where he painted murals and worked in stained glass.

December 10, 1889, 107B Quattro Fontane.

Giacomino develops very well. He is really the most pleasant tempered jolly little fellow I ever had to do with. He exemplifies my theory that it is the old people who ought to take charge of the children. I am sure at 25[1] I sh[oul]d not have had the patience with him that I have now, nor have had leisure to enjoy his frolics. I think he has come in a fortunate time when I need something to enliven the house.

1. CPC's age when her son James was born.

1890

January 20, 1890, 107B Quattro Fontane.

I am busy with a young clergyman who came to help Nevin. Mr Monroe Royce[1] universal favourite. He was taken so ill I put him on the big sofa & kept him 24 hours till he could move to the Church Home where the trained Nurses can do better for him than I—but I go every day for a couple of hours to him except today, when I am coughing and pumping with carbolic. . . .

Giacomino was 3 years old 3d of Jan[uary] the day before I reached the Psalmist's term of life. He is a jolly little fellow, and decidedly more amusing & less troublesome than a dog, & so far pays no tax.

1. Supply minister temporarily replacing Robert Nevin.

February 9, 1890, 107B Quattro Fontane.

I have been shut up for a month as usual with catarrh. There has come a throat, nose & ear doctor and I went to him because my breathing has been so much obstructed these four years. He examined my nose, & discovered in one nostril polips. I was horrified, but forthwith decided to have them out. With cocaine he removed two the first day—and I breathe so much more freely, [than] I thought I c[oul]d do. But there is one more, quite large & way far in, almost in the throat. So I had a second bout, but did not succeed in lassoing it. And the cocaine affects me so much, that

I shall have to put off completing the treatment till I have finished the portrait of Mrs Hill. Did I tell you I was painting her? A handsome woman Miss Mintzing of Charleston married 20 years ago to a rich NewYorker. She is very fine & full of pretension. . . .

A lot of Boston people are here and others whose company I should enjoy if I were not imprisoned by this eternal catarrh. It has been so far five years now. Nearly all winter I can't go out of the house except by some fluke once in a while. But never when there is rain or wind!

May 14, 1890, 107B Quattro Fontane.

The sickness has fallen upon me. No sooner went Willie and came Miss Goodridge than the weather being very warm I thought it time to change my winter flannel shirt for the intermediate silk one. I felt nice—and cool—but a nice cool air blew upon me and I began to feel very unwell—went back to the flannel, but for the fortnight Miss Goodridge stopped I was more unwell all the time The moment she left the house I collapsed with a violent pain in the ear—sent for Aurist[1] & crawled to bed where I staid ten days in great pain. An abscess which kept on paining after breaking—and general misery I have now been out of bed three days—& the pain has nearly gone—but my head feels like a cotton bag, and I am quite deaf. Dr Bettman assures me that will wear off. Be warned by my sad experience not to take off a winter undergarment before May is well come in. . . .

There was a grand charity Ball last week at the Villa Borghese. They say the statues lighted up especially the Pauline Borghese under a rose coloured light were exquisite, and the dancers moving among those works of art lent & received a grace unknown before.

1. Specialist in diseases of the ear.

June 8, 1890, 107B Quattro Fontane.

I told you in 163 what an awful time I had with abscess in the ear. It seems it was going about, and I came off better than many, owing to the skilful treatment of Dr Bettman, a new young practitioner specialist for nose, throat & ear. He is from Cincinnati—is most kind, and puts off the subject when I speak of his bill. Lucky for me; for the tax gather[er] has come to collect taxes on me as an artist for twice more than I have gained in a year. They set an arbitrary sum as what you are supposed to have gained. I have protested, but I don't know how it will end.

On the very first day I was going out with Mrs Field in her coupé the card was brought me of Mrs Porcher Postell.[1] It seems she found Milan too cold, and she had been all winter at Florence where she says she got good lessons, and she had run down for a week to see Rome, and had come with her bag straight to me, and asked me to recommend a lodging very cheap. I was appalled—but Esterina suggested a room belonging to the woman Willie will recall who came in to help—and Lorenzo took her valise there, & I made out a programme for her, and had her come back to dinner. She is rather passée, has been pretty is lively & energetic, and self reliant. I was really so ill it was a great effort to attend to her. But I did what I could—laid out each day for her, & had her to dine each evening, and I got the Woods to go about three times with her—but when at the end of the 4th day she told me she had concluded to go the next, I was greatly relieved. I was so afraid she sh[oul]d fall ill on my hands. I got a note from her from Florence that she was off for Dresden. She has a brother in Washington who helps her on her tour. It was strange to have her talking to me of the Postells as my nearest relations; I who never have felt the ties of blood to them except as very galling.[2] From her account they all flourish in Georgia much better than we do. . . .

[Ben Allston] is moving to Union, and he finds it hard to pull up stakes and depart with no better prospect than Union[3] affords. Still I gather that it is better than Plantersville and affords more look out for the children. It is like a story some one told me of coming in the old time to board with a family in Rome who lived on the third floor of a retired street. Several years after he returned and found the family installed on the lower floor, and the father explained his daughter having grown up they moved down a floor that she might enjoy the advantage of looking out of the window. That was the Roman bourgeois idea of entering into society.

1. A distant cousin by marriage who was studying voice in Europe.

2. CPC's mother was only one of the Postells whose attributes rankled.

3. Allston had just moved from the rectorship of the Episcopal church in Plantersville, South Carolina, to that in the somewhat bigger town of Union, South Carolina.

[July 1890,] Chartreuse di Pesio vicino Cuneo.

Here I am up a tree! Literally there is no road beyond this old monastery in the Maritime Alps.[1] It is an immense structure built by the Carthusian monks who were dispossessed by the French Consulate when it over ran Piedmont.[2] Sold for a song to a rich family of Turin they turned it into a hydropathic establishment—which prevented its falling into ruin. Now a brisk french widow from Nice keeps it as a summer boarding house. The Hydes spent last summer here and I decided to come with them now. Clem [March] wrote for me to go with him to Sorrento, and as I c[oul]d not refuse when he comes so far to get me, I agreed to go in August, dreading the journey the length of the Peninsula in mid summer.

But now I am reconciled to it by the cold I have encountered here. Mrs Hyde says it is much colder than last summer. The rain came on last night and the mountains that seem quite near at hand are covered with snow. There arrived this morning a cavalry regiment making its exercises on the frontier,[3] they have 10 or 12 howitzers with them, and were all dripping wet. They were let into the great court, parked their horses in circles with chains, & spread out their overcoats to dry. Fortunately the sun has come out, & their hats & jackets are drying upon them, many lying asleep. Under my window is a round of the horses with their heads in their nose bags crunching their corn. The men were served out [of doors] with biscuit wine & a small bit of dried beef. The Officers had lunch at our table and are now gayly singing to the piano. In an hour they will depart, dragging their cannon up the mountain to learn the way to do it when France next pours over the border.

It is very picturesque in this old building, with long arched galleries open on one side to the air. The Monks were very rich and built their cells so large that they make very spacious modern bedrooms. The chapel is contiguous—and a priest comes every Sunday from Chiusi [Chiusa di Pésio] to say mass. Meanwhile the door stands hospitably open all the time, and in the morning I take my book and go there to say my prayers, there being clean modern benches, more comfortable than the concrete floor of my room. The gardens are large and shady, and I sit out all day in the sweet, light air, where the Linden trees are in bloom, and the sound of the rushing Pesio is always in one's ears. If it would only get a little warmer it would be perfect. The best summer place I have ever been in. . . .

Esterina behaved very well about leaving Giacomino. He was asleep & we got off without the parting agony. And she has not so far worried me by lamentations. It is only 5 days ago. I hope the little fellow will keep well at Ceccano Lorenzo's paese.

I have just been to see the artillery train move off. It was very pretty to see them winding down the road, but if they take as much time to limber up and get under way in action they will come in at the end of the fight. there were 24 guns with 6 horses to each and 12 men.

1. Just inland from the Italian Riviera.
2. Napoleon Bonaparte, as first consul in the post-Revolutionary French government, had led the armies that invaded northwestern Italy in 1800 and there defeated the Austrian army.
3. Chiusa di Pésio is about nine miles from the French border.

August 4, 1890, Gênes, Grand' Hôtel de Gênes.

Clem [March] came to Pesio to fetch me, and stopped four days in that beautiful place, though I must confess it rained most of the time and some French girls sang in such shrieks as nearly distracted us. We came to Genoa to take the Archimede of the Florio Rubattino to Naples. We steam out tomorrow ev[enin]g at 9—lie all day Wed[nesday] at Leghorn and then on to Naples that night, hoping to arrive in time to catch the little steamer for Sorrento Thursday. Thus we shall have taken one week for the journey from Pesio to Sorrento! We might have gone Saturday night and have been there by this time. But Clem was disposed to stop three days in Genoa, and the heat has not been intolerable, and as he pays the scot in travelling I have nothing to object. When we get to Sorrento I pay for myself—such was our bargain when he asked me to go with him. He is as amiable and amusing as ever. I wanted to spend July & Aug[ust] at Pesio, and Sep[tember] at Florence, but I cannot be indifferent to the pleasure of Clem's company, & the compliment he pays me in desiring it. And when I get to Sorrento I will yield to the charm of that climate. . . .

Here I broke off for dinner. After just as we were going to the Giardino Italiano for ices—the rain came down, & Clem took up a N York Herald (of Paris,) of 31st July and there saw the death of Mr [George L.] Schuyler, and at the same time an outbreak of cholera at Valencia Spain. We were quite upset and demoralized—and did not know whether to give up Sorrento and we telegraphed back to see if I c[oul]d get rooms again at Pesio—the house being now full. It stormed all night, and I feel very sorrowful about G L S. But now Clem has come to propose we adhere to our purpose and go on to Naples tonight by the Rubattino Archimede. It does not follow that cholera will come to Naples, even if it be bad at Valencia—and he could get away on the first alarm. So I think we will keep on, instead of running to Venice which we thought of or Annécy where is C[ounte]ss Gianotti in a hired Villa on the Lake.[1]

1. City in east central France, about twenty miles from Geneva.

August 13, 1890, Hotel della Sirena.

We took the Archimede Tuesday 5th at 9 PM. Lay all next day at Leghorn taking in freight It was not hot under the awning and we were amused to see the variety of goods hoisted aboard by five cranes; ranging from Railroad iron to bonnet boxes. We were two nights and two days from Genoa to Naples—getting to Naples in time for the 5,45 train to Castellamare & a carriage thence brought us to the Sirena at 9 PM. We had just taken a week from Pesio! having stopped four days in Genoa to get the Archimede wh[ich] is the best Rubattino boat. Clem had come out in her 8 years ago from NYork to Gibraltar. Clem is always amiable and kind. He of course rolled me as he calls it from Pesio here. But now I resume my own bill. . . .

Lorenzo has won lire 200 in the lottery and forthwith he arrived yesterday with Giacomino so we are all grand complet.

September 28, 1890, 107B Quattro Fontane.

I had a very pleasant time with Clem. He was very gay, and he put me to my speed I assure you. He had enough of Sorrento by end of Aug[ust] when it turned from extreme heat to delightful cool & we went to Naples and then came to Rome—which I found so cool there was no use going farther, and here I am three weeks before my usual time. But I find myself involved in a most unpleasant incident that occasions me the greatest pain and anxiety! When it is over I may tell about it, but not now. Suffice that I am very much worried. Alas! little but worry is my portion If only Willie and you were prospering, I sh[oul]d not care for what happens to myself. Mme de Hegerman[n] is transferred to Sweden, and she was packing & going when I returned to Rome. She is one of those pleasantest to me, and I regret them extremely. They went to take leave of their Majesties at Monza.[1] The Queen gave her a superb brooch, large sapphire set round with diamonds, & engaged them to come back yearly & spend part of their congé[2] in visiting them at Monza or Rome.

1. A village about nine miles northeast of Milan.
2. Leave.

October 17, 1890, 107B Quattro Fontane.

Dr Bettman succeeded two days ago in hooking out the last polyp from my nose—which have been causing me so much trouble for four years. It was not until I went to him last winter that I knew what was the occasion of all this I called catarrh. The polips were so deep seated it was exceedingly difficult to extirpate them—and it would take much cocaine and several hours at a sitting—many times failing to get hold on one. The cocaine leaves me quite upset for a day or two. Now at last the last one of 11 has been removed—and provided they do not grow again I will be much more comfortable. You need not mention I have had this trouble.

October 26, 1890, 107B Quattro Fontane.

You are right in your surmise that the disagreeable episode relates to Lorenzo & Esterina. They have got entangled with the police, and it will be very difficult to exculpate Lorenzo, who has been guilty of the most stupid folly, but nothing else—although his complicity is terribly involved.

Esterina has a youngest brother an unfortunate fellow left on the town at 9 years old when their parents died & the elder ones had to fight for their living & the little girls were taken as you know by two Princesses & educated in convents. But poor Luigi [Servadei] nobody took, the city educated him with vagrants & turned him out at 14 reading & writing but without a trade. He went to a shoe maker where he barely had bread—I used to help him 12 years ago, & then he was drafted and I heard no more till about 4 years ago he reappeared as a cobbler in a little hole down by the Tiber—suffering so much with his eyes that a Doctor I sent him to said he w[oul]d lose them sleeping in that damp hovel. So one way or another I have dragged him along ever since, letting him sleep in the entrata[1] when he was unable to hire a little room under the roof here—& he had the scraps.

A year ago a first cousin of Lorenzo came to Rome as a wet nurse. Mme Maldura[2] saw the advertisement & asked Lorenzo to send her to her daughter Mme Polidori, where she gave great satisfaction & the baby thrives: but the Polidoris forbid her receiving any visits, so L[orenzo] & Esterina seldom saw her passing with the baby. Lorenzo returned with Giacomino from Sorrento 2nd Sep[tember]. I arrived 6th not being expected to stop the house was all dismantled & Lorenzo had to bestir himself to sweep my room & get me a place to rest. Esterina went to her bed and was fast asleep. Just then the <u>balia</u> (as a wet nurse is called) rang at the door, Lorenzo opened it, she went into the kitchen & produced two carte registrate—that is coupons one for lire 200, the other 1000—she said she had found among some papers in a basket at the Polidoris. Lorenzo said it was impossible she sh[oul]d <u>find</u> such things—she persisted she had. He told her she must take them back & put them where she found them—she said she c[oul]d'nt because she had torn up the cera[3] & they w[oul]d suspect her, or she w[oul]d burn them rather than put them back. At that moment I rang & Est[e]r[ina] being asleep he came to me hastily putting the papers in his pocket. I kept him a good while, & when he went back the Balia was gone. The more he considered the more he saw the notes were stolen, but he did'nt want to have Polidori's money burned, and he still less wished to denounce his cousin by carrying them to Polidori or to the Questura.

He believed the woman had been ignorant of what she was doing—and his idea was to make her come to him, and persuade her to put them some where in Polidori's house before the subtraction sh[oul]d be discovered—& if she refused compel her to take them away. He c[oul]d'nt go on such a mission to Polidori's where he c[oul]d'nt see the woman except in the presence of her mistress. He gave a woman of Mme Maldura's 50 cent to go and tell the Balia to come to him. So she did one morning, & by chance I went to the door thinking it was Clem. Esterina was just telling the woman Lorenzo was out & she must come again; she ran off before I c[oul]d ask after the bambina. When after two days more she did'nt return Lorenzo began to get desperate to quit himself of the notes. He sent this Luigi to watch for her at her own door & tell her she must come. She told Luigi she could'nt & they might burn the notes for her—or to give them to Luigi. Thereupon Lorenzo gives them to Luigi to carry to her to do what she pleased but that he sh[oul]d wash his hands of them. He actually was fool enough to think that so he was out of it. Luigi at sight of the notes lost his his [*sic*] senses—gave to an old woman the 200 & sewed up the 1000 in an old shoe. The old woman took the note to a changer by chance hard by the office of Polidori who is a notary. The notes were numbered & Polidori had long before had them noted. The old woman soon told whom she had got it from, was arrested, & of course Luigi.

The first I knew of all this was a police officer coming politely to inform me that Servadei domicilated in my house had been taken for passing stolen notes. Thereupon Lorenzo told me the whole story—and went into an awful fright when he found how horrid I considered his position. I went off at once to a legal friend who sent me to a lawyer who says he will get Lorenzo through. He was been once interrogated, & told the whole thing as he did to me. But he has to appear tomorrow on charge of complicity—and he is in an awful state. Meanwhile Mme Maldura told me the other half. Her preposterous daughter had made a <u>nascondiglio</u> that is a hiding place for these notes, which was no other than to sew them up in an old stocking & put them in the Baby's cradle! When she missed them 10th Aug. they took up the other woman, & the Balia also was interrogated denied & did all she c[oul]d to fix it on the other. But there being no proof found she was discharged. Polidori said she c[oul]d'nt suspect the Balia, because (forsooth) she had showed her the nascondiglio and told her it contained Lire 1200. Thus putting this overpowering temptation before the eyes of the ignorant contadina. Then on account of the milk for the baby they tried all they could to screen the Balia. The questura let them keep the Balia until they c[oul]d get another and when they did it was St Michael's day—& some how the woman was allowed to go off free to Ceccano. And so far we don't know if they have taken her.

Lorenzo has his savings & lottery gains amounting to L5000—which he expects to pay to the lawyer provided he can get off. But his agony is awful. And with his impatient character the scenes in all the ups and downs are terrible! I have suffered these two months more than you can imagine—and now comes the crucial point. Malduras turned upon Lorenzo that he must have known his cousin was a bad character, & drove him to fury one day. But they now blame themselves that holding Lorenzo responsible for her character they did not tell him of the robbery as soon as it took place. Had he known that, he w[oul]d not have been taken in by the Balia for a moment. It is a wretched affair. I suffer enough, but I c[oul]d'nt bear all my friends talking to me of it. I have taken precautions not to have it go into the better newspapers here. The tension is dreadful. Sh[oul]d Lorenzo be sent to prison he will come out a pernicious ruined man.

1. Entryway.
2. The wife of CPC's landlord.
3. Sealing wax.

[Unsigned draft of a letter to the acting minister at St. Paul's Episcopal Church in Rome enclosed in a letter to James Carson]

November 2, 1890, 107B Quattro Fontane

My Dear Mr [Monroe] Royce,

I wrote & sent off a letter to you just now, and then I answered one from Baron Osten Sacken a friend of 30 years with whom I have always been at issue on the subject of religion. He being a man of science and often trying to <u>open my eyes</u> to what he thought wiser and <u>truer</u>. If you will notice These scientists call Truth that which is only material Fact. Truth is intellectual moral fact—not material. I think in all these discussions with the Baron I must have made some impression, for his letter speaks of books he has been reading, and he says "It is the religious aspect of their lives which interested me most. Take Card[inal] Newman, Ch. Kingsley, Charlotte Bronte, Miss Martineau[1] all of them intellectually and morally people of the highest excellence, and yet, falling out on questions which are above all human intellect and knowledge!" To this I answered what I do not know that any body has said—but if it is mine I give it to you and you may use it as a corollary to what we were speaking of. "These people fall into confusion for the original sin of coveting the knowledge—of good and evil." They demand to penetrate into the dealings of God with man. Why they say does he let sin and evil exist? Can he be merciful and see the unmerited sufferings of his creatures. There is no answer given any more than when Pilate asked what is Truth. And so they fall away and are confounded.

We have come to look upon the Apple of Eden like the Apple of the Hesperides,[2] a mere old world myth, whereas it is a living active truth, the unhallowed clutching at what it has not pleased God to reveal. When I studied Plato I saw he had risen to the utmost height of the human intellect. I know of nothing approaching him, and he points so clearly to the Revelation of a God above all other Philosophers that he seems inspired with a higher revelation than he could have got from the Egyptian priests. But he reaches his height by a chain of reasoning hard to follow & easily lost if a single link be not apprehended. But Jesus comes and says I know—and it is all simple and any one may take hold on the truth to live and die by. Only they must take his word for the mysteries that are not to be revealed to mortal eye. In vain do wise men kick against the pricks, they cannot tear down the veil, and they cannot make a living religion to square with their notions of what God ought to be.

I have gone on writing all this which is not a copy of my letter to Osten Sacken. To him I only said the falling out of these eminent persons is owing to the original sin of seeking into the knowledge of good and evil, which is debarred to man.

1. John Henry Newman (1801–90), a founder of the Anglican Oxford movement who in 1846 was ordained as a Catholic priest and was subsequently involved in a number of theological disputes, the most celebrated with Charles Kingsley (1819–75), an English cleric and novelist. Charlotte Brontë (1816–55) was best known for her *Jane Eyre*. Harriet Martineau (1802–76), the English writer familiar to Americans from her travel books about the United States, was highly sympathetic to antislavery reform.

2. The golden apples that Ge, the Greek earth goddess, gave to Hera at her marriage to Zeus were guarded by the Hesperides, the daughters of Atlas.

November 23, 1890, 107B Quattro Fontane.

You are very good and generous about poor Lorenzo. I hope he may be let off without imprisonment. But it is an anxious time and I have hard work with his crises of despondency & despair—and the lawyer is a shark. He c[oul]d'nt fly now—nor if he be condemned, for they w[oul]d demand his extradition. But sh[oul]d he be subjected to even a month's imprisonment his pride will be so cut up he will want to go away—and he thanks you with all his heart. The case I hope will be tried next week & be disposed of before Xmas.

December 14, 1890, 107B Quattro Fontane.

The ice & snow that have enveloped Paris—and have visited Venice and Milan, have come down upon Rome. Yesterday the fountain of the Tritone was frozen hard with long icicles hanging from the Triton skull—and all my visitors came shivering in: including Grace & Charles [Bristed] who is here for a month's recess. The roads North are more or less blocked. . . .

I am afraid Mme Folchi[1] has gone too far ever to come back. Her husband did all he could to restrain her standing up for her loyally—and when he could do no more he shut his eyes, on account of the children. But she has become so audacious the Folchi parents said she sh[oul]d no longer stay in the apartment she had in casa Folchi. Not content with going out to meet her men, she allowed herself to be caught by her husband in flagrante delicto[2] in her own chamber. Moreover she has long been contracting debts (although it is said) she took money. Mrs Heywood [her mother] will not pay for her any more, and she has been nearly killed by the scandal, and she stops in Paris. It being impossible for her to face Rome while the trial for separation goes on. The Catholics have no divorce but they have a legal separation. . . .

Lorenzo's affair has not yet been brought to trial—they now say it will be 29th Dec[ember]. It is hard to meet the holydays under such apprehension. He is very grateful for your good will. I hope he will escape without a day's imprisonment. If he be sent for a term I am sure he will want never to show himself in Rome more. It is pathetic to see how thin he has grown, and so much subdued in temper. But he cooks all the better. Giacomino is the pleasantest little inmate I ever had. He is very jolly & intelligent, but he does'nt catch English at all.

1. Lily Heywood Folchi, an American by birth, had married a Roman.
2. Legally, "in the very act of committing the crime."

December 18, 1890, 107B Quattro Fontane.

I have so much to bear already and I so long for rest and peace, before I go hence and am no more seen. My next birthday tells off one of my extra years. Papa was 74—his father 75[1]—Mamma 70—only Aunt Adèle has had a lengthened term. God knows I do not desire it. But I do pray for tranquillity, and if possible that I may come to the last restored to my sons.

1. CPC misremembered her grandfather's age. He was 79 when he died.

1891

January 20, 1891, 107B Quattro Fontane.

The relief of Lorenzo's absolution is very great. The thing has taken down Esterina's pride considerably, which is a very good thing. Giacomino is the light & warmth of the house. I don't know how I sh[oul]d have got through these anxious months since Sep[tember] without him. It is very cold. Snow loading the roofs, and much fire needed. Bettman hooked two more polipi out of my nose. It is very painful operation, but the relief is immense. Good bye my dear James, I must refurbish our motto. Our utmost strength when down to rise again, And not to yield though beaten, all our praise.

February 10, 1891, 107B Quattro Fontane.

Lorenzo got off with the skin of his teeth. When the Judges absolved him 31st Dec[ember] after that long agonizing day, neither he nor I could believe it, nor recover our spirits till next day. I began to breathe freely. Then the villainous lawyer sent to terrify him with the fear the Public Prosecutor w[oul]d appeal against him! and they must have more money to quash it—and actually forced Lorenzo to give fr[anc]s 200 more! I believe it was all a fetch,[1] for if they c[oul]d buy off the Attorney Gen, for 200 fr[anc]s the farce of holding trials w[oul]d be exploded. As it is he is impoverished having paid 1200 fr[anc]s. He goes quite shabby, and

Esterina wears her oldest clothes, and has not <u>even</u> got a new frock for Giacomino. The restraint on her vainglory is one good result after all.

It seems queer I sh[oul]d have taken it so to heart. But had Lorenzo been incarcerated for a month even, on such an accusation, it w[oul]d have broken his pride and would have stained his <u>papers</u>, on wh[ich] it must have been recorded, and had he wished afterwards to emigrate he could not have shown a clear certificate. To have him go, and leave Esterina on my hands would have been to put me in a miserable position, her lamentations w[oul]d have made her utterly unbearable; and poor little Giac. How could I have turned him out? . . .

Carnival has been resurrected, & was very fine. But I never went to the Corso. The streets are resounding tonight with the last veglione.[2] Tomorrow we go into ashes.

1. Trick or strategem.
2. Masked ball.

March 2, 1891, 107B Quattro Fontane.

I have just resumed my painting. All the time of the Lorenzo trouble I was so nervous I could not paint; nor could I paint when the cold was bad, for I had to abandon the studio and stick to the sunny side of the house, for all which I have burned an awful quantity of wood. Giacomino continues [the] bright spot in the house. Poor little fellow, I grieve to think he will soon grow into a common boy and must take his chance with the people of whom he is born. He has naturally such a charming disposition, that I hate he shall come to their level. But I can't help it.

April 24, 1891, 107B Quattro Fontane.

I am glad to have y[ou]r letter this day, for I am very nervous, and I need a pleasant stimulus. I have on my back a mole like that Willie has on his throat, I am sorry to say. This mole about 6 years ago got irritated & Dr Aitken gave me a little wash[?], it subsided. But about three weeks ago it began to grow higher, and my clothes hurt. It is like a thorn sticking in me. I consulted my devoted Bettman & he thought I ought to have it cut out. So I sent for young Dr Van Master who has been studying in Baltimore with Edward Miles[1] and Julian Chisolm![2] And it is decided to make the operation this afternoon. There is a great provision of antiseptics & linen—and they will be here in half an hour. He says it will take but 10 minutes to cut out the thing & sew it up, and then some ten days to heal. I shall take chloroform as I have suffered enough pain in my time.

1. Probably Francis Turquand Miles (1827–1903), Charleston physician who was appointed to the chair of anatomy at the University of Maryland after the Civil War.
2. John Julian Chisolm (1830–1903), Charleston-born surgeon and ophthalmologist who taught at the University of Maryland 1869–93.

April 30, 1891, 107B Quattro Fontane.

I wrote you just before submitting to the little operation that caused me much apprehension. And I instructed Esterina to add on the outside my letter the result when it sh[oul]d be over. Because I was put under chloroform from which I suffered several days. The wound is healing very well, but I am much pulled down by it. It will be several days more before I can go out or put on a close fitting gown. My two young surgeons Van Master and Bettman have been most kind. Van Master would take no pay. He is only 22 years old graduated last year at Baltimore,[1] & went off yesterday to be assistant to a great surgeon at Berne. He will one day be a man of reputation

1. From the University of Maryland School of Medicine.

May 10, 1891, 107B Quattro Fontane.

The wound in my back has been slow in healing. It was doing beautifully & quite closed on the first intention—but Van Master had to go away so he took out the stitches, and the skin not being strong enough for the strain on the back, it opened, and I have to wait for it to close more tediously. It is just at the waist band, so I can't put on a close fitting dress to walk out. But in three days more it will be quite healed—I am glad to get rid of the thing. It was always getting bruised by the towel.

July 6, 1891, 107B Quattro Fontane.

Here I am still in town although the heat oppresses me very much, and this summer I wanted to stay a long time at Pesio, and paint the lovely wild flowers. But C[ounte]ss Gianotti has been ill a month with rheumatic fever the result of grippe, & bringing out latent heart trouble. With her accustomed resolution when she found herself in for a long illness just at the time she is used to carrying the children away, she w[oul]d'nt keep them in Rome, but packed them off with the governess to a Villa near Florence, and she has taken out her sickness in the solitude it is the habit here to impose on the patient, who needs be patient indeed. I am the only person suffered to see her. The Count was obliged to go yesterday to Venice on his service to the King, and he c[oul]d only go relying upon me to be at hand in case of any change or emergency. So I go and sit down by her couch, the only thing for me to do, and I remember the hours and days Charlotte Hamilton and others patiently sat by me, and gratitude to them carries me through. The poor dear Constance is very weak & very patient. She cannot even read her letters. When the Count returns we will get her off to Leghorn or Pegli[1] where the sea air will bring her up.

I hope I shall not break down as I have done twice that I stopped in Rome after first July. There are many persons still in Rome. . . .

They say both Mrs Strong and her companion Mrs Riley died from the effects of morphine injections wh[ich] they habitually used. That seems the most deleterious sort of intoxication of all. Evelyn[2] has evidently those at her back who pay, how else c[oul]d she have moved for a new trial, which however the Court has refused her. Now is to be seen who will push the Public Prosecutors to pursue for perjury. The scandals are all odious. The Gordon Cumming affair[3] is inexplicable in any light you could put it. That Miss Garner in an impulse of generosity sticks to "her own stricken deer" is not so astounding as his towns coming out to greet him as a hero, and give him a triumph! That such things can be, shows a deplorable depreciation of the moral sense. Presently some poor wretch will think the public conscience is asleep, and he will venture on some peccadillo, and be caught up and be made a scapegoat to satisfy morality. It is a bad look out for the P[rince] of Wales—and recalls to me the "affaire du collier"[4] which so bespattered poor Marie Antoinette and hastened the downfall of the french monarchy. And now Parnell's[5] impudent marriage with Kitty O'Shea! Let us all take heed how we stand in these slippery days.

1. A seacoast town some six miles west of Genoa.
2. Gladys Evelyn was an English woman whom William H. Hurlbert had taken to the "sunny south" and who had then launched a breach of promise suit against him.
3. Sir William Gordon Cumming, a colonel in the Scots Guard, was found guilty of cheating at baccarat at a high society house party attended by the Prince of Wales, later King Edward VII, and his cronies. The prince, a rash gambler, had raised the stakes well beyond his friend's ability to pay.
4. A scandal about a diamond necklace in 1785.
5. Charles Stewart Parnell was co-respondent in an 1889 successful divorce suit for adultery brought by Capt. William O'Shea against his wife, Katherine, whom Parnell married in 1891.

July 26, 1891, Certosa di Pesio.

Giacomino was left with Lorenzo. I am afraid he will have a hard time, and it is especially hot in Rome; but since the trouble last winter Lorenzo has taken Ceccano in horror and will not go there. He thought the village took part with his cousin the woman who stole the money in some way holding him to account for her misdeed, and he swears he will never go near any of them again.

September 27, 1891, Florence.

I had a pleasant six weeks at Pesio. The climate delightful, I painted wildflowers all the morning, and walked three hours every afternoon with my friends Mrs Coale & Miss Bell nieces of the original Choate.[1] Now I am busy in the Uffizi copying the Great Madonna of Andrea del Sarto[2] for Mr

Caroline Carson, copy of Andrea del Sarto, **The Holy Family.** *Courtesy of Ashton and LaVonne Phillips.*

Miles. He had an engraving of it in the old times that I copied in lead pencil. I never come to Florence and see the great original without thinking of Mr Miles, so I proposed to him to do it in Water colours for him, and he agreed—and sent my letter on to Lynch Hamilton, who forthwith wrote me a charming letter, and says he too eagerly expects the picture.

It is a picture so much in demand one has to make application years ahead for leave to sit down before it. This I did not know, and came primed & headed to the Conservator, who politely told me it was impossible to accord permission as two artists were copying it and there are 12 waiting their turn. But I got the custode[3] of the hall on my side and assured him I c[oul]d see from a longer distance than most, and my friends were so and so—and at last he yielded, and there I am in the very middle of the room with my easel, and everybody circling around. However I am getting on very well, and I hope to make a beautiful copy. But it will take all October.

1. Rufus Choate (1799–1859), Boston lawyer and United States senator from Massachusetts from 1841 to 1845.
2. CPC had earlier copied del Sarto's *Holy Family* for herself.
3. Guard.

November 10, 1891, 107B Quattro Fontane.

I have got safely home on Nov[ember] 3d at 1,15 AM. The trains from Florence leave at the most inconvenient hours. 6½ AM, or 7 PM. It was the latter I took as 6½ AM means getting out of bed at 4. I was all the time busy in the Uffizi painting the picture for Mr Miles. It was a great undertaking, it is 4 ft high. I was at the door when the gallery opened at 10 AM, and I sat uninterruptedly till 3, mostly till 4 when the Gal[lery] closes. Then I went home to Simi's pension had tea and something kept from lunch, but I was too tired to eat, I lay on the sofa 15 min, and then forced myself to go to walk. In the ev[enin]g I played patience & went early to bed—none of my friends returned to Florence till nearly the end of Oct[ober]—so there was nothing to interfere.

I held out well for 20 days, but then I began to give out. I took some biscuits & cake with me, but it did not avail. My digestion revolted at the ill usage and refused to endure any more. Nonetheless I worked on for 14 days more, and then I had to give in, and come away. The main part of the picture however is done, I have only to work up the back ground wh[ich] I can do better almost at home in my studio. It cost me $200 stopping in Florence including the expenses on the painting. So I hope Wm P [Miles] will be willing to pay handsomely for it. Mrs Hyde was detained by a sick relative in Switzerland, and only arrived in Florence as I was leaving. We c[oul]d just embrace as she got out of the R[ail]R[oad] carriage and I stepped into her place. Two of my kind Newberys who were in Florence insisted on coming to help me off. Walter seeing to my luggage & the great case in which the picture is packed was a great relief to me who was so sick & tired. He & Katy put off their dinner at the hotel till 8 O'clock that they might come to me. Lorenzo met us—he had got a friend to stop in the house with the sleeping Giacomino. Soup was ready & my bed wh[ich] I was mighty glad to get into. By taking pepsine with my food, and charcoal pillules I am getting straightened out—and I hope soon to be as fine as when I came from Pesio. . . .

I went to lunch today with Annie Porter in the new apartment she is furnishing. It is on the very <u>acies</u> of Rome at the Castro Pretorio.[1] Very pretty and very out of the way. The excellent Woods are doing very well, and I dined with Mr Greenough Sat[urday] ev[enin]g. So the winter has begun its usual round although the Reverendo [Nevin] has not returned to his flock.

1. The Castra Prætoria, site of the Roman barracks for the imperial Prætorian Guard in the northeast edge of the old walled city, was therefore "acies," that is to say "on the very front line of battle of the city."

1892

January 3d, 1892, 107B Quattro Fontane.

I have had a very good Xmas except that my friend Dr Bettman was laid up, but he is out again & we took a walk Monday 4th my birthday by the way. I had Wood the V[ice] Consul to dinner and he staid till 11½, so I repented.

6th

C[ounte]ss Gianotti sent me a superb basket of flowers. Xmas I had a number of presents very good except my young man Mr Russell Pardon Cooke sent me a large box of fine bon bons, which turned out to be all fondants,[1] which I loathe. I restrained the expression of my vexation to him. . . . But I put by the box and sent them at New Year to the unhappy Brilacqua children, who I dare say were made sick by them.

Mrs Hurlbert is here very quiet. She does not tell where Hurlbert is. It is said the English extradition law would cause his surrender by every country except Spain. I think his lawyers gave him away. They told him there was no case, and they clearly prepared none. They evidently went into court with the vaguest notion of the matter in hand and Sir Ch[arle]s Russell only woke up at the end and made a very good speech for Hurlbert after he had given him away in the beginning by his "alternate plea" He evidently learned the case through the pleadings when it was too late to avail his client. Even if the letters had been written by Hurlbert (which I don't believe) there was no promise of marriage in them, and his lawyers ought to have got the judge to throw the case out for want of proof without going to trial. To go and stand the suit for perjury would cost him much money wh[ich] he has'nt got, and Mrs Lee says she will not allow her sister's money to be given up to pay lawyers. It seems Mrs Lee has the power; without her signature Kitty cannot dispose of her estate. The letters now purporting to come from Wilfred Manning demand thousands of pounds and Mrs Lee told me she would not give up her sister's money to pay Wilfred Manning to come forth. I do believe it is all a got up job and conspiracy. There certainly never was a man with such a proclivity for getting himself wound up in mysterious entanglements.

1. Thick, creamy sugar paste.

Caroline Carson's grave in Il Cimitero Acattolico di Roma. Photograph by William H. Pease, 1992.

February 10, 1892, 107B Quattro Fontane.

Mrs Hurlbert says her lawyers write her very encouraging letters—and Mr Story says they are working up the clues, and find it is a much wider spread plot than appeared on the face of the proceedings. Evelyn evidently has backers who paid the expenses of her suit, wh[ich] are enormous in England, and Hurlbert is not to show until they have got together such overwhelming evidence that no costs at least will come out of him. . . .

I am going to have Bishop Potter[1] to lunch tomorrow and the Lancianis[2] & Terrys—Lorenzo gets into such an excitement that he has made his chicken pie today! I am afraid it will not be so nice when baked tomorrow. Giacomino is as amiable as ever and Esterina has rather more sense. She got into one of her tantrums a while ago and I dismissed her so positively that she was convinced I was ready to do without her, and to let the whole of them go. She has been very much more reasonable since, and I mean to pull the reins tighter hereafter.

1. Henry Codman Potter (1835–1908), Protestant Episcopal bishop of New York.
2. Rodolfo Amadeo Lanciani (1846–1929), an archaeologist specializing in Roman antiquities, and his wife.

March 9, 1892, 107B Quattro Fontane.

I will copy the Confederate flag for you when I have leisure. I am very tired now and have to rest after finishing the Madonna delle Arpie,[1] The Replica, I mean. It looks splendid in the frame, and it will be sent off this week. I am thinking if I shall or shall not, have it taken out in N York and exhibited at the Water Colour exhibition.

1. Andrea del Sarto, *Madonna of the Harpies,* which she copied in the Ufizzi.

April 12, 1892, 107B Quattro Fontane.

I wrote [Willie] the sad collapse I have made. The pain and discomfort are very great; but the torture is diminished by the treatment I am undergoing

Dr Montechiari is a very superior man. When Dr Weir Mitchell[1] was here last year and examined into his treatment of Mrs Crowninshield's complicated case, he pronounced Montechiari equal to the best, and said in US he w[oul]d not go out as a physician, but reserve himself for consultations. He pulled C[ounte]ss Gianotti through last summer. He has had the chief surgeon Duranti[2] to consult over me, & they have settled on treatment without the knife. If this tumour were cut out, almost surely a bigger one w[oul]d come in its stead. It has not ulcerated which is favourable It is a hard angry looking lump, which burns like a coal of fire, and darting pains to my heart. But with the use of Déclat's preparation of Phenic, Iodine &c and daily subcutaneous injections relief is obtained from acute pain. Although Montechiari does not flatter me it will ever go away altogether, but be reduced to a tolerable condition, I believe it will go away—like those others. They were inert however and did not give the local pain this one does that has seized on the nerves of the back. Of course I have to give myself up to the nursing this lump. I cannot paint, for the less I use my arm the better. I can write without trouble, but not raise the arm much, nor lift any weight. I have had a little straw hat made to go over the lump & keep anything from pressing on it. The Doctor is very much tickled at the invention.

My friends all rise up to comfort me. Grace [Bristed] is devoted & takes me to drive in her comfortable carriage I go to lunch nearly every day with one or another—and I can walk very well—but I get tired by night, so I don't go to dine except with Constance [Countess Gianotti]. Mrs Young has sent me an elegant bl[ack]silk loose cloak to walk out comfortably. Mrs Delano forthwith said this must increase my expenses and she sent me $300 to help on. Mme Cortazzo who has come into her fortune, insisted on paying the bill for the medicaments sent from Paris. Dr Montechiari gives me to understand he will have me pay little, or nothing just as it suits me best. But with Mrs Delano's subsidy I expect to pay a moderate retribution. He comes however every day, and at the best it will be a long weary thing. Nevertheless I sh[oul]d be a mean wretch not to be comforted by so much kindness, and to murmur at my lot.

At first I was plunged in despair, and I supposed I sh[oul]d pass the rest of my life under the influence of morphine injections, which bring one to a miserable pass. But the Iodine of soda, & the phénique control the pain. And I have adjusted this cross to my shoulder, and I hope to bear it with patience. I have trusted in God, and I hope never to be confounded either in my own person or in my children.

1. Silas Weir Mitchell (1829–1914), Philadelphia physician, neurologist, and novelist.
2. Francesco Durante (1844–1934), surgeon and pathologist with a specialty in cancer, was the director of clinical surgery at the University of Rome.

May 15, 1892, 107B Quattro Fontane.[1]

I have suffered less pain the last few days, but the tumour looks as ugly as ever—though it does not ulcerate yet, and it requires incessant treatment and daily hypodermic injections of iodine & phenic, alternated with Sublimate of Mer[cury] which burns like fire. So my whole wretched body is sore with little wounds, and ribs ache as much as back. Nonetheless my digestion & appetite are good, and I can walk, and am the better for walking. . . .

I still hope the tumour may come to a head, and assume such a shape I need not stay all summer near the Doctor. Some urge me to go now to Paris. But all my friends there are just scattering for the summer, and most likely Déclat himself. I have just written to ask him. I c[oul]d not get in any hotel the comforts of my own home, & I w[oul]d rather stop here till July. Mrs Cortazzo will send for you and Willie.

1. This is the last letter CPC wrote to James Carson before she died of cancer on 15 August 1892.

Index